To Judy and Bob —
Much affection.

CLOSE
YOUR
BOOKS

Selected Sermons and Writings of

RABBI MARK S. SHAPIRO

With an Introduction by Rabbi Karyn Kedar

Edited by
Stephen A. Shapiro

BJBE

Table of Contents

Table of Contents

Acknowledgments

I'm deeply grateful to the students, colleagues, and friends who added their words to these sermons. They touch me deeply. Their contributions appear within the text as *Shulayim*—footnotes.

My loving thanks to:

My brother Ben and sister-in-law Barbara, the best of siblings. They encouraged me to take on this project. Our parents would have *kvelled* to see how much we love each other.

Our son Steve, who has worked long and hard to make this book a reality. What a wonderful man! His Rachel is a gem and a loving daughter. Their beautiful daughter Natalie, the #1 granddaughter and songbird, worked at transcribing the sermons, making it a family project.

Our son Eliot, the consummate *mensch*, knows how to be loving and gentle and available. His wife Ellyn takes the "in-law" out of daughter. What would we do without her, her good sense and her loving nature? Their gift to us, grandchildren Noah and Rose, keep giving *nachas*, and they light up the stage for us.

David is a loving support to Hanna and me, bright, lots of fun, always available. We count on him.

Hanna, "The Lovely Hanna," has lovingly kept me on a kind of straight and narrow, always a challenge. She's as lovely as when I first met her on the shores of OSRUI!

–MSS

Introduction

Rabbi Mark Shapiro has always been clear: A Reform synagogue is a vibrant and unpretentious community where people matter, social justice is an obligation, and values define the true character of an individual. In whichever way you encounter B'nai Jehoshua Beth Elohim (BJBE), either by entering the building or meeting the people at an event, you feel it in the air, the traces of kindness, comfort, peace, and commitment. People show up. They show up to study, to pray, to make sandwiches for the poor. They show up to pitch in, to stack chairs, to say thank you, and to welcome people they have never met. BJBE is known as the down-to-earth congregation, the place where the individual matters and community comes first. The place engenders life-long learners who know that the well of *Torah* can never run dry. BJBE is the place where social action is not a program, but rather in the DNA of the community.

This is the congregation that I inherited. BJBE was formed by a beloved rabbi, Rabbi Mark Shapiro, whose vision and deeply held beliefs created one of the most extraordinary congregations in the country. As I reflect on his life's work and his legacy, eight principles emerge as the foundation of his rabbinate:

Live in a world of values. "Judaism is a way of life replete with special words...words like justice, mercy, belief, understanding, holiness, goodness, truth. 'Help us apply these, Rabbi'—that is what today's Jews ask." (RH 1965). These words, written decades ago, are still essential to who Rabbi Shapiro is and strives to be. And we still ask of our rabbis to teach and help us live the intangibles. To make life meaningful, purposeful.

To be good is to do good. Rabbi Shapiro teaches us to believe in the power of righteous acts; to speak out, to march, to give, to behave in a way that is worthy of Judaism's highest ideals. He believes that righteousness is attained every time we care enough to stand for something greater than ourselves. That is why he chose the verse "Know Before Whom You Stand" to be on the Sanctuary wall of 901 Milwaukee Avenue, in Glenview, Illinois. That verse remains on the walls of our Chapel in Deerfield, Illinois. We may have moved locale several times, from the West Side of Chicago, to Glenview to Deerfield, but we always took us, with us. This phrase, chosen by Rabbi as our guiding principal, reminds us that the smallness of the human condition can be transformed when we perform acts of love and kindness.

Be a mensch. "Being a *mensch*," in Rabbi Shapiro's worldview, is the key to a rabbi's success. Integrity, "being the same person on and off (the *bimah*) is a worthwhile goal." At the end of the day, he teaches us all that we are judged not by our knowledge or wealth but by our kindness.

Empower the individual and put community at the center. Empower the lay community to be stewards of their congregation. Rabbi Shapiro urges us to excel at Jewish learning. Many a person was tapped on the shoulder to become a teacher, a leader, an advocate of those in need. He was their rabbi and teacher, and they were charged with making BJBE kind, courteous, and grounded.

Torah is the greatest joy and most important gift of all. Rabbi Shapiro feels a great pull between his books and the wisdom of *Torah* and the needs of the people. He would say that people always win. And I know him to be a deep and dedicated learner, a lover of the Hebrew language, a reader, and a faithful student.

Humility. Appearances do not matter. Rabbi Shapiro never had much regard for status or flash. BJBE has an aura of genuineness. In a larger community that often gives into excess, he teaches modesty. And in a world that could be complicated, he strives for simplicity. He felt that his role was to be the non-anxious presence in our complex lives.

Children matter. Rabbi Shapiro dedicates himself to the children. I often hear of the times when his youngest students sat on the floor in his office while he was sitting on his rocking chair answering their questions. He was an important part of that generation of rabbis whose passion for Jewish camping established a successful network of Reform Jewish camps. It was on the lawn of OSRUI that children and teens fell in love with *Torah* and learned the obligation of righteous deeds. So many of his "kids" wanted to grow up and be just like him. He raised many disciples who have become rabbis, cantors, and educators, and today's leaders.

Words have power. The carefully crafted sermons in this volume still inspire. They are at once a historical snapshot of American Jewry and forever timeless. When we read the words, we can hear that voice. Reassuring. Thoughtful. Rabbinic. Kind. Authentic. Caring. The voice that guided us through a journey that elevates and inspires. His message is that we need to build a world that is just, that is attentive to what really matters, that is humble, that is kind. "I always felt like Mark was talking directly to me. His wisdom comforted me. He speaks the truth but doesn't preach it." (Rabbi Reni Dickman)

These eight principles are a start at defining the legacy of Rabbi Mark Shapiro. First and foremost, my job as the Senior Rabbi of this generation of Congregation BJBE has been to remain faithful to that legacy. I am profoundly grateful to have inherited a community that is aspirational and caring and engendered a culture of love for the clergy. He was and remains a servant to the Jewish people. He is a rabbi's rabbi. May his words live on as a reminder to those of us he has guided and be a true teaching for generations to come.

–Rabbi Karyn D. Kedar

The *Torah* in Our Trunk

By Steve Shapiro, Editor

Many people—hundreds and even thousands—thought of MSS as their own personal rabbi. As you'll read in some of the wonderful contributions to this book, many others still do, more than 15 years after he retired from the *bimah* at BJBE. Some in these pages will even refer to him as a "rabbi's rabbi."

At this point, I think of a line from *Fiddler on the Roof* where one of the young women in Anatevka discusses setting her sights on the rabbi's son. "We have only rabbi and he has only one son…"

Or in our case, three sons. To Eliot, David, and me, our rabbi was our father. But bottom line: He was and is just "Dad," and now "Grampa."

People sometimes asked me how I felt having a rabbi as a father. I honestly never knew how to answer that question. Because I could legitimately ask them the opposite question—what's it like NOT to have a rabbi as a father?

How best to describe what life was like as MSS' oldest son? When I was growing up, before BJBE had its own building, the congregation famously made use of a number of buildings in and around Glenview. The office was above Classic Bowl on Waukegan Road in Morton Grove, services were at a number of churches over the years, and Sunday School met in different public schools in the area. The *Torah* needed to be mobile back then, so it lived in the trunk of our car—a Ford Galaxie, if I recall.

If you were to ask me, as a seven-year-old boy, why cars had trunks, I would have told you that cars have trunks because people needed a place to keep their *Torah*. It made total sense to me—it was as much a part of my life as Cap'n Crunch cereal and

Luis Aparicio.

That was my reality—the life that I knew. Didn't everyone have a *Torah* in their trunk?

Walking and Talking

And the real reason that I never knew how to answer the question about what it was like being a rabbi's son was this: MSS—though a beloved rabbi—was a real person: human, playful, smart, expressive, funny, loving—and human. He was good at many things, but at others was decidedly more average. Once when our new neighbor watched Dad struggling to build a *Sukkah* for the first time in our new house on Harrison, he noted that building shelters—even temporary ones—was not a particular strength of MSS when he said, "I don't think that shed's gonna last too long."

My father isn't bigger than life. He's not unapproachable. He's a real person, just like the other fathers in the world. He made eggs for breakfast, sent us to our rooms when we misbehaved, played catch with us in the front yard, and yelled—and even swore—when he got angry.

In reading this collection of his sermons, you'll notice how he set a fairly high bar for how he hoped his congregants would conduct themselves in their daily lives—as Jews, as family members, as a community, and as individuals. He talked the talk—an insightful talk that revealed how well he understood the lives, the struggles, and the needs of people, his congregants in particular. He had high hopes and an optimistic outlook.

But how do you preach a higher ground and live a normal life at the same time? It's a bit like a tightrope, I believe, with its own built-in tensions.

As his now-adult son, I have grown to understand the depths of the tension that I know he felt when he delivered his sermons. I now know that sometimes he struggled with that message. He wondered—to himself, mostly, but occasionally to others whom he trusted—how people would feel if they ever found out that he didn't quite walk the walk that he talked about so often. That he, himself, was imperfect, human, normal?

There was the time, for example, when he went to the emergency room one night after experiencing some chest pains, and they decided to keep him overnight for observation. When one of the hospital chaplains he knew came by to visit him, he was a bit embarrassed, and asked the chaplain not to tell anyone that he was there. "Ah," said the chaplain. "You don't want anyone to know you're human, eh!"

I believe we all have a tension between the life that we live inside our skin and the one we show to others. When we see other people who seem strong, confident, and capable, we sometimes compare our insides—our insecure, scared, inadequate insides—to those confident-looking outsides, and we invariably come up short. Perhaps we even feel like impostors.

I have come to appreciate that tightrope MSS sometimes walked—that perhaps there was too wide a gap between the talk he talked and the walk he walked. Did people know that he likes bacon? That sometimes he found board meetings frustrating? That he wasn't really an expert on the *Talmud*? That he liked to have a cocktail with dinner? That sometimes when we were on vacation we didn't light the *Shabbat* candles? That our family faced some of the same family struggles that he addressed from the *bimah*?

Did people care? *L'hefech*. The opposite is true. I believe they loved him even more!

People may have called MSS many things over the year, but I never heard someone call him an impostor. I have heard people call him human, insightful, and truthful. And a truth I know is this: Real people have real-life struggles, even in the rabbinate. That's what I love about him—his struggles, his imperfections, and specifically that tension he felt between what he said and how he acted.

Of course, it wouldn't have really mattered if someone "outed' him upon discovering that he likes bacon. People respected him because he shared enough of himself that they got to know the real MSS. Not all the details of his life, not all of his *mishagass*, as he would say, but enough so that they recognized his humanity. When he finally found the personal courage to share details about his struggles with depression, for example, it didn't turn people off. They appreciated him even more.

That's why his words—the ones in these sermons and bulletin columns—will still resonate and impact their readers. Those who are reading them for the first time will find that they're learning from someone who could be their friend, their neighbor, their card-playing companion, the guy they see working out at the Y, or the guy sitting in front of them at the ballpark yelling for the Sox manager to yank his pitcher out of the game. Or the guy who invited the youth group to his house at the end of every summer, teaching them how to play round-robin ping pong.

The walk that MSS has always walked may not totally measure up to the talk that he talked, but that made his message even more accessible. It made his words even more appreciated. They didn't come down from on high, but they came from a beloved peer, a regular guy who showed, time after time, that he understood our struggles and our tensions. Because deep down, he faced them too. And in his actions, he was letting us know that while it was good to strive for a certain life, it was important for all of us to recognize our own humanity, which sometimes meant realizing that it was OK when we fell short—that we could forgive ourselves and love ourselves even when we didn't measure up entirely. Be yourself, from top to bottom, from strengths to weaknesses, when you live your life and when you preach from the *bimah*. Talk the inspiring talk, and walk as best you can, and accept yourself even when you fall short. I think that's a pretty good way that you get to be called a "rabbi's rabbi."

Rav Todot, Many Thanks

Putting this book together with MSS has certainly been a labor of love. Together we have chosen a relatively small number of sermons from the many hundreds—and perhaps thousands—that he has given since the late 1950s. We chose sermons that are still relevant today, though some of the details may have changed in the ensuing years. But the challenges Jews faced in contemplating the presidential election in 1968 turn out to be the same issues that we contemplate as Jews in 2016. His perspectives on Martin Luther King, Jr., one of his personal heroes, are particularly interesting to us today, in part because of the historical value of his words, but also because of how much we still today struggle with issues of racial justice.

There were some logistical challenges, of course. My daughter Natalie drew the difficult task of trying to decipher his scribbles as she typed the sermons from pre-digital paper copies. The punctuation and spelling MSS used over 45 years in the rabbinate changed from sermon to sermon and needed to be made consistent. And MSS was a frequent user of ellipses…because the sermons were originally meant to be spoken, not read. But the advantage was that I got to read so many of the words that my friends and I grew up with—some that I remembered and many more that I had never heard.

And I got to read—and occasionally edit—the wonderful contributions from others for this book. It was no small task convincing MSS that this book would be better with those contributions from so many of his former students, colleagues, and friends. He was hesitant to go along with the idea, concerned that this would seem to others to be a vanity project. (Who writes a book and invites others to heap praises upon him?) But this book came together for many reasons, one of which was that so many people would want to own a copy of it or, perhaps more importantly, many would continue to be moved and inspired by his words.
In an attempt to calm his concerns, I remember invoking the words of BJBE's Rabbi Brian Stoller, spoken from the *bimah* during High Holidays 5776, when he suggested that we shouldn't wait for eulogies to say wonderful things about those we love. The words of so many contributors only serve to remind us all of what MSS brought to those who trusted him enough to invite him to guide them along their journeys. And he gets to see what they wrote.

We received a tremendous amount of support and enthusiasm for making this book happen, from current congregants to former BJBE-ers to those in the Facebook group, "I am a Jewish Leader and Mark S. Shapiro was my Rabbi" that Ira Wise started some years back. We're grateful for the support of Rabbi Kedar, the rest of the BJBE staff, the Jacobson and Splansky families, and the BJBE Board of Directors, for stepping forward to help fund the production of this book.

I hope you'll love reading this collection as much as have I loved putting it together.

B'shalom,
–SAS

Foreword

My brother, Mark Shapiro, was a unique congregational rabbi—
unique in that he was just so good at so many things. He was a
wonderful leader, teacher, counselor, scholar, and more. And he
also gave great sermons.

When you were at a BJBE service, you could sense the congregation's anticipation as sermon time grew near. When Rabbi
Shapiro said, "Close your books," you knew you were in for
something special. And he made it look easy. It was like watching
an athlete at the top of his game. A Mark Shapiro sermon was like
a perfect golf swing: great set-up, great finish, simple yet powerful.

Simple yet powerful. Those words, in particular, describe
Mark Shapiro's sermons. And by simple, I only mean that the
message was clear and uncomplicated. Mark didn't use his sermons to show how smart he was or how erudite he could be. He
had a message to give and he gave it. And always the message was
meaningful and insightful, whether it had to do with Judaism,
political action, ethics, or just the human condition.

And always there was humor. Our father, Marvin Shapiro,
was a salesman all his life; he was also a very funny man. He often
said that he used humor to engage his customers and help make
the sale. I saw a lot of our father when Mark gave a sermon. In a
way, he was a salesman and what he was selling was his message.
And he often used humor to engage the listener. I think he made
the sale every time his sermon moved you or provided an important insight or called you to action.

Here's a tip for you if you were fortunate enough to hear Rabbi Shapiro give a sermon:

Don't just read these sermons; rather picture in your mind's eye Mark on the *bimah* and listen to him talking to you. You'll hear the familiar cadence and rhythm, the cajoling, the soft words of wisdom, and the loud demand that we Jews must be righteous.

Here are some things you will see:

The deep breath and pause. That means, "I've told you a lot. I'll stop for a moment to let us catch our collective breath."

The tapping of two fingers on the lectern. That means, "Listen to this. I'm about to tell you something important."

And my favorite—the expression on his face as he begins a sentence with the word "Look." This, as you knew, was a time to pay attention.

A final word. These sermons were given over a period of some 45 years. If you read them chronologically, you will get a real sense not only of Mark's development as a sermon giver, but also as a rabbi, a thinker, and a human being.

So sit back, relax, and read (and hopefully see and hear) Rabbi Mark Shapiro at his best.

This is a real page-turner. Enjoy.

–Ben Shapiro

Beginnings

Shabbat Shuvah 5719/1958
Jonesboro, Arkansas

*As a student at Hebrew Union College, MSS served as
rabbi in a number of small Jewish communities, including
Bogalusa, Louisiana; Kokomo, Indiana; and Schulenburg,
Texas. He served as student rabbi at Temple Israel in
Jonesboro during his fourth year in rabbinical school.*

WE LIVE IN A WORLD OF EXPERIMENTATION, testing
and change. Never have the words of some homespun
philosopher been truer—"If you didn't like what we
have today, then just wait a minute." Textbooks are coming
out with experimental editions, fashions are changing with
extraordinary rapidity, medical science is moving forward every
day with lightning speed, and discoveries are occurring that our
great-grandfathers would not have believed.

If you have seen a diagram of the U.S. Rocket Testing Base at
Cape Canaveral, the importance of experimentation in modern life
is even more strongly impressed upon us. It seems like the ancient
Greek gods are with us again when we see testing spots reserved
for Atlas, Jupiter, and Thor; and then, of course, the secret areas
where none but the most trusted and necessary workers are
permitted. Cape Canaveral seems like a world where everyone's
watch is running at double-time, experiment after experiment,
change after change.

And sometimes I wonder if the congregations that are served
by student rabbis on a bi-weekly basis mustn't feel as if they were

living in the midst of Cape Canaveral. A new student rabbi every year, some of us, frankly, wet behind the ears. It must be difficult to have someone new every year, with different ideas, wanting to change this and that, waiting to experiment with a poor helpless congregation. It's easy to be in favor of change and new ideas, but when one has to put up with it year in and year out, it must get rather wearisome. It's like the group of teenage girls in Birmingham who were planning in January for a dance they would hold in May. One suggests that the theme be outer space. "No," said another. "Everyone will be tired of that by May."

Not only is the congregation subject to a new person every year, but there are other recurring problems that we know only too well. Size is a constant problem. With few members a congregation simply cannot do what larger congregations can. Almost all of the congregation's work must be done on a volunteer basis, which certainly is a hardship on many. Yet Abravanel said, "The fact that the heavenly bodies are large while man is small is no proof of their greater importance." We should know that with all the problems that must attend every small congregation, we are truly the strength of Judaism, for only we can truly be a congregation.

The *Talmud* tells us that we must not begin with a tale of woe. We know there are problems, but let us consider that for every problem we have a strength that makes that problem solvable.

We have what no sprawling, spreading, monster-size congregation can ever have—we have unity. And unity, togetherness, is one of Judaism's most important commands. The *Talmud* is so interested that men live together in harmony that it asks the following riddle and gives this rather startling answer. Two men are walking in the desert. They have but a little water between them. It is enough water to keep one man alive, but if they split the water both will die. What shall they do? The *Talmud* answers, "They shall split the water and both die for it says in the Bible that thy brother shall live with thee, and if he cannot live with thee, you must die together."

Though we prize unity, we might be tempted to give a more practical, and in the long run, more humane answer. Yet the fact that Jews have lived together and died together has been the cohesive force which has kept us alive as a group.

We can be united as few congregations in the world can, we can know each other. What would the rabbis of old, what would our great-grandfathers have said if they were to see the 1,500-family congregations that abound in our big cities? What would they say to a congregation where the rabbi cannot know every member? Where each member does not know every other member, where two percent of the congregation must do the work of the other ninety-eight percent who are not interested or will not be interested? As Brandeis said, "The curse of bigness has prevented proper thinking."

But thank God, we shall never be simply numbers or names on a mailing list to our fellow congregants. We will never be merely ships that pass in the night to one another. Instead, we are a congregation, knowing one another, loving one another for our individual virtues, bearing with one another for our individual failings. We are the true congregation.

Not only is our size the factor that has united this congregation for years, but it is also our real source of strength. We can each speak our mind so that the other may hear. There is room for us to work side by side, whether it be for the education of our children, planning for our own religious and educational needs, or joining with one another on the joyous and sad occasions of life. We must be a do-it-yourself congregation and there is no one who works so hard, so valiantly, as the devoted person who works for the love of helping his own Jewish community.

Now we are beginning—beginning again for the 61st year. It is my privilege to serve you this year. There is much that I hope to bring you, there is much that I know I shall take away with me. As unity has been our strength for these many years, so let it now be our strength.

Eloheinu v'elohei avoteinu—our God and God of our fathers—May our year together be a year of toil and accomplishment, a year in which the hearts of the parents will be drawn to the hearts of the children. A year where the heart of man will be drawn unto his fellow man, a year where all our hearts may be drawn unto Thee.

Shulayim: Phyllis Steiner

"Close your books."

That short instruction from my rabbi heightened my attention—here comes his sermon. I'm excited, as it always seems as if his words are directed only to me. How does he do that? After the sermon is finished, I look around to see everyone nodding their heads at each other, giving a secretive "thumbs-up" as a silent grade. Walking out after services we are all talking about the words of wisdom imparted to us and we'll be talking about the sermon on the way home and even afterwards. But the messages are so dear that I must own them, adding this year's sermons to that swollen folder of treasured words next to my bed, so I can read them again, and again. The messages are classic in that they are as powerful and as fresh as if they had just been written.

Phyllis Steiner has been a BJBE congregant for many years and served in several staff positions, including Family Education Director.

Tz'dakah Means Righteousness

Rosh Hashanah 5726/1965

*In 1965, MSS marched in Selma, Alabama, one of hundreds
of clergy who joined in support of Dr. Martin Luther King,
Jr., and the black communities in the South. Social justice
was important to him, and he felt that Jews had a special
responsibility to demand justice for communities of color.
In this particular sermon from the 1960s, he talks about
applying the principle of Tz'dakah to encourage a greater
understanding of the effects of racism.*

JUDAISM IS A WAY OF LIFE REPLETE WITH SPECIAL WORDS, words hallowed by centuries of usage—words like justice, mercy, belief, understanding, holiness, goodness, truth. Rabbi Shimon could say that the world stands upon some of these words, chiefly in his view learning, prayer, and goodness, and no Jew ever questioned the propriety of those words as goals.

The need of the modern Jew is not for more words or for different words. The need is for someone to take these value words and relate them to our day, to our lives, and to our problems. "Help us apply this, rabbi." This is what today's Jews ask.

Let us on this morning of a New Year try to apply one word, *Tz'dakah*, which means righteousness or sometimes justice. Let us apply it to our day and to this hour.

How to apply it may be difficult, but where to apply it is evident. There is yet a growing injustice, a glaring lack of righteousness that exists in our midst. The crisis of white and Negro in America is not solved, not for all the legislation and all the marches. The bloodshed of Watts only proves it. There is a great inequality in the land, a great lack of *Tz'dakah*—justice. If you doubt it, then read that the unemployment rate among white males has never been lower, yet never higher among Negro males, and we know the importance of a job and an income.

You have heard about the civil rights struggle before—from me, and from others. But it has not gone away, it does not. And today the feeling of some that the problem is solved makes it all the more crucial, for it is not solved.

America's Negro community has begun to feel the depth of its disgrace and has begun to organize to make changes in the social order. What shall we do? What does *Tz'dakah* ask us to do?

First, *Tz'dakah* asks us to examine our own feelings.

And if we do so, is it not true of you and me that we have a subterranean and lurking hatred and fear of Negroes? Let us not be quick to deny it. I think it is almost impossible for a white, middle-class Jew to have grown up in this American age without acquiring some of America's basic and neurotic outlook toward men of dark skin. The attitude that they are dangerous, should be avoided, isolated and locked away from our world.

The rabbis said that within each of us exist the *Yetzer Rah*, the evil instinct. It has taken a different form in different ages but in this age it assumes the form, among others, of unreasoning animosity toward Negroes.

We get nowhere at all until we admit it. I spent the summer living in Chicago's highest-level integrated community. My family and I lived there with a daily commitment to the *mitzvah* of civil rights, and yet I felt the anti-black man *yetzer* stirring within me even there.

One late night in August I saw a Negro man walk down the street in front of our Woodlawn Avenue residence, and I saw him look at the house. My imagination quickly made that man into a potential housebreaker, thief, and rapist. And I was afraid. Yet I know that the same actions on the part of a white man would not have aroused such emotion within me!

I am confident that this is not merely my *mishagass*—that it is ours, and that America has given it to us. Norman Podhoretz, a dedicated liberal, more ethical than most of us, wrote the following in an article entitled "My Negro Problem and Ours." Podhoretz said:

> "I now live on the Upper West Side of Manhattan, where there are many Negros and many Puerto Ricans. And there are nights when I experience the old apprehension again and there are streets that I avoid when I am walking in the dark, as there were streets that I avoided when I was a child. I find that I am not afraid of Puerto Ricans. But I cannot restrain my nervousness whenever I pass a group of Negroes standing or sauntering down the street. I feel ashamed and guilty—but the fear and hatred I still feel for Negroes is the hardest of all the old feelings to admit."

Is he not speaking for us, too?

When four Negro girls were killed in church, when Negroes in Selma were assaulted by men with clubs on horseback, we felt sympathy for the underdogs and anger at the assaulters. But what about the riots in Watts, when the aggressors were Negroes? Were we as angry at them as we were at the white state troopers? No, most of us were enraged at the Negro rioters, as if they were rioting directly against us.

And when that police chief of Los Angeles gave his revealing evaluation of the situation, saying. "Now we are on top and they are on the bottom," how many of us secretly applauded the racism which breathed in that offhand remark?

We hate murder, but I am afraid that deep down, we hate blacks murdering whites much more intensely than we hate whites murdering blacks.

That is the evil within us! An evil emotion which we did not create, but which dogs our footsteps nevertheless. You and I know that it is wrong. We know that it is a child's fear and a child's hatred, not a man's. And for the sake of *Tz'dakah*, for the sake of justice, we as Jews must see it, and try to uproot it or subdue it.

How to subdue one's evil inclination? The rabbis of the *Midrash* suggested that if the evil instinct should accost you on the road and suggest all forms of wickedness, you should drag him off to the house of study where he will become subdued, in other words, drag him off to be educated.

And the racist instinct within us should get an education, too. It should be shown what's really happening in the world of slum-locked Negroes, and how deeply the inequities go.

So, drag that instinct off to the high-rise apartments which dot the Chicagoland inner-city scene, and look closely enough to see that these are not at all like Prairie Shores or 1000 Lake Shore Drive. Notice that there are three children for every adult jammed into these structures, and notice the postage stamp size of the playground. Look at the runways rising high in the air, runways which must be both yards for the adults and yards for all the kids. Learn that garbage collection is hit or miss, more miss than hit, and that the elevators can stand in disrepair in these 16-story buildings for days on end, and then you may understand why the Negro community refers to its high-rises as Alcatraz instead of gracious living high-rises!

Speak to youngsters around the playground. Ask them what they want to be, and hear them respond that they all want to be janitors, for the building janitors are the highest ranking professionals that they ever see, and represent the highest ranking job to which the Negro child thinks he can aspire. No aspirations for doctor or lawyer as we would undoubtedly get from our children. There is some lack of *Tz'dakah* here, some lack of justice.

Go to the South Side and watch youngsters involved in a recreation program. The leader is playing a game which almost all children know and love, the game of "make up a story as you go along." The leader begins the story and then stops. "Now go on with it," you say to the six-year-old at your side. The Negro child says: "But I don't know the story." There is no story already made up, says the leader. "You can make it up your own way."

The child does not understand; none of them do. None of them can conceive of a story that is just being created, and so they can only repeat the same response: "I never heard this story before."

Now if a six-year-old with a decent IQ cannot play this game, something is very wrong somewhere; for this child there has been no *Tz'dakah*. Yes, the schools should help her, but studies show that while the average Negro youngster enters school with an IQ at a relatively normal rung, it actually goes down in the first three years of grammar school, while the IQ of youngsters in more middle class neighborhoods goes up. Why?

For more reasons than we yet fully understand or want to, but here are some: Because the teachers available to slum children are often the least capable or the greenest. Because some teachers who go to teach in slum schools come with a patronizing, sometimes already biased attitude, a few wearing actual or invisible gloves all day to avoid contact with the school building, the youngsters, or the neighborhood. Because some teachers approach their slum classes expecting them to be unable to learn much and thus unconsciously help in making it true. Because, all protest to the contrary, less is spent per pupil in slum schools than in middle-class or even lower-class white schools.

There must be some basic *Tz'dakah* lacking here.

The Negro youngster is given a primary reader inhabited by white Dick and white Jane, happy white children who use their graded and dull vocabulary in a sterile suburban atmosphere of home and lawns and trees. Some white youngsters can have trouble relating to Dick and Jane and their cousins, but what of Negro youngsters? Detroit tried to solve the problem and create a primary reader for Negro youngsters. Unfortunately the heroes turned out to be Dick and Jane in blackface, Negro Dick and Jane in that same suburban somewhere which was still never-never-land to slum kids.

Of course it is not all the fault of the school. Of course these youngsters come to school the very first day with a disadvantage, the disadvantage of their homes. Economically low-class homes, slum homes, black or white, are not verbal homes as middle-class homes are. There is very little conversation or dialogue or enrichment in slum homes. The slum child's world is woefully small. Two thirteen-year-olds, living at Roosevelt and Blue Island, a mile-and-a-half from the heart of Chicago, had never been to the Loop before they went to march with Dr. King this last summer. And the educators say: "The more a child sees and hears, the more he wants to see and hear."

This deprivation of the slum-child, preschooler, and school-goer is certainly far from *Tz'dakah*. Someone must care about evening up his life for him.

Walk the streets of the West Side, if you dare, and find out what a police car means. To you, to me, to most of us most of the time, a police car means something secure and protecting. The policeman works for you, and is ready to help you. Not so to the West Side Negro. To him the policeman is the representative of the whole societal structure which makes him a second-class Chicagoan.

A crowd of Negro youngsters gathers at a corner. A police car moves in next to them. "Keep moving boys," says the voice with the badge. "Keep moving."

Keep moving... to where? Where can a slum teenager go and be left alone? Where but to drink or to marijuana or to jail—the usual road.

I have seen crowds of youngsters on suburban corners, and no police car rumbles up and tells them to "keep moving, boys." There is a glaring lack of *Tz'dakah* somewhere in all this.

Take that racist instinct of ours to the scene of the most tragic hours, to the ghetto of Watts, California, home of the people who clean up after the middle class, who carry the bags of Los Angeles, and who lose even those jobs when the machines take over. The first reaction of many of us is to say, "How much do they want? How dare they loot and destroy property and break laws?" What is overlooked by most is that the rioters of Watts burned their own neighborhoods and their own homes. Looting took place in Negro neighborhoods, not white neighborhoods. And hatred of one's own environment does not grow without some grounds and does not grow overnight. What is the cause? Let Dr. Kenneth

Clark of NYU try to explain:

> "The inmates of the ghetto have no stake in respecting
> property because they do not possess it. It possesses them.
> Property is an instrument by which others exploit them.
> Stores in the ghetto overcharge for inferior goods. Ghetto
> people may obtain the symbol of America's advertised
> higher standard of living: radios, TVs, washing machines,
> cars. But only through the most usurious extra carrying
> costs. They do not respect property because property is
> almost invariably used to degrade them."

And anyone who looks to prove that need not go to Watts.
Look in the windows of credit jewelry stores in the black belts
and see the gaudy bangles which are passed off as valuable items
and which bear expensive price tags. Some defend the merchants
by saying, "That's what these people came to buy." But a better
day can never come if we keep condoning the actions of those
who exploit a slum dweller. Too many of these merchants get rich
on him; not enough care about enriching his life. And there is no
Tz'dakah in any of this, neither in Watts nor on Chicago's 63rd
Street.

Our lack of *Tz'dakah* is not merely something to regret. It is
something to fear as well. For the other ghetto areas of the land
are riots waiting to happen, awaiting only the spark which will
ignite.

So what can we do today? Realizing the inequity, subduing as
best we can that part of us which remains neurotically hostile to
dark men, what can we do about bringing *Tz'dakah* where it is
needed?

In small part it is to do as it has been done, to pass laws and
ensure the right to vote. But to say that from today on we will give
the Negro equal opportunity everywhere, and that is the end of it,
is to delude ourselves that *Tz'dakah* is easy. It is not. Nat Hentoff
points out "that to give the Negro equal opportunity today, and
only that, is like offering a man who has one leg the right to enter
a race with a man who has two." To say that qualified Negroes

will get good jobs sounds very principled and moral, until we realize that 300 years of no opportunity have made hardly any Negro men qualified. What about them?

Jews often react to this by saying, "Well, what about us?" When our fathers came here they had some strikes against them, too—their names, their beards, their strange ways. Somehow they got into the race and didn't do too badly.

What we forget is that our ancestors had something else to stand upon, which Negroes have lost, and that is a tradition of manhood and learning. We had a 4,000-year history to lean on, and America allowed us to remember it. But the slavery system stripped the Negro of his name, his African history, and heritage and values. Only today are we, along with the Negro himself, beginning to understand what a dignified intellectual history Africans had. But white America took it away from the black man and left him naked of yesterday's glory, clothed only with today's humiliation.

So we Jews cannot say with any sense of *Tz'dakah* to the Negro: "We'll give you a shot at it, as we were given. Go out and make the grade." The Negro has no tools for making the grade, and no campaign of self-improvement in the Negro community. No barnstorming by Willie Mays and Thurgood Marshall is going to succeed without outside help and understanding. The Jews in the Warsaw ghetto were doomed to extinction when they began to fight for their lives. They had no rifles, few guns. The Negro child in a slum school, as the Negro male in the job market, has no weapon to wage the struggle, and his defeat in the handicap-free race is also a foregone conclusion.

What is *Tz'dakah* in this day? It cannot be letting the healthy race with the sick and applaud ourselves for giving everyone a fair chance. Judaism never saw justice as being so inflexible. When we read the injunction about a man who gleans his harvest we see that he must leave everything he cannot gather in his first harvesting to the poor. Does it not belong to the landowner, you might ask? If justice is strict and blind, it does. But our tradition gives justice compassionate eyes, and decrees that a part of what the rich man owns actually belongs to the impoverished. When we read about the offerings that Jews were asked to bring to the priest in order to atone for themselves, we see that the law asked much more of the wealthy than of the underprivileged. Here too, *Tz'dakah* was the justice that understood the difference between men.

And so we must be prepared to give more than simple mathematical equality to the Negro who is the unwilling invalid of modern America. Difficult as it may be for some rugged individualists to swallow, we will have to adopt preferential hiring practices, and give the needy a head start in many other areas. Industry has a community responsibility for schooling, but particularly in slum schooling, and that surely means ninety percent Negro schools. The demand of *Tz'dakah* today is to right old wrongs, to atone by giving extra help to those who have gone without it for so long.

And is it only to ease our conscience that we must carry on this work of *Tz'dakah*? No, not completely. We do it to build a new kind of society for ourselves and our children. I am not happy to live in a world where I must always be running away from the expanding numbers of slums and slum dwellers. I do not want to uproot myself every six or eight years to move farther and farther away. There are not enough expressways or developments in the world to keep me forever away from having Negro neighbors. So we need a world which has decided not to run away any more from poor men, from black men, from sick men, nor from the invalids of society. We cannot afford the expense of running away, for it costs the purse greatly, and it costs the soul even more dearly.

A world of *Tz'dakah* today means a world of justice triumphant. Knowing ourselves, knowing our inner hatreds, we can yet build a world which breathes *Tz'dakah*.

Lo alecha ham'lacha ligmor, v'lo ata ben chorin l'hibateil mimenah. It is not incumbent upon us to complete all this work. But neither are we free to withdraw from its demands.

May the God who told us what *Tz'dakah* means, be with us and give us strength.

Amen.

Elijah was at Our House

April 8, 1966

Who is this mythical prophet Elijah who somehow visits all of our Seder tables each year, and for whom we always leave a cup of wine? MSS had many ideas of what a modern-day encounter with Elijah might look like, including a real-life encounter in the early '80s with a man named Jack. But that would be almost 20 years after he delivered this Pesach sermon about what it means for us to open our doors to Elijah the prophet.

AT SEDER TIME, YEAR AFTER YEAR, someone in everybody's house is bound to ask, "Does Elijah really come in when we open the door?"

Now that should be an easy question to answer, but often it isn't. Frankly, I have different answers every year. Some years I just let my brain take over and say to everyone that Elijah's coming isn't something we really expect, that it's only an idea that we're expressing, an idea about opening the door to everyone who is hungry or in need or doesn't have a home of his own in which to celebrate Passover.

But some years I forget about the logical part of my brain, and let my imagination and my heart take over. And in such years I like to imagine that Elijah really could walk into our homes if he wanted to, invisible certainly. He wouldn't make speeches, shake hands, or maybe not even drink the wine, because if he drank all the wine that Jews set aside for him he wouldn't be able to find his way around.

And when I imagine that Elijah could really enter our homes, I imagine something else. I imagine that we wouldn't know until afterward whether he was there or not. Maybe later that night or the next day or the next week, we would look around at one another and we would suddenly smile and say, "You know... he was here, wasn't he?"

It reminds me of a story I once heard of a man who bought a house. The house had remained unsold for years, because the people of that area believed it was haunted. But this man didn't believe in ghosts or haunted houses, and he liked this large rambling old mansion with its expanse of lawns. So he bought the house. And after he signed the mortgage the real estate agent told him. "You know, the people in the neighborhood say that the ghost is a rather friendly ghost anyway. And by the way, they all say that when you see the ghost you won't realize it till afterward."

Well, he laughed a little and he said he didn't mind meeting any ghost whether he knew it then or later. And he went around exploring his property, and getting acquainted with his neighbors. He talked to the lady who lived on the north side who had some dogs for sale and she said that she had never seen the ghost but she had heard about it. The new owner stopped at the little farmhouse on the west of his new house and he met an old gentleman, a farmer, who said his name was Horace, and who said he had lived in that area for many years. The farmer said that he didn't believe in the ghost either and he invited the new owner back to visit him the next week, when the farmer would have some fresh apples for sale. The newcomer visited the large old home just east of his new property and met the Harper family. All of them had heard rumors about a ghost but they had never really been bothered by it, so they weren't concerned. They invited him to stay for lunch that day and all of them became good friends.

The newcomer liked the Harpers so much that he stopped over to see them quite a few times that week. About a week later he was at the Harpers' and he said to them, "Why don't we all go over to see that farmer, Horace, and see if his apples are for sale yet."

"How far away is it?" asked the Harpers.

"Far away?" said our hero, "Why it's just a few yards from my front lawn. You know the farmhouse, the farmer, that nice old gentleman who's lived there so long."

And the Harpers didn't say a word for a moment.

And then Mr. Harper cleared his throat and said, "That farmhouse hasn't been lived in for 30 years."

"But I met Horace!" said the man. And he raced out of the Harpers' house toward the farmhouse where he had seen the old gentleman. He burst in the front room of the farmhouse and ran into cobwebs and stale air. There was no one there. There had obviously been no one there for years.

And then the real estate agent's words came back to him. "They say that he's a rather friendly ghost anyway. And by the way… they all say that when you see the ghost you won't realize it until afterward."

I always liked that story. And it reminded me of Elijah's coming in. I don't think you know till afterward that he's been there.

You'll know that he has been there by seeing what he leaves behind.

But don't look in the corners to find it… it's not an *afikomen*, candy, or *matzah*. No, Elijah doesn't leave calling cards like that. But if we can imagine that he really could come, the gift that he would leave would be a special feeling. Not a feeling in the air, not a cloud, but a feeling in you and in all the people in your family.

You only know afterward whether or not he's been there. And how do you know? Well, we have to ask how you feel the day after *Seder*, or three days after, like today, or a week from now. How you feel about the rest of the people who live in your house. When your father tells you that you can't have something you think you want, do you raise the roof and yell or go off in a corner to brood? Or do you know that Elijah's been there because you feel that father knows best, and that even if you're not happy at being refused, you know that you're loved? How do you feel about your big brother or your little sister? Does it seem to you that they are as bad and as irritating as they always have been? Or can you more easily say, "Well after all, he's older or she's younger, and I guess that all of us are different." If you can say something like that, then Elijah was there.

And what of us adults? Is the kids' noise getting worse and worse? Does the *afikomen* hunt give us nothing more than a massive headache? Is the Passover *matzah* a burden instead of a treat? Do you talk to one another in grunts? Or have we got a new feeling about all our loved ones, understanding that children are simply that, children, not little adults, and that we have to judge our husbands or wives by their own standards and not by ours? If we have this new understanding and judgment then afterwards we can know that Elijah was there.

How do you feel on waking up in the morning? Is it with a groan, and a mumbled curse? Is it with an aching head that you confidently expect will get worse as the dreadful day goes on? Do you mutter a prayer that we can somehow get through the daylight hours again? If so, he didn't make it to your house, or maybe you closed the door too soon. But if somehow the hardest morning can be just a little exciting, if you can praise God for the dreary day as much as for the brilliant one, if you can wake up and think lovingly of the loved ones that will surround you that day, then Elijah was there, really there, in your house.

And how do you feel about your life—your school life, your housekeeping life, your synagogue life, your breadwinning life? Is it just one thing after another, never quite getting ahead, outgo always beating income by three lengths at the wire? Or is every experience in your life just another chance to flex your muscles and your mind and accept the challenges as if they were fresh starts every morning? In baseball the season begins over again each year, and the A's and Astros don't start with any handicaps in the standings. Last year is forgotten, and if necessary we can forget yesterday too. If we find ourselves feeling this new way, then surely Elijah was at our houses, though we did not know it till now.

The greatest secret of all is this, however: If he can come into our lives, he can come anytime we open the door… at holidays, after holidays, and in between holidays. He will come whenever the right door, the door of our hearts, is opened. He will come and leave his gifts with us, and later we will look around at one another and suddenly we will say. "He was here, wasn't he?"

Was Elijah at your house? If not will you let him in now? Open the door wide. Open it wide.

Shulayim: Roy Splansky

Since the day my life began, I have considered Rabbi Shapiro to be my rabbi. I mean this literally—I am told that he officiated at my bris in 1963, just a year after he joined *B'nai Jehoshua*.

I didn't attend religious school at BJBE. It's not where I had my *bar mitzvah*, nor where I was confirmed. It was, however, my second temple, the one where generations of Splanskys and Sabaths—my grandparents, great-grandparents, aunts, uncles, and cousins—attended. It was a place where I had many friends from OSRUI and youth group. It was also where I found a rabbi with whom I felt a personal and inspirational connection.

I have fond memories attending services at 901 Milwaukee, sitting next to my great-grandmother Stella and listening to sermons unlike no other, sermons with messages I could relate to. I remember my mother talking about how much she liked Rabbi Shapiro and how she felt a spiritual connection with his words.

I always felt special at BJBE, and appreciated how Rabbi Shapiro took such an interest in my life. It was for these reasons that I joined BJBE shortly after college graduation. He helped me begin my life with Karen 25 years ago, and has remained important to my family in the years since.

And I continue to love his sermons. Rabbi Shapiro has a wonderful gift of delivering a strong, important message with a gentle voice. We were entertained and enlightened. Often we laughed and we cried and sometimes we did both at the same time. We were also challenged to be better human beings, to be kind to one another and to do the right thing. Sometimes he told us what was right, but most of the time he didn't have to—we just needed the reminder.

"Close your books" became a welcome and familiar phrase spoken to us in his warm, friendly voice. What was really being said was, "Pay attention and open your mind. This is important." It was a simple expression packed with a direct message, a foreshadowing of what was coming.

So turn off those phones and computers. Open THIS book. This is important.

Roy Splansky joined BJBE in 1989. He and his family have been actively involved in the synagogue ever since.

Wonderland

Yom Kippur 5727/1966

---

*Over the years, MSS shared insights on many stories and
tales that were considered Jewish ones. But he also found
lessons in many of the mainstream stories, movies, books and
even TV shows of the time: "The Wizard of Oz," "Harvey,"
"M*A*S*H," and his favorite book as a child, "Tarzan of the
Apes." In this sermon, he shared his thoughts on another of
his favorites, Lewis Carroll's "Alice in Wonderland,"
asking aloud: "What would Alice think if she showed
up in our world today?"*

THE JEWISH TRADITION OF LAW, RITUAL LAW, and
case law, is known as *Halachah*. The Jewish tradition of
legends is known as *Aggadah*, and stands for all the stories,
narratives, and fanciful interpretations contained in the corpus of
Jewish writings.

Halachah, the law, seeks to give and to administer a
direction—what shall we do, at prayer at holidays, on rising and
retiring.

Aggadah, the tradition of stories, seeks to give not so much
a direction as it seeks to unearth the truth, the truth about man
and God and being Jewish. And so during these holidays we have
been dealing with *Aggadah*, not necessarily Jewish *Aggadah*, but
those stories which tell us something about what it is to live in
these days, what it is to be human, stories which dramatize our
predicament and our hopes.

It is, as we have noted, not accidental that certain stories have become beloved of every generation of the English-speaking world. A story grabs our hearts and our imagination because it tells the truth, a truth that we recognize either consciously, or sometimes, subconsciously.

And of such stuff is the classic, maybe the great English classic, written by an English schoolteacher, a math instructor, the Reverend Dodgson, known to us as Lewis Carroll: the wondrous story of *Alice in Wonderland*.

And I think that of all the English classics, Alice is the least understood, for most of us have dismissed it as nonsense. Lovely nonsense, rib-tickling nonsense, beautiful English tongue-in-cheek nonsense, but nonsense.

But what is it really about? I think it is about us. I think it speaks a truth and offers a direction.

For the story is about a seemingly imaginary Wonderland where the absurd rules. And yet the heroine, the Alice who makes the journey into the hole in the ground, through the sea of tears, into the land of the King and Queen of Hearts, always following that elusive white rabbit... this Alice is not absurd at all. She is a proper English schoolgirl who tries to remember her etiquette and her schoolbook wisdom when faced with the most irrational of situations. Alice, in a world of the absurd, gamely holds onto her sanity, though everyone tries to steal it from her.

And part of our involvement in the story is our whispered encouragement to Alice. "Hold on," we say, "hold on to the reality. Don't become insane or absurd like everyone else or you'll never get back home. Keep going and keep entertaining us, but hold on to your sanity."

And so she does. When she shrinks to twelve inches she searches for a way to get back to normal height, just as she does when she grows an enormous neck. When she is giant-sized, a bird flies at her and says, "You are a serpent bent on stealing my eggs." And Alice, looking certainly more like a serpent at that point than anything else, replies with full conviction, "No, I am a little girl." And though she cannot convince the bird, she never forgets her own identity.

She sees a cat in a tree which begins to disappear, leaving

only a grin. And no one else finds this at all strange, but Alice has a firm hold on reality and so she says, "Well I've often seen a cat without a grin, but never a grin without a cat. It's the most curious thing I ever saw in my life." And so we agree it is, for that is the reality.

She goes to a tea party with a Mad Hatter, which is an absurd affair, yet Alice always asks intelligent questions. She becomes involved in a senseless croquet game with the Queen of Hearts who keeps shouting about chopping someone's head off for hardly any cause. Eventually, Alice is put on trial in the most ludicrous court imaginable and is accused of crimes of which she has no knowledge. It is all absurd—entertaining and absurd. And even in court Alice tries to keep her reason with her, and as the story ends, Alice shouts to the Queen's soldiers, "You're nothing but a pack of cards!" And she awakens from the dream.

Alice in Wonderland is not merely a nonsense story. It is a tale of the absurd, in which reality and unreality are constantly and intentionally reversed, in which up is down and down is up, black is white and white black.

And therefore *Alice in Wonderland* was ahead of its time. For it is only in our day that writing about the absurd has caught hold of literature and particularly of drama. And thus we have today a rash of plays which no one can understand rationally—plays like *Waiting for Godot*, *Tiny Alice*, some of the off-Broadway happenings, and underground movies. All dramas absurd in themselves, irrational, yet trying to demonstrate that the world in which we live is equally absurd. Therefore, *Alice in Wonderland* is more a story of our day than any other.

What absurdities do we live with? More than a few. We live in an age which multiplies weapons in an attempt to gain world peace. We run for the moon while the Earth's problems are far from solved. We pay lip service to ideas which certainly do not affect our actions or run our lives. We pay lip service to honesty and the clean democratic process, while at the same time we know how much of our political life is colored by corruption and syndicate influence. We spend fortunes for funerals and scrimp on the needs of the living. Much of our life is therefore as irrational as the March Hare who solemnly posed riddles to which he had no answer.

Yet Alice kept looking for the answer, even to the most absurd riddles. Alice represents the hope that man in an absurd world could yet find the way to reasonable and responsible living.

So, what do you think Alice would say if she came to our world?

Imagine that the hole into which she fell deposited her not into the kingdom of the Queen of Hearts and the White Rabbit, but into the kingdom of American Jewry 1966. Would it have appeared a rational world to her, or would she have been just as astounded as she was in Wonderland?

I think she would be astounded, if she were as reasonable a little girl as she appears to be in her own story. And I am thinking of two areas of our present-day thinking that would seem absurd, and in a way they are related.

First, our Alice would find a Jewish community, rather prosperous, comfortable, relaxed, and even a trifle apathetic. She would find us this way some 25 years after forty percent of the world's Jews had been wiped out in that unspeakable Holocaust for which we have had to coin a new word... the *Shoah*, the senseless destruction of six million men, women, and children.

And Alice would see most of us living our pleasant lives, acting as if it had never been. Maybe she would ask a representative American Jew a question, maybe a question like this.

"Dear Sir, many of your people were slaughtered like cattle barely a few years ago, while the whole world looked on with not too much concern. Yet I do not hear you telling about it, nor living your life any differently than before. Has this not changed anything for you?"

And she would probably get a response like this: "Young lady, I wish you wouldn't start talking about that. You sound like a rabble-rouser. I've seen enough of those gory pictures and programs about the Nazis. I don't even let the kids watch it because it might give them nightmares. That's gone now, so forget it! And anyway, things are swell in America. The Catholics are talking nicely to the Jews, the Protestant minister and the priest and our rabbi have lunch together."

And if our Alice were aggressive, she might go on, "But sir, didn't you learn anything from that Holocaust?"

And our present day Mad Hatter might respond, "Learn anything? I've learned that the person who asks too many questions and reads too many papers and books can get very depressed. So I stay away from all of it."

And Alice would feel at home in an absurd Wonderland.

Admittedly, I among others have counseled you to ignore George Lincoln Rockwell and those of his type. But this is only because a battle against Rockwell would be a waste of energies that we should be using more profitably. But I cannot myself ignore, nor can I suggest you ignore, the possibility of catastrophe reoccurring.

Yet there are people who do hide in the sand. There are parents who are dead set against their youngsters hearing anything about Nazi Germany because of the anxiety it would create. There are those who want us to paint Jewish history as a nice nursery tale of heroes and fine ideas and to ignore the realities of what it has historically meant to be a Jew. They want us to teach that man is a fine upright creature, incapable of doing great intentional harm to another man. They want us to teach Sinai without also teaching Auschwitz.

But they fail to recognize something important, something suggested by the contemporary author Elie Wiesel. For Wiesel says that there was a revelation of truth at Sinai and there was a revelation of truth in the Nazi death camps. And I think he meant this: At Sinai the commandments were spread before humanity, and men realized how they could rise, they could be just and merciful and honest, for that is what God asked of them.

Yet the revelation at Auschwitz showed how far man could sink.

Alice, holding on to her sanity, would ask how we can ever forget, or why we would want to forget? She would point out that our wounds have healed far too soon. She would ask why we have fallen so quickly back into the apathy towards our faith that was characteristic of the pre-Nazi German Jews. She would ask why we believe that America can do no wrong. She would wonder why some of us still insist on going to interfaith activities looking for a kind word, instead of as representatives of a people who should be receiving the atonement of others, not apologizing for its continued existence.

Alice would find the apathetic post-war Jew as absurd as a Cheshire Cat, grinning when there is nothing to grin about.

And what would she say—WHAT WOULD SHE SAY?—about our world and us during the past three months, these past three months of Negro civil rights activity in communities very close to home? She could certainly not miss seeing some overtones of Auschwitz right around us. For the crazed people who spat at nuns and threw rocks at little children had descended to the level of animals. And contrary to popular opinion, it was not merely the roving bands of renegade hoodlums who threw curses and rocks. Women living in the area, dragging their children along by the hands, were also among the spitters and cursers and rock throwers.

And Alice would be able to see the reactions of us, we American Jews, supposedly intelligent, supposedly sensitive to human suffering. And what would she see?

She would see us hardening our resistance toward the Civil Rights Movement in the past few weeks. We, who had been sitting on the fence, somewhat sympathetic to Dr. King and his movement in a self-satisfied way.

And this means many of us in this auditorium.

You know it. Many of you have drawn the line at open occupancy in your neighborhood. Many of you have said, "This is going too far, all this street march agitating."

A great number of people who were only too happy to see their friends and their clergymen marching for voter rights in Selma, have now become opponents of the same kind of marches in their areas. They undoubtedly reason that Selma was far way and Gage Park is too close.

They go on to say that the marches only stir up trouble, only bring out the beast in people and only give the Nazi-types an opportunity to wave swastikas. And deep down they are probably saying that they do not want a free, open society.

Now what would our Alice say of this? Accustomed to the absurd by her adventures with the Queen of Hearts, Alice would feel right at home. Wonderland all over again, she might say. It grows more and more curious.

For how can people rationally cheer for civil rights in Alabama and hold back when the locale switches to urban and suburban Chicago? They cannot say that the South is worse, for the rock-throwers in Chicago were as violent as those among Southern whites. To have one philosophy for Selma and another for Chicago would seem to Alice a replay of the absurd croquet, in which the ground rules keep switching without announcement.

And how about the argument about "not stirring up trouble," or the principle of "see-no -evil, speak-no-evil, hear-no-evil," the argument that says that marches are wrong if they stir up hostility? Alice would find this wonderfully absurd. For hatred smoldering can be more dangerous than hatred expressed. Social progress is made by exposing our prejudices for what they really are, by making us see ourselves rationally.

But Alice would probably have the best laugh over the last absurdity. To see Jews who do not want a free society, open for everyone in housing and employment and protection. For our one hope as Jews for security is at last to be in a society which not only preaches equality but which enacts it. Our only hope is for a society where throwing rocks at minority groups is not only illegal but unacceptable. If the civil rights movement is given room to breathe, it just might make America mature overnight, more mature than any other society has ever been. It just might make America into the first society which does not use scapegoats. That is a dream, granted, but for us to turn away from the very movement which is working towards that end is the height of Wonderland absurdity. The prejudices of this generation do not have to be the biases of their children and grandchildren. And that is our only real hope for an America secure for our children.

In Wonderland, Alice alone was sane in a world peopled with Mad Hatters and March Hares and Cheshire grins without

Cheshire Cats, in a world where you could have your head chopped off for no reason. And while Alice kept trying to make sense of Wonderland, she had to wake up in order to regain her reason.

But the absurdities with which we have been living, and which we to some extent have been creating, are not a dream. We will not wake up to sanity. We must find our way there, in waking life.

And maybe on this *Yom Kippur* we are capable of seeing absurdities as never before. Maybe today, removed from the phone and the job and the apathy and the habitual prejudices... maybe today we can see that our Mad Hatters are indeed mad; that our religious apathy and our racial bigotry are not only immoral and un-Jewish, but hopelessly and insanely absurd.

Maybe we can regain our reason before it is too late, before the Queen of Hearts begins to look reasonable, before the nonsense verse of the Dormouse starts to be intelligible, before we too begin yelling, "Chop off their heads!"

Others have called us the wise people of the book. May God bring us back to our wisdom, our book, and our senses.

Finding
the Treasure

Family Services, Sept. 22, 1967

---

*MSS reserved special stories for family services, monthly
Shabbat gatherings with content that was appropriate for
younger folk. Prayers, rituals, and traditions were explained.
Children were invited up to the bimah with him during their
birthday months, and they marched up to the front of the ark
as he said, "(Insert month here) is a terrific month to have a
birthday." His family service sermon was more of a story-
telling, as is this one, a tale about the rabbi who dreamed of
finding a great treasure buried in a far-off place.*

B ECAUSE OF THE DIFFERENCE BETWEEN the Hebrew
calendar and the calendar we normally use, the High Holy
Days come quite late this year. *Rosh Hashanah* doesn't fall
for over a week-and-a-half yet, although in some ways we feel that
the Temple year has started already, with schools and activities.

And in some ways it's good for the holidays to come late,
for that gives us a better opportunity to prepare ourselves, to
get ourselves in the best frame of mind to enter those High Holy
Days.

This evening I have what I would call a story-and-a-half,
which says something about getting ready for the Holy Days.

The whole story is about Rabbi Isaac son of Rabbi Ezekiel
who lived in the town of Krakow, and if you think you have

ever met someone who was poor, well you never met Rabbi Isaac son of Rabbi Ezekiel. He was a scholar, not a worker or a businessman, and frankly, people used to take advantage of him. The grocer would cheat him, the butcher would overcharge him, and Rabbi Isaac, whose nose was usually in a book, didn't know what was happening. Eventually his clothes became rags and his little hut became not much stronger than a leaning *Sukkah*, yet Rabbi Isaac never lost his trust in God.

And one night Rabbi Isaac had a dream, and in the dream he saw himself. It must have been he; his clothes were like rags and his beard was gray and black and uncombed. There he was walking down the road to the large city of Prague, which contained the palace of the King. And in the dream Rabbi Isaac goes to the bridge that leads to the castle and he stops underneath the bridge, takes out a shovel from beneath his cloak and starts to dig under the bridge. He digs a little while and his shovel strikes a box. He unearths the box, opens it, and finds it filled with silver and gold. And then he awakens.

He stretches and yawns and says to himself, "What a dream for a poor man to have, finding a chest of treasure under the King's bridge in Prague!"

And the next night he dreamed again, and the same thing happened. He was walking to Prague with the shovel, stopping under the bridge, digging and finding the same treasure. And the next night the same dream. Three times in a row—exactly the same dream.

"Once," said Rabbi Isaac, "the dream could have come from the garlic I had for supper. Twice, it could have come from the onions. But three times? Didn't our saintly teacher say that a dream repeated three times comes from God Himself?"

And he took all his few belongings, including an old shovel, gathered them up and began the journey to Prague which was a walk of a day-and-a-half, at least.

And as he approached Prague, he saw in the distance the castle of the King and the bridge leading up to it. There under the bridge was a spot which looked quite a bit like the spot in the dream where he had found the chest of silver and gold. But as he prepared to go down there he saw a large sign: "No Trespassing! No Digging at All!"

And there was a guard standing right next to the bridge, whose job was to see that people obeyed the sign. Rabbi Isaac didn't know what to do. Every morning he came to the bridge and walked around it till evening, hoping that the guard might leave it for a little while, but he never did. Finally, the captain of the guard approached him.

"You have been walking around this bridge for quite a while now. Are you waiting for someone or looking for something?"

The captain seemed like a fairly kind man and Rabbi Isaac decided to take a chance and tell everything. He told the captain of the guard the whole story of the dreams.

"And so you see," he concluded, "having the same dream three times made me feel that it just might be true, so here I am."

The captain of the guard, kind as he was, began to laugh at the story.

"So you wore out your shoes just to come here, did you? Poor, silly man. You know, the same thing happened to me once, though I had sense enough to stay right here and not waste my time on wild goose chases. Last year I had the same dream three times, and it was quite a bit like yours, to tell the truth. I had a dream in which someone told me to leave Prague and go to the small town of Krakow and look for a rabbi by the name of Isaac son of Ezekiel. Then I was supposed to dig under the old stove in his little house and I would find a treasure. I had the dream three times. But imagine—ME going to Krakow to find the house of Isaac son of Ezekiel. Half the Jews in the world must be named Isaac, the other half Ezekiel, or so it seems. Anyway, I was smarter than that and stayed home."

Rabbi Isaac listened intently to the story. He bowed to the captain of the guard, and hurried off down the road to Krakow. He made the day-and-a-half trip in less than a day, raced to his hut, and began to dig under his own stove and, there came a thud. He dug faster and faster and unearthed a chest just like the one in his dreams, filled with gold and silver.

And with that wealth, Rabbi Isaac, so the story goes, built a small synagogue, a House of Study and Prayer, which they called The *Shul* of Reb Isaac, son of Reb Ezekiel. And they say it is still there.

Now I am quite sure it didn't happen just that way. But what counts is this: Rabbi Isaac learned that what he was looking for wasn't far away.

Amen.

Shulayim: Rabbi Reni L. Dickman

I always felt like Mark was talking directly to me. I remember sitting in those orange velvet chairs listening to the story of the people in heaven who could not bend their arms, and so they fed each other. That's the first story I remember hearing from Mark, my first memorable "aha" moment.

As a teenager filled with angst, his wisdom comforted me. Once in high school, I was having a hard time cleaning out my bedroom closet, which was filled with letters, pictures, books, and lots of old schoolwork. Mark happened to call, and I shared my struggle with him. He heard me and said, "We can only get rid of things when we are ready." So true.

I always loved the way he wove Hebrew words into his conversations and sermons. It made me want to weave Hebrew into my life too. At my confirmation, Mark spoke to me in front of the Ark. He said that he hoped I would think about becoming a leader among the Jewish people. I'm not sure if he meant **CFTY** board or rabbinical school, but I listened.

Mark's humor is classic. His voice is one of a kind. He speaks the truth but doesn't preach it, and he always seems to know what people need to hear. Several years ago, after a High Holy Day sermon, my mom said, "I could hear Mark's voice in your sermon." There could be no higher compliment.

Reni Dickman serves as Rabbi at Sinai Temple in Michigan City, Indiana, and teaches at the Chicagoland Jewish High School. She was ordained at HUC-JIR in 2003, and was confirmed at BJBE in 1988.

A Great Man

April 5, 1968
One Day after the Assassination of
Dr. Martin Luther King, Jr.

---

*The special connection—a combination of admiration,
respect, and commitment—that MSS felt to Dr. King comes
out in this sermon, a eulogy delivered just days after King was
killed in 1968. Once again, he challenges his congregation
to recognize that the Jewish community bears a unique
responsibility to help continue King's work.*

A GREAT MAN HAS BEEN SHOT DOWN.
We knew him. He was a leader, a speaker, a man of
courage. He led organizations and galvanized movements.
But he was more than a fundraiser or an orator, he was a
Christian. When he sang "black and white together" or "we'll
walk hand in hand," he didn't mean it as a political or tactical
gambit. He meant it because he believed God wanted it that way.
To him the goal and reason for the goal were so simple. "Let's
practice it," he said. We all know the words, they're in everyone's
religious vocabulary: freedom, fulfillment, equality, sharing,
justice, love. It's what God asks.

And I think this is why he, more than anyone else, was able
to awaken the churches and synagogues of our land. Before King
decided to lead boycotts against bus segregation in the South,
even the liberal religious groups in our land were apathetic. Jim
Crow was bad, you always could preach about how bad it was,
and Northerners could congratulate themselves that lavatories in

Chicago or Newark weren't segregated. But King came to Chicago some six years ago for the conference on Religion and Race, and he turned us on. He found the words which cut through the wax in our ears and the hardness of our hearts. And later that year, in Washington, he stood in front of the indescribably awesome Lincoln statue and told us of his dream, that one day even Alabama would be a land of brotherhood, that one day his black children would be a real part of this nation, not hostile to whites, but joining with them to build.

Jewish social action owes more to King than to any rabbi. He opened us up. He gave the movement a mouth and a vocabulary and he gave it a soul.

But of late, King had often been a loser. He hadn't changed any of his dreams or ways, but new backlash was brewing. His march into areas of Chicago was surely no different from the marches elsewhere. But many of us were too afraid, and some of the white liberals deserted him in Chicago because we said he had gone "too far, and what was he after, anyway?" And almost in retaliation the hard-core of alienated Negroes combined with some Negro intellectual strength to question King's non-violence, asking whether it would ever make the white community straighten its crooked heart.

So King began to lose ground with some of us, because he was bringing it closer to our homes, and with some of the Negro community because he could not bring home enough accomplishments. He got a few swimming pools in Chicago, eased out some slum landlords, had a summit agreement with Chicago leadership which died a slow easy death. But nothing really changed. And he began to lose his hold on the movement, the movement that was by now a mass of splinters.

Yesterday he was killed by a sick Caucasian, but the truth is that he was wounded seriously by all of us in the last few years. We knew he was the best, but we said that we were not sure if we could support him, and we thought he'd better spend his time educating his own people instead of consolidating his advances, not realizing that all of us desperately needed him in the forefront, to keep the struggle for equality a religious battle and not a declared war. We forgot that he was not the extreme edge of the movement at all, but was the voice of everyone's conscience, the real voice of justice, one of the few men who could say to his people, "It's not burn baby burn, but learn baby learn," and make them believe it.

King said, "Violence won't get anyone anywhere." But fewer were believing him because they could ask, "What has non-violence gotten you and us, Dr. King? A few scraps from the table, but not a seat."

Listening last night to Roy Wilkins discuss the destruction that broke out sporadically after the murder, the point came home clearly. The announcer asked Wilkins, "What can you as Negro leaders say to the young blacks who are destroying and burning as their response to the death?" And Wilkins said, "Nothing. We can say nothing." For if we say that violence doesn't get us anywhere, they will yell out: "What did nonviolence get Dr. King? Why should we be saints? He was, and they killed him."

But I don't think we can talk about Dr. King without recognizing the fact that he recently stepped into the issue of Vietnam. He became a dove, he gave of his time and influence to speak against our involvement in Vietnam. And he did so not just on a racial basis, not only because he felt that America was using Negroes to fight a war against Asians in Vietnam, not only because he knew that the money expended in the war could have gone to fight the despair in the ghettos, but because he, as a Christian, found that war unjust. Many of his advisers told him that the Vietnam issue was not for him, that it would weaken his basic civil rights effort, that it would lose him some friends and some financial support, direly needed by his Southern Christian Leadership Conference. And he knew that was true, yet he decided anyway to speak his conscience. A leader who speaks the truth as he sees it, even when he knows it may lose him friends and supporters and finances... that is a leader.

And what happened in this very week of his death? The dissent that he joined and helped to shape, the dissent from the war, has become the growing feeling of all Americans, conservatives and liberals. The movement for de-escalation has carried the day. The Administration actually changed its course and its mind. For a change, King would have been almost in the majority. For a change, he might have had an accomplishment more tangible than a written agreement or a promise. He might have had that dream come true.

So where are we all now? First, we are grieved, but truthfully, the emotion that immediately engulfs our grief is our fear. What will happen now? Is this the last straw? Will there now be rioting like never before? Will the death of the non-violent man spark the greatest violence we have yet known? What is the answer to it?

I think that the answer is the same answer, the one we've known all along. The answer is written all over the Kerner Report and over every reasonable report which has been submitted to America regarding the race issue. Make the despair of the ghetto the main concern of America. Do it out of altruism or out of Christianity or out of Judaism or out of secularism, or out of good economics or self-interest or just because you're deathly scared that the violence or its backlash will destroy your possessions. Let America forget about moon travel and controlling Asia and saving face and just save itself here and now. Let us tell our representatives that we will have no more stalling while America burns, that somehow we must find the money to do everything at once.

In response to King's death, white America must do something beyond urging black America to keep cool, something instead of buying guns and planning vigilante groups. Our representatives must be told by us that we want the Kerner Report implemented, that, if the pilgrimage to Washington envisioned by King, actually does go on, we want them to listen and respond because those will be the voices of responsible people. Our representatives must be told that there has been enough shilly-shallying on how much civil rights they can afford to give. They must be told that we must leave the war in Vietnam quickly to find a peace at home.

And for us Jews, somehow we must try it again, hard as it is… try to uproot from our midst the racism that lives in some of us, and the apathy about racism that lives with most of us. We must lay down all our rationalizations about why we don't want *schvartzers* living next door, and as Dr. King was a Christian before all else, we must be Jews above all else. And a Jew opens his heart to the strangers and the despairing for he was a stranger in despair in the land of Egypt.

As we grieve, so may we be awakened.

Amen.

Hurry Up, Noah!

October 25, 1968

Many people looked forward to hearing MSS share his interpretation of the Scriptures. He always seemed to be able to take a story from the Tanach and help people understand its themes and apply them to present-day life. Noah, builder of the now famous ark, was a challenging character to understand, and this sermon helped to make sense of Noah, saying that perhaps he was more like each of us than we care to admit.

THIS EVENING WE READ A SECTION of the story of Noah. And to tell you the truth, I have problems with Noah. I don't quite understand him. I don't find it easy to relate to him, or to identify with him, because he seems so good and believing, sort of like Albert Schweitzer and the Dalai Lama rolled into one.

Now I don't have this problem with most other characters in the Bible, and I imagine you don't either. Adam is easy. We put ourselves in his shoes right away. His wife gives him advice, which he takes, then he tries to get out of his crime by telling God that it was Eve's fault or the snake's fault or God's fault.

Eve is easy. She just has a bit of vanity in her, a desire to try new things even if she's not supposed to, highly human traits for men as well as for women.

Even Cain isn't too hard for me to identify with. After all, he was jealous because God had accepted Abel's offering but not his, just as any brother would—and does—feel jealous if special approval is given to the other brother.

And Abraham, who often falls from grace, is easy to identify with, and so are Isaac, and Jacob, and King David who couldn't control his libido, and Solomon who wanted to be wise but who also wanted to be rich and well-known. They're easy to relate to, because the same emotions plague us.

But Noah is hard, very hard, at least the way he's described in the literal words of the Bible.

First, he seems to have been the only man in the world worth saving. Everyone else had to die, but Noah and his family would live. How had he gotten to be so good? How could he have saved himself from becoming just a little corrupt, like all the rest of the people of his time?

It's as if the teacher said, "The rest of you have to stay after school, because you've been bad, but Sammy can go home on time because he didn't do anything wrong." It's pretty hard for the rest of the youngsters in the class to relate to Sammy who didn't do anything wrong. And so it's hard for us to relate to Noah. Maybe we think, "Had we been there we would probably have been left outside the ark, too!"

And then there's something else about Noah that's hard for us. And that is his great faithfulness, his great, unquestioning certainty that this strange prediction about a flood, spoken by a God heretofore unknown to him would really come to pass. Not a thought in Noah's mind to the contrary, no reservation about whether it would really happen, or that everyone else would be exterminated save himself alone. One might almost call it a monumental naiveté.

And then God's command to stop everything and start constructing the ark, which asked him essentially to change the whole course of his life and go into general contracting. Didn't he have some doubts about it? Didn't he wonder what others were thinking of him, a grown man, sane at least until then, beginning to make his backyard into a shipyard, miles inland? It sounds like the work of a *Chelmite*, and Noah must have realized it looked silly and that others would laugh uproariously. And didn't he mind that just a little? And wasn't there a time, ever, when he doubted that the whole task was worthwhile?

And so one day it starts to rain, and God says to him, "This is the rain which will begin the flood, so get all the animals together and all your children and grandchildren and get into the boat." And so, according to the Bible, Noah does. In he gets when the rain starts.

And that's hard to accept just as it is. For then, the rain undoubtedly looked like any other rainstorm, and up to that point rainstorms always had an ending much before they turned into a flood, and the next day the puddles usually dried up.

So wouldn't you think that Noah might have had a thought something like, "Tomorrow—if by some chance I'm hearing voices instead of God's voice, tomorrow it may stop raining, and the sun may come out and people may come around and look at us all here in this ark and on dry land, and I may look like the world's first and greatest idiot."

I cannot believe that Noah would not have had some thoughts like these, thoughts which were not recorded in the Bible. For if all he had was certainty, then I cannot identify with him at all.

And in looking through rabbinic interpretation of this story, we find something to support our feelings. For a certain Rabbi Yochanan, reading the story of Noah, said this: "Only when the water reached Noah's ankles did he enter the ark."

Now, this interpretation makes Noah look more like us.

According to Yochanan, Noah had some real doubts, just as we would have. At the last hour, he worried that the voice had just been a dream. He wasn't willing to take that final step into the ark until the water reached his ankles, until it was obvious that this was more than an everyday garden-variety rainstorm, but one which said, "Noah, hurry up!" He wasn't disobeying, exactly, it was just a gap in his certainty, the certainty we had assumed to be unbroken. Rabbi Yochanan's interpretation makes Noah human again. He waits until his knees are dripping wet.

But the comment does more than that. Yochanan was not out merely to pick on the only man in the Bible who seems to be perfect. He wanted to say something positive, not just to debunk.

He wanted to speak about Jewish faith, then and now.

For most of us agree that a religious man is a man of some trust and some faith. The prayers we read say it, the hymns we sing say it, and we accept it.

But what is that in Jewish terms? It is not what most of us think it to be. It is not demanding that we sign on the dotted line for a series of beliefs about God and theology which we can henceforth never question. It is not being able to say: "I believe with certainty, every moment as strongly as every other moment, that there is a God, that all things are worthwhile." Nowhere in the tradition does it say "Thou shalt always believe X, Y, or Z."

In Hebrew the word for faith is *emunah*, which is much more connected with one's actions than with one's beliefs. It does not mean constant certainty about things. It means choosing a starting point; it means staying on path, or close to it, even when the going is hard.

This is one of the dilemmas with which we begin our 10th grade curriculum. What must a Jew believe? And it's so much harder to discuss than it would be, I imagine, in a Christian environment. There are no hard and fast answers for us. There is no belief which causes one to be expelled from Judaism if it is rejected. There is hardly a belief which would find consensus among Jews. All the attempts to define Judaism through creed have been dismal failures.

The only attempts which have been somewhat accurate have been attempts to define Judaism in practice, to point out the Jewish road of observances, to show where a Jew starts, and to suggest some priority of loyalties. "What must a Jew believe?" is no reasonable question. "What must a Jew DO?" is at least discussable.

Noah, as Rabbi Yochanan saw him, knew he had to build the ark. He did. He knew he had to follow the basic course God set out for him. But I think that as he built that ship he wondered and he worried about the outcome of it all, and he pinched himself and he questioned his motives and maybe even his sanity. And even when he waited outside that boat, not quite willing to enter until the water got a little bit higher, he was still a man of faith,

Jewishly speaking. He knew what he was going to do. He was merely undergoing an eclipse of certainty, as do you and I more often I suspect than Noah did.

To have doubts is what makes us human. To be willing to stick to the course even when doubts assail us is what makes a Jew a Jew, a little bit like Noah.

Amen.

Shulayim: Rabbi Deborah Kaiz Bravo

Over my 18 years in the rabbinate, hundreds of people have inquired as to what or who influenced me to become a rabbi. Without hesitation, the first part of that answer is always the same—my childhood rabbi. Rabbi Mark S. Shapiro is a true rabbi's rabbi, and his teachings, his demeanor, and his emphasis on building relationships and getting to know people has greatly impacted the rabbi I have become today.

I remember sitting in the pews at the old BJBE listening to his sermons and wondering what he would teach us next. I could always rely on his three-pointed sermon: tell them what you are going to say, say it, and tell them what you said. It was always direct, with good, tangible examples, and it was never longer than it should have been. His sermons taught me how to love Judaism and how to question Judaism, and I strive to bring some of those lessons into my own sermons.

I was also deeply influenced by Mark's commitment to the Hebrew language and his desire to send so many of us to Olin Sang Ruby Union Institute (OSRUI) camp. He spoke about camp from the bimah regularly, and he made sure we all could manage to go to camp. His emphasis on the language was a great influence on my love of Hebrew and desire to become fluent in our sacred tongue at a young age.

When people tell me they never met Rabbi Mark S. Shapiro, I tell them he was one of the great rabbis of this generation.

Deborah Kaiz Bravo, ordained from HUC-JIR in 1998, is the spiritual leader and founder at Makom NY: A New Kind of Jewish Community in New York. She was confirmed at BJBE in 1985.

Election
Problems
for Jews

Nov. 1, 1968

---

*How should members of the Jewish community go about
deciding whom to cast their votes for each year on Election
Day? Do we vote as Jews first—or as Americans first? And
what are the issues that we need to address as priorities in
choosing for whom to vote? MSS wrote this sermon about the
presidential election in 1968 among Nixon, Humphrey, and
Wallace, but its message can easily be applied to the issues
our world faces today.*

THIS IS A BIG WEEKEND FOR America in general. Election
Day looms closer, the computers are poised, the pollsters
are making their final canvasses, and the invective and
propaganda and pre-emption of TV time all reach a crescendo.

Now most religious groups stay away from specific
endorsements of candidates, and that is as it should be. Instead,
religious groups usually take a more general tack and advise their
people, if their people are listening, to make sure to vote and vote
on all the issues, and listen to all the arguments carefully and read
as much as you can, and then cast your vote in accordance with
all the knowledge you have been able to amass.

In other words, religious groups usually talk about elections in very general terms, staying away from individual evaluations and often even skirting issues.

But Jews have concerns at election time that are not necessarily the concerns of other voters. We have dilemmas that are not shared by other voters. And we should really be aware of our special concerns and talk about them openly.

We should talk about the question of the "Jewish vote."

Now that question really has two sides, as seen by the candidate who assumes that there is such a Jewish vote, and as seen by the Jewish voter, who must decide if he is going to vote as his Jewish interests dictate.

In a well-known survey of suburban Jewry, Jews were asked whether a good Jew would vote for a candidate just because the candidate was Jewish. And almost everyone seemed scandalized by the question. "On the contrary," most said, "anyone who did that would be a bad Jew." And the impression was that the good Jew would have to vote strictly as an American, for the proverbial best man, and not let religion get in the way at all.

And I think that most of us, if we were asked about it, would be equally vehement that our Jewishness should not enter into our vote, only thoughts of who is the best qualified.

But how strange is it that, coincidentally, Jews just happen to find other Jews almost always the best qualified, or candidates who favor a Jewish point of view on an issue the best qualified. Can it be that Jews are actually the best qualified so many times? Could it be?

The truth is, of course, that the candidate who recognizes the existence of a Jewish vote, is much more realistic than those of us who don't like to admit it.

In the first place, most of those who run for lower offices are completely unknown to us, and if one has no knowledge, a "Goldstein" will probably look good to a self-respecting Jew who rationalizes it by saying, not, "He's Jewish, he must be good," but "He probably needs my help to 'even out' with the people who might vote against him because he's a Goldstein."

There is a Jewish vote. Republican Jacob Javits has received it for years, even though New York Jews are generally Democrats, and when there is no Jew running, a certain candidate will usually get the Jewish vote. The Kennedys have received it, Johnson got it in '64, simply because Jews have seen these men as more attuned to Jewish values, and more willing to be supporters of Jewish causes. It doesn't always turn out that way, but that is the way Jews see it on Election Day.

So this Jewish vote—for Jews, or for those who look like friends—is of course a reality, and most of us, underneath the rationalizations, know it to be true.

And I would like to take it a step further, and say very candidly that it is not a bad thing at all. For the ideal America is not the America where people are all the same, with the same interests and demands, but the ideal America is the pluralistic society in which the many groups are represented in government and therefore many needs can be expressed and heard, including Jewish needs.

When the Arab-Israel war seemed imminent a year ago June, it was the Jewish members of the House who first brought the issue to the public attention. When Orthodox Jews want the opportunity of keeping their Sabbath instead of the Christian Sabbath, it is usually Jewish legislators who work for passage of the proper legislation. When pressure from the top is needed to keep the lid on anti-Semitism, or to ensure equality for Jews in any area, it is Jewish elected officials who are usually the most sensitive and most understanding, and who can bring the matter to their colleagues most effectively. Jewish security in America cannot be divorced from the fact that Jews can and do hold office at various levels of government. It is good for the Jews, and it is also good for American pluralism.

How good it is can be clearly seen by how much the Black community wants it. Bayard Rustin, a black strategist, says that the black man needs the same kind of political clout that other ethnic groups have had and used for so long, and electing black officials who will be particularly responsive to the needs of the Black community needs no apology.

This is why the Black community is struggling to produce a black vote, responsive not to the ward heeler and to the machine, but responsive to black needs. And this is why, it seems to me, black leaders all over the country have finally come to endorsing a candidate. None of the three aspirants for the White House is completely a hero to blacks, and they could have decided to take no sides or suggest staying away from the polls. But they have decided that it is more important for blacks to show a unified voting strength, and thus we see endorsements from such as Mrs. King, Rev. Abernathy, and Jesse Jackson.

But the example that they are trying to emulate is ours. Malcolm X used to say—among other not-so-sweet sounding sentiments: "We've got to learn to be more like Jews."

So I think we need not apologize if we are drawn to the Goldsteins or to candidates who seem more amenable to Jewish causes.

With, we should say, one strong exception.

All the candidates, all of them, are very much aware of ethnic votes, and thus aware of the Jewish vote. And all of them would like to salt it away.

How do they hope to do it?

Very easily. First, they try to say a good word about Israel. They make speeches about "that brave little nation over there" with references to "the wonderful progress" they've made. A European Jewish newspaper recently published side-by-side interviews with Nixon and Humphrey and one could not outdo the other in generalities of praise for Israel, generalities of how they will bring peace to the Middle East, and how they will re-arm Israel soon.

How do candidates try to secure the Jewish vote after they have said these good words for Israel? They show up at an Israel Bond dinner, or a synagogue dedication, or have themselves photographed in a *yarmulke* or eating a bagel and saying *Shalom*. They talk about their good Jewish friends, and try to get a rabbi on the dais with them. These are the standard gambits.

But it should be said that the whole business of support for Israel is really a smokescreen. You and I know that whether a given candidate is really proud of Israel is not going to determine the policy of this country. Our nation happens to be pro-Israel because it suits the international policy of America to be pro-Israel, not because the administration is proud of what those brave people are doing. And to let ourselves be fooled by such nice words and flourishes is to act like geese. Surely, anyone who allows his vote to go to a candidate because of the bagel-eating or glad-handing with synagogue officials has sold his vote dirt-cheap, and has exemplified the worst and least intelligent aspects of the Jewish vote.

I do think that Jewish issues should influence our vote. But it must go far beyond just Israel, and who can say shalom the most accurately. American Jews have got to be deeply concerned about what is happening in our cities, and whether or not they can survive. We care because we are often the victims of the struggle between repressive government and upwardly striving lower classes. The survival of the city is a Jewish issue, not only a Jewish issue, but one which is going to affect the movement of Jewish life, and the survival of Jewish institutions in both the city and the suburb.

And which candidates have really considered the problems of racism in this country? Which candidates would be best able to neutralize the growth of the Wallace-ites? That is an important question for Jews. There is hardly a Jew I have spoken to who does not see the danger of Wallace-ism as one of the real concerns of '68. We are smart enough to know whom he looks like and acts like and speaks like. We know that from the podium he does not say "Jew," but we know that there are some who hear "Jew," and some of his followers who are willing to hate anyone for the right price.

Who will neutralize this rising tide of dangerous people who have simple answers to hard questions? That is a Jewish issue in the election, too.

There is a Jewish vote, because there are Jewish concerns and because Jews identify with one another. It is a vote that is wanted and sought after. Let it not be sold cheap, not exchanged Esau-like for a bowl of soup or a smile at Israel. Let that Jewish vote, which we hold, be used with intelligence, and with a sense of priorities, and in full knowledge of the crucial questions confronting our nation.

God, help us be that wise.

Amen.

I Am
with You

November 29, 1968

*How can we, as Jews, better understand our own
relationships with God? That question was a continuing
theme that MSS addressed through his sermons, helping us to
learn the lessons of the Bible, interpret teachings of scholars
and understand the meaning behind many of our traditions.
Most important, he often spoke about how we might better
recognize how God plays a role in our daily lives, as in this
sermon that looks at Jacob's famous dream in which he,
himself, sees God.*

THE NAME OF TONIGHT'S PORTION is *Vayetze*. "And he
went out." It is the continuation of the ongoing story of
Genesis: Here the subject is Jacob, and the story bears
retelling.

Jacob is basically a teenager, maybe a young adult. Esau, his
twin brother, is violently angry at him and Jacob is forced to leave
home. And here he is, out on the road, really lonely for the first
time in his life, not knowing much about what the world is really
like, trying to put on a brave front, but shaking a bit behind it all.

As the sun begins to go down, Jacob is about to spend his first
night away from home. He looks around for a pillow, realizes that
pillows are only found at home, contents himself with a mossy
rock, and after a time, falls asleep.

And he has that famous dream, of the ladder, going up to heaven, with angels going up and down on it. But it is not only angels, for the Bible reports that in his dream Jacob sees God Himself. And God says, "This ground on which you are now lying I will give to you and your children forever." And God goes on and says what may be the most important words of the dream: *V'hinei Anochi Imach*. "Remember, I am with you. I will not leave you."

Now if you are psychologically minded you may say that this is not an unusual dream for a young man. What would he want to hear? Certainly words like these, "I am with you," because he had just severed relationships with an important piece of his life. And yet as the Bible tells it, the experience is more than just having a dream which projects the fulfillment of our need. For he wakes up, and instead of shaking his head and forgetting the dream, as most of us do—instead of saying, "What a crazy dream"— he says, "Surely God is in this place too, with me right here, and I did not know it. How awesome is this place." He is nonplussed, astonished, struck with awe, and knowing even the young Jacob, that is an unusual situation for him. The feeling of the dream holds over into the waking hours... He is not alone. God is with him.

And so in this story, we are dealing with one of the key bricks in any structure of religious belief—Judaism as well as most other faiths: The belief that even when man looks to be alone, he is not alone.

And we should have some empathy for Jacob, for certainly we have lived through moments like these in Jacob's life. We have known loneliness, the days when four walls are speechless and the ordinary sounds of the world only emphasize the silence round about us. We know what it is to feel a hole in our lives, an absence of something important and someone or something dear. We know what it is to be lonely.

But Jacob comes to feel that there is no such thing as ultimate loneliness. He comes to feel, or let us say that he comes to believe—with a belief that seemed like knowledge, that God was with him, and would be with him. That there was always a

Presence somehow with him which could be addressed as You, Thou, one which might respond—if only with assurance—that the Presence was there.

I do not know how Jacob came to such a belief. And you do not know either, nor do we really know how we come to agree with such a belief, if we do. We do not test it on a computer or weigh it on a scale or submit it to a jury of our peers. Suddenly, we are aware that we are not alone, as simple as that, and henceforth no loneliness and no darkness is quite so forbidding. It is not rational, it is not irrational. It is above and beyond what we normally think of as reason.

Rabbi Abraham Heschel says it well: "The traditional way of thinking about God in philosophy has been to proceed from the known to the unknown. Our starting point is not the known, but the unknown within the known, the mystery inside the rational world. We sense more than we can say. When we stand face to face with the grandeur of the world, any formulation of thought appears as an anticlimax. If one would think at all about God, he must realize the mystery in the world is incomparably greater than what we know about the world."

"We sense more than we can say," says Heschel. Think for a moment of a picture or a sculpture… think of the Picasso in downtown Chicago if you like it. To experience that sculpture or any decent work of art is not a verbal experience. It cannot be duplicated in words. If it could, there would be no need for visual art.

And so, our ability to explain why we know that we are not alone is no ability at all, but it does not negate that experience. There is a Thou in the world to whom we can address ourselves when there is no human being there, a Thou who in His own way also addresses us. That is what Jacob felt, and that is an experience available to us too.

But it is also true that Jacob did not use that experience in the most exemplary way.

He heard God say, "I am with you, and I will be with you." He made his own translation of those words, and in his mind they were transposed to say, "I am on your side Jacob, and I will be on your side, and I am ever your Helper, concerned that things will go well for you." And we know that he heard the words that way, for he went on to say: "God, if You really do remain with me and if You do protect me on this journey and give me bread to eat and clothing to wear, and I do finally return home safely, then You shall be my God, and in return I will always set aside a title for You."

In other words, Jacob heard God say, "I am with you" and mistook Him for a kind of genie of Aladdin's lamp who would henceforth be in the control of the master, Jacob.

When we hear God saying, "I am with you," if we do, when we become sure that ultimately we are not alone, it does not mean that God authenticates or underwrites everything we plan or everything we want. When a father says to a child, "I'm here," it does not mean that everything is allowed, that the child may do as he pleases, and that the father has become the servant. No, the father will go on making demands on the child, and getting angry and being preoccupied from time to time and being, in the child's eyes, extremely unjust occasionally. When the father says, "I'm here" he promises nothing more than that.

And so with God. He does not allow Himself to be used, just because He says, "I am with you."

And you know how many people have made that mistake. "God is with us" has been used not only as balm for the lonely but as a sword in the hand of the worst animals history has known. The general says, "God is on our side!" as he sends soldiers to battle. The John Birch Society says, "God is with us" as it attacks the public schools and sex education and fluoridation and the U.N. The Inquisition said, "God is with us," and the DAR says, "God is with us," and General LeMay says, "God is with us," and God knows He cannot be on all of their sides, otherwise He is not on His own side.

So Jacob did not quite understand that God was not a genie. And he also did not quite understand that though God was ultimately near him, and with him, there would be times when the loneliness would seem absolute again.

And that is something for us to be aware of. Our sense

of God's nearness, of His availability, is a rising and falling awareness. It is like trying to tune in a station located in a distant city. It comes in, you catch it for a few moments, then it begins to fade, and the static takes over.

And so there are times when our awareness of God's nearness is overwhelmed by human static, when despondency wants to carry the day. And the sureness we want is just not present.

But the static has not disproved the existence of the station, nor has the station ceased to exist. If you stick by the radio, the station fades in again, often more strongly than before. We may miss what we wanted to hear, but if we keep listening they will say it again.

And I believe, so will He.

So Jacob feels God's nearness, is struck with awe by the dream, and then makes two errors in thinking that God is His servant and that God's presence will always be as clear as it is right then. But something he does right. For the Bible says that early in the morning Jacob took the stone that he had put under his head, and he set it up as a pillar and he gave that place a new name, Beth El, a name that has come into common use for synagogues.

He felt that God was with Him, and he did something—something in response to that knowledge, something that changed the world just a trifle. That is, to me, the most Jewish element in the whole story. For Jews, to say that there is a God is only half the story, maybe in a final analysis the less important half. What counts is what we do about it, how we respond to Him.

You see, in Catholicism, saints become saints because certain visions were vouchsafed to them. Once the vision is authenticated, once the Vatican can be certain of the facts, then the beholder of the vision is canonized. And so the little girls who said they saw the Virgin at Lourdes are given a special kind of holiness.

That is not our way. Moses is not the hero just because he spoke to God and spent 40 days with Him on Sinai. Moses has stature because he came down from the mountain and gave the tablets to Israel, because he responded to his experience of God in a concrete way. And we do not talk of him as "Moses who saw

God," but as "Moses who gave the law."

And therefore, if we can come to have a confidence in the God who is always there, it is not enough to rock softly in the bosom of that lovely certainty. We must somehow respond actively. We must share the love that we feel, spread the consolation that we experience. Not only God help me, but God through me help others. And that is what the rabbis meant, when they said: "If a man says that he loves God, but cannot stand human beings, do not believe him at all."

"I am with you," said God to Jacob—not on your side always, not in your control, not always clear to you—but I am with you.

God, send us that message too, and may we deserve to hear it. Amen.

Shulayim: Rabbi Aryeh Azriel

Mark Shapiro gave me great opportunities, opening doors for me that eventually led to my becoming a rabbi. From him I learned of inspiration, courage and love.

I first met Mark before campers arrived during the summer of 1973 at OSRUI. I had just come from Israel for the first time and was confused and unsure of my role at camp. Rabbi Shapiro practiced his Hebrew with me the entire summer. It was love at first sight!

One year later I was invited to Chicago as a *Shaliyach* for the Reform Movement, working with youth at some local synagogues. Those were amazing years during which my friendship with

Mark and Hanna deepened. When I began dating Elyce, they befriended her as well.

After we were married, Elyce and I returned to Israel to start our life in my homeland. It was a difficult year full of disappointments, unhappiness, and frustrations. Hearing about our situation, Mark invited me to come back to BJBE to work as a teacher and youth group leader, even finding additional work for Elyce and me at other temples, making it possible for us to live in Chicago. During those years, I felt his trust as I taught youth and adults. He is the reason I decided to look at the rabbinate as an option for me and the family that I was planning to have.

Mark Shapiro was and is a rabbi's rabbi. Thanks to him, I spent 33 years in the rabbinate, and recently was able to retire happy and satisfied.

Aryeh Azriel taught at BJBE and, along with his wife Elyce, was youth group advisor, in the 1970s and '80s. He was ordained at HUC-JIR in 1983, and retired in 2016 after 28 years as senior rabbi at Temple Israel in Omaha, Nebraska.

The World is Not *Hefker*

Yom Kippur Kol Nidre 5734/1973

What are the sins which we—the global "we"—need to keep in mind each year at the Day of Atonement? How does each of us apply the solemn language of the Machzor to our own lives and experiences? MSS talked about this topic in light of the disturbing revelations of 1973—the Watergate scandal, which would bring both impeachment hearings and the eventual resignation of President Nixon.

IN SOME AVANT-GARDE SYNAGOGUE SOMEWHERE, so up to date that their liturgy regularly keeps up with the events of the world, they are probably now speaking a revised version of the *Al Cheit*, confessing "the sin which we have sinned against Thee." Don't you imagine it going something like this?

AL CHEIT: For the things which turned out to get us into hot water though we didn't realize it at that point in time,

give us a pass, God.

For the so-called sin which wasn't that bad because we got caught before we could do what we planned...

be lenient, Lord.

For the error in judgment we made when

others gave us the wrong information, and
failed to ask us the right questions,
                    God, be understanding.
For the mistakes others say we made and which
we may have made but only out of a sense of
loyalty and only when bad people frustrated us,
                    Aren't those mitigating
                    circumstances
                    Ribono shel Olam?
For the things we did which could not have
been quite so illegal or immoral as they say,
because we were so sincere.
For the justifiable lapses and so called excuses,
undertaken with clean hands and pure heart,
FORGIVE US, GOD for we have already
forgiven ourselves. And let us get back to the
task of running the country's and the people's
business.
                    Dismissed. Adjourned. Amen.

There is, of course, a dilemma. To speak this evening about
anything connected with Watergate is predictable, probably
redundant, and cannot add much in analysis or insight to that
which we have already read, heard, and said ourselves.

Yet to disregard it on this day of introspection and evaluation
is to do Judaism a disservice. Jewishness is not an isolation ward.
Judaism intersects real life. We in America are the most powerful
and influential Jewish community in the world and we are
committed to the health of America. Therefore, crucial American
history must be allowed to intersect *Yom Kippur.*

But let us do it our way. Let us put aside *Time* and *Newsweek*
and all the reams of political analysis. If our heritage is a real way
of life, it should provide us with some handle on Watergate, a way
to extract a personal and national lesson. On *Yom Kippur*, let us
talk not as Sam Ervin or even as Sam Dash, but just as Jews.

Let us talk for a moment about some words.

Hebrew is a language of strong straight words. It is a

simple tongue which speaks clearly. When Nathan the prophet
confronted King David after David had committed adultery and
then had the lady's husband killed, Nathan did not say,

"M'lord, let us examine some of the motivations, the possible
alternatives and the degrees of guilt."

Nathan spoke two of the shortest most inescapable Hebrew
words.

Atah Ha-ish. "You are the one—You are the man." And
David, maybe in response to the directness of the accusation,
confessed simply. *Chatati L'adonai*, he said. "I have sinned
against God."

Similarly, the words we use in the *Viddui*, in *Al Cheyt*, are
strong and unvarnished. We ask God to forgive us for *chozek
yad*—for "heavy-handed acts." We ask forgiveness for *dibur
peh*, for word of the mouth. We ask forgiveness for things which
were done without knowledge or under duress, and we make no
legalistic distinction between them.

The strength of the Hebrew language gives little comfort, but
some security. When we use words with that clarity, either to God
or to one another, we are somehow forced into truthfulness, into
saying, "guilty" or "not guilty."

In contrast, one of the most disturbing things about the
Watergate crimes and their subsequent defense has been the public
murder of language. Reducing real criminal events to laundered
language only produces moral stupor, and being tired of the whole
complicated thing.

And unintentionally the hearings have contributed to that
smoke screen, by allowing the investigation to appear like a
lawyer's exercise class.

But something happened! As when King David stole Uriah's
wife and had Uriah killed and when Nathan said: "You did it"
and the King said, "I am guilty." We all know that breaking and
entering happened at the Watergate Hotel, that the people's time
and money and business was hustled away from us. When Bobby
Riggs hustles, he at least tells us ahead of time that he is a hustler.
But men who feigned altruism took their almost limitless power
and almost stole the country, and hardly anyone says the word

guilty. They talk about meetings and plans and fears and reports and high sources and impressions, but nobody says, "I did it." And they have been talking a long time.

Often, people are described as being sincere or well-intentioned. That is a language we all understand. Sincere, or well-intentioned, means that a man acted out of good motives; he thought it was a helpful thing he was doing, there was no gulf between what he really wanted to do and what he did. When a man is described as sincere, it is intended as a defense, and a number of us find it convincing. Yes, a handicapper who's "real sincere," how bad can he be?

But being well-intentioned is Jewishly no defense at all. Christianity finds intention more important. Did you intend to do evil? Did you believe it was wrong? If your thoughts were evil, that's a lesser crime. But Judaism, in line with the directness of the Hebrew language, cares mainly about outcome. "Well intentioned" is a cop-out phrase, designed to blur the edges of reality.

And if we have been subjected to the public assassination of our language, what can we say about the homicide directed against logic? How have they defended the Watergate events and the White House horrors? It has been said by a highly informed source that the accused were only responding to the excesses or the expected excesses of the other side. In clearer words... the social upheavals of the '60s, the campus protests, some of the violence, Kent State, Hoffman-Rubin, SDS—these were the ultimate cause of Watergate. That they preceded it in time is indisputable. That they were the ultimate cause is like saying that the Sox lost their first two games because Dick Allen broke his leg. It does not compute.

The assault on logic continues when they defend the much-discussed break-in to Ellsburg's psychiatrist's office. It was defended on grounds that Ellsberg's crimes made the Watergate crimes necessary. That does not compute either, and the real aim of that obfuscation is to say, "Ellsberg stole and the plumbers stole—Let's call it a Chinese standoff, and speaking of China let's talk about that instead."

But the truth is that Ellsberg photocopied some documents and made them public to inform us. The Watergate plumbers were prepared to steal an election and keep their activities secret to deceive the public. The incredibly wide difference between these two acts is so obvious that they could be linked only by people far more interested in deception than in truth.

Now when we squirm at all this, we are not merely talking Watergate. We are not just purist prudes or enemies of Mr. Nixon. The ability of our government, pre-Nixon, to do what most of us did not want it to do, was based on manipulating words and logic. Had we been offered a referendum on the question, "Shall we interfere in Vietnam's civil war by sending our army there," the answer, even years back, would probably have been "Of course not!" But the question was always put, especially in the early years, "Do you support our policy in Vietnam? Shall we continue fighting Communism there?" And for many years, most people did not realize that all those different questions referred to one horrid reality and they said yes. Now, as correspondents travel through North Vietnam and parts of the South, and report on the havoc we wreaked there... the civilian life we spoiled, the present state of political repression in Mr. Thieu's regime. Now the reality behind all the words is too apparent.

And you and I? We still have minds and consciences. We still know right from wrong when we see it clearly. We even might do something about it in our personal and civic lives, if only leaders would stop murdering language and logic.

Now this is all a moral Jewish concern over Watergate and related matters... we care about truth and falsehood because the *Torah* taught us to care. And that caring we share with Americans of all other faiths.

But there is also a peculiarly Jewish dimension to our concern about Watergate, which has not been discussed much at all in the media. And that relates more to Jewish survival, at least the climate for healthy Jewish survival in America.

You are aware that the Watergate crimes and mindset are being defended as our government's way of reacting to a conspiracy, a holy mission to combat secret internal enemies. As Seymour Lipset and Earl Raab point out, throughout the testimony before the Senate committee, there runs this self-justifying description of Watergate's background. In testifying, they return to the disruptive demonstrations of the past, trashings, bombings, civil disobedience, much of it conducted by supposedly shadowy figures who were never apprehended. It is suggested that the average American didn't recognize that all these events were related. Of course the FBI determined that they were not, though the FBI would have been happy to find evidence that said there was a conspiracy. But the executive branch, say Lipset and Raab, was sucked into the conspiracy theory. It was congenial to past prejudices. Therefore the executive branch could not even believe the CIA when it said that Ellsberg was acting alone out of what he thought was patriotism. The White House had to believe that Dan Ellsburg was a conspirator too.

This is an old, frightening American pattern. When confronted with frustrating changes in society—emancipation of the young, changing moral standards, demands by minorities—we simply believe it to be an anti-American conspiracy. The KKK was a way of reacting to change in American society and for them the sources of the conspiracy were "Bolsheviks, foreigners, Jesuits, and descendants of Abraham." Because of the supposed threat, all defenders of the country against a conspiracy, from the Know-Nothings through Henry Ford and Joe McCarthy and beyond, all of them felt justified in taking the law into their own hands. "We had to do it to save the country," they say. Watergate fits.

The danger signals in all this are apparent to descendants of Abraham. Conspiracy means secret plot, anonymous people masquerading as friends but possessing other loyalties. It is the backdrop against which anti-Semitism is ignited and sometimes blazes. Most of the anti-Jewish material produced for mass consumption, from the Soviet Union to the Arab States to the Liberty Lobby, pictures Jews involved in some international plot to overthrow nations and take over.

Now minority groups have their greatest security in democratic societies which legislate equality and then make the law almost holy.

But any can move toward circumventing the law, because someone in power feels that he cannot fight conspirators and still obey the law. That calamity is for minority groups, and you know which one makes the best scapegoat.

The lunatic fringe always rumbles about us anyway, Watergate or no. They write hate letters to congress about Kissinger the Jew, and they even show up to give acid testimony against him. They accept the Arab line which says that Israel wants Soviet Jews to emigrate only for Israeli expansion and to squeeze out the Arabs, and therefore they can applaud the Austrian government's unbelievable action of this past week. When the government also believes in conspiracy, then fringe lunacy grows strong. And to the extent that Watergate reflects this, Jews have a right to be personally concerned.

So, as Jews, in concert with others, we abhor Watergate's attack on truth… and as Jews, we see in it a subtle danger to us.

And as Jews, we understand it. Maybe better than others. Simply said, it does not surprise us! We have known that man is corruptible, ever since he broke God's first commandment. We may be indignant over Watergate but not surprised. We know that high office may bring out the best in an occasional man, but we know also that the opposite is equally true, that it is easy for little men, as most of us are, to think little thoughts even in the biggest jobs.

Some liberals wail and wring their hands as if the end has come—the White House is polluted, the country is irredeemably soiled, we should all burn candles or build an ark.

We know better. *Pirkei Avot* said it clearly long ago. "Be careful of the ruling authorities, for they befriend you only when it is in their interest, not yours." And yet a rabbi could conclude, "Pray for the welfare of the government, for without it, men would swallow one another alive."

People are corruptible, and no one is as heroic as we would like to paint him, yet government can be led only by people. We know the Messiah has not yet come. Some people take a Christian bias into politics and lament in astonishment over how bad things can be after Jesus came and showed what would be. Jews know that history is as yet unredeemed; that the pettiness of Watergate is more a picture of us than *Profiles in Courage*.

We are fairly pessimistic about man. We learned it and had it engraved in our flesh too many times to forget it. If German music-lovers could have built gas chambers, then statesmen can turn thief. Isaac Bashevis Singer, the great Yiddish writer, sprinkles this Jewish pessimism throughout all his stories. And when interviewed recently, he said, "Yes, I'm for social justice, but I believe that no matter what people are going to do, it will always be wrong, and there will never be any justice in the world. Even the Bible keeps repeating that one can expect very little from a human being... even if he tries to do good, sometimes it comes out wrong."

Yet Singer has not caught quite all of the tradition. Not captured the passion of a people who know that the Messiah is not here yet long to force his coming, a people who can also rage at injustice, burn with indignation and vow to work for a society which will do more than keep men from swallowing each other alive, Herculean though the task is.

Maybe it is seen best in this vignette: A student was talking about how saintly his *rebbe* was. Last week, he said, my *rebbe* was sitting at the window, and heard a noise in the yard. A thief was stealing some of his firewood, and immediately my rebbe threw open the window and yelled "Hefker," which means "ownerless property." My *rebbe* declared his wood *Hefker*—ownerless—in order to keep the thief from the actual crime of theft.

The other man listened, and then responded: Your *rebbe* seems to you a saint, and to me he is a fool. My *rebbe* taught us to say: *di velt iz nit hefker*—"things do have owners—and the world is not for stealing."

The world which has owners and may not be stolen is the only one we can live in safely.

God, give us wisdom to nurture THAT world.

Amen.

Shulayim: Rabbi Amy Memis-Foler

Back in the spring of 1993, shortly after being accepted as the next associate rabbi of Congregation BJBE, I received an Israeli aerogramme letter from Rabbi Mark S. Shapiro. It began in his inimitable upper case print,

"Dear Amy: This is your first(?) BJBE challenge—to read my scrawl. I'm trying hard but it will probably deteriorate. I'm much better at relationships than penmanship."

So true. This letter included some of what he and Hanna were doing in Israel at the time along with wise advice as I was about to enter this journey into the rabbinate at BJBE. He mentioned some of the important people to know and contact along with other logistics, but also therein was one important sermonic message. In telling me about one particular person, he wrote, "Just be yourself with [this person] (and everybody)." Rabbi Mark S. Shapiro excels in relationships, and that is due to Mark Shapiro being himself, which is one of the first and timeless sermonic lessons he taught me.

To this day before I begin a sermon, *d'var Torah* or story I still say, "You may close your books." To avoid loud slamming shut sounds, the variation I have used for the younger kids before I tell a story is, "You may *gently* close your books."

Amy L. Memis-Foler is Rabbi at Temple Judea Mizpah in Skokie, Illinois. She was Rabbi at BJBE from 1993–2001.

Jonah

Yom Kippur Afternoon, 5735/1974

---

*The lessons in the Book of Jonah have always been connected
to the theme of atonement, which is why the Haftarah portion
gets read each year on Yom Kippur. In this sermon, MSS
wonders: What exactly were Jonah's transgressions, and
how do they relate to each of our own personal ones? In this
interpretation, MSS looks at the secrets that Jonah concealed,
and how they came to be revealed, challenging us to consider
our own struggles with the truth in our lives.*

CAN YOU IMAGINE HOW MANY SECRETS there are in this
room? How many people know something that they won't
tell, wouldn't tell to a stranger, not even to someone very
close?

And how many of those secrets are really secrets? How many
of them do other people know anyway, even though you haven't
told them?

How many would be quite as horrid, in the light of day, if
they were known? And how many people would feel a lot better if
they could tell at least someone?

Can you imagine how many secrets there are in this room, and
how many of them really aren't secrets at all?

I think of that now because there's a prayer in the service for
the Day of Atonement which talks about secrets. It's powerful, I
think. We say to God, "God, do You not know all things, both
the hidden and the revealed? You know the secrets of eternity

and the hidden thoughts of every living being. You search the innermost recesses and probe the deepest impulses of the heart. Nothing is concealed from You, nor hidden from Your eyes."

That is powerful stuff. Powerfully distressing, maybe, but also powerfully comforting. Distressing, if the secrets are embarrassing. And yet powerfully comforting to know that SOMEONE already knows—God.

Nothing is concealed. That is one of the messages of *Yom Kippur*.

And maybe that is why tomorrow afternoon we will read from the Book of Jonah, the man who thought he could conceal it, and get away with it. Not quite as many of you will be here tomorrow afternoon when we read it as are here now… so let me remind you of the story of Jonah.

His father's name was Ammitai, and that comes from the word *emet*, meaning truth, and truth comes to play a very important part in the story. His name was *Yonah*, and *Yonah* means a dove which can fly away, and that plays an important part of the story, too. That's all we know about Jonah when he gets the message from God. It is very clear.

"Jonah, go to Nineveh, that great city, and proclaim judgment upon it, for their wickedness has come to My attention."

Poor Jonah was to go and tell Nineveh that God disliked their wickedness. Which promised to make him as popular as selling Israel Bonds on the main street of Damascus. For Nineveh was the sin-city of its day, Las Vegas honky-tonk, con-man infested, Mafia-run. Think of the worst from top to bottom, and that was Nineveh.

You knew what Jonah had to be thinking. "Find yourself another boy, Lord!" But he didn't say it, didn't even let on that he was unhappy. He listened, reacted internally, made some secret decisions, and then dutifully went home for an overnight bag.

He played out the part. Nineveh was a ship's journey away, at least the first leg, so it was not unusual that he went down to the docks to find a ship going in the direction of Nineveh. There were many ships leaving that day, some going toward Nineveh, some going the opposite way, like to far-off Tarshish.

How convenient: The ship which would start him out toward
Nineveh was docked right next to the one going to Tarshish.
Why, it was easy for Jonah to walk toward the one ship and, at
the last moment, jump lines and buy a ticket for Tarshish. He
looked around. There was no one he knew. No one had spotted
the switch. He bought steerage. Better to be away from the deck
where people were seen.

(The "sting" had yet to come.)

He feels that his escape is assured. He goes to his space in
steerage, and contentedly falls asleep. He sleeps so well that the
beginning of the storm does not wake him. The sea churns, the
ship tosses, Jonah sleeps on.

The sailors are in a panic. They have never seen a storm quite
like this one—something strange and eerie about it. The sailors
pray to the gods of the sea and the gods of the wind, and being
pragmatists too, they also give their gods some help and begin
flinging the ship's cargo overboard, for the ship is in danger of
sinking.

Jonah sleeps on.

Finally a sailor, looking for the last bit of cargo to throw over,
sees Jonah and awakens him. "Man," he says, "how can you
be sleeping so soundly? Get up, help, pray to your special God.
Maybe He will save us."

The sailors are all convinced that someone on board is "a
Jonah" and they cast lots by dice or spinner or Ouija board, and
the device answers that it is clearly Jonah at whom the sea is
raging.

Jonah might have known it. Nothing is concealed or hidden
long. And caught is caught.

"Yes," he says, "I am fleeing from my God who gave me a
hard job I didn't want. That's the truth."

"But how can we stop this storm?" ask the sailors.

And Jonah, trembling, thinks he knows what the answer is.
"Get rid of me, heave me overboard, and the sea will calm. For
truly, the punishment is directed against me."

And so they do toss him overboard, like the cargo. But it
turns out that the storm is not so much a punishment, but rather

a way of getting Jonah back on track. For the story says that God provided a great fish, maybe a whale, to swallow up Jonah and carry him back to dry land, and spit him back on the shore, not too far from his home. And with this fantastic twist, it is clear that the story of Jonah is an allegory instead of an historic incident.

Jonah, bedraggled, somehow thumbs a ride home, and hardly has time to dry off when God's voice comes to him again:

"Jonah—about that job. Maybe you didn't quite understand me the first time. Nineveh—not Tarshish. Get to it, quickly now."

What a guest preacher that ancient prophet Jonah would make on the subject of deceiving, of things finally catching up to you. What an interpretation he could give of those verses, "Nothing is concealed from You or hidden from Your eyes." How well he knew that all things stand revealed at last.

Oh, we know it too. Maybe not as exhaustively or exhaustingly as Jonah, but we know it too. Was your mother always able to tell when you were shading the truth? You thought you were lying with a straight face, as casual as you please, no stray body motion to give you away. She knew when you were lying, as if you had a giant Sox-o-Gram printed right on your forehead that said, "I'm lying, I'm lying," and shot off a Roman candle or two to call attention to the message.

Nothing is concealed or hidden forever.

And how many examples you can find in your own personal life to prove that? The prejudice you tried to hide eventually slips out. The small lie needs protection from larger ones, and eventually the fabrications tumble, revealing the original untruth. We are all eventually like the little boy who tried to sneak a stray cat into the house under his shirt, and it kept putting its tail out through his collar, his sleeve, his buttonholes, his shirt-tail.

How can we not know that after the national events of these past years? Richard Nixon just never heard the right sermon from the visiting clergy he invited to the East Room, never heard that sermon he so needed about nothing remaining always concealed or hidden. Or if he heard it he failed to apply it. Or maybe he did and didn't like it, and maybe that's why he eventually closed up the private chapel.

With all the power that men can give to another man, and he had it—even he could not forever conceal the truth. No matter how far he retreated into his own private depths, no matter how many fan-bearers denied access to the truth and then simply denied the truth, no matter. Nothing is concealed or hidden forever.

And if you think that a whale is a pretty unbelievable agent of revealing the concealed and setting things on track again, you may be right. I think so too. But is it much more unbelievable than the actual agent of revelation in the national drama? Who would have believed that a man would have taped it all, his private moments and phone calls, his own incriminations? Who would have believed that a technique designed somehow to preserve imagined greatness for the future would be the ultimate and ironic agent of downfall? More contrived than a Greek tragedy, it seems. Who would have believed that this most private of men would suddenly become more public than any other public figure? That the man who so laid himself open for public viewing and listening would in the end have his profanities, his indecisiveness, and his deceptions all revealed word by word by word?

Is it not almost as unbelievable as the whale?

In a sense, that lonely man has received the ultimate punishment. When you have lived in the whale's belly for three days, what more can they do to you? And when your deepest, most embarrassing secrets are mass-distributed, what disgrace can a nation add—or would we find necessary to add?

The *Machzor* says:

Nothing is concealed from You O Lord, or hidden from Your eyes.

For Nixon, that turned out to be the *emes*, and the end.

Yet for Jonah it was the beginning of the way back, and maybe it is for us. Jonah had tried to deceive God, had taken the wrong ship, going the wrong way. The storm hit, the sailors suspected Jonah, but they wanted to hear it finally from his mouth. And as the storm broke upon him, and all signs pointed to him, he told the truth—yes, he had been given a mission, yes, he was fleeing from it, yes, the storm must be on his account.

And when the bedraggled Jonah gets home, God simply says, "Jonah—about that job—get on it… now." No more storms or whales. Jonah had spoken the truth and could return to his mission.

Truth marks a new beginning. Remember Portnoy and his complaint? He spends the whole book telling his psychiatrist the truth about himself, much of it unsavory, ending in a final wail of self-revelation. And then the doctor says to him at the end of the book, "Now, may we please to begin, yes?"

Real new beginnings come after the real truth.

But saying the whole, real truth is frightening, and before we say it we run down a thousand side alleys.

You know, there are people who need help—family help, counseling… people who need it very much, so many that it is almost like an emblem of belonging, certainly no longer a stigma.

And help is available, and works most of the time, or at least enough of the time if we really want it to help.

Why do people resist then? Is it the inconvenience, the time, the interruption of pattern?

I think it's a fear that the truth will be known: that concealed things will be revealed. Like Jonah, deep in the hold of the ship, the truth about how we feel and what we think can be hidden behind years of boxes and crates and tarpaulin covers. We don't want it to emerge into sunlight. We fear it'll blind us, destroy us, destroy others, or destroy relationships.

Jonah told the truth, finally, and though he thought it meant his destruction, it only served to put him back into life.

And in the proper situation, when done in a circle of skilled concern, telling that truth is not blinding, not destructive. More often it is the beginning of healing, saying, "I'm lonely," or "I don't really like what I'm doing." "A lot of the time I'm afraid." Truths like those, hidden in steerage, can be faced. Others can love us just as much, maybe more, after hearing them. Truth is the beginning of healing.

The *Machzor* says, "Nothing is concealed from You O Lord, nor hidden from Your eyes." And so that line in the prayers is initially frightening, but ultimately comforting. Nothing is hidden... He knows it already—our worst lies, our selfishness, our anguish. And that should give us strength to speak other truths on other days, and make us feel more whole.

Lord, nothing is hidden from Your eyes.

Amen.

Returning to
the Eternal

Yom Kippur, 1975/5736

---

*Cantor Cory Winter spent ten years working with MSS as
Cantor at BJBE, beginning with four years from 1975–1978,
and then again from 1996 until MSS retired in 2000. During
the first High Holy Days that they worked together in 1975,
Cory found one of the sermon topics to be particularly
challenging. In the BOLD type interspersed within the
sermon, he shares his recollection of both his reaction to the
sermon and its role within their personal relationship.*

I KNOW THAT I HAVE SAID THIS BEFORE, but I have an
ongoing feeling that *Yom Kippur* is hard for Jews. I don't mean
the fasting. Actually, I think that *Yom Kippur* is hardest on us
liberal Jews, and there are some of us who do nibble a little.

It's hard on us because we resent it. The service on *Rosh
Hashanah* is about hopes for a New Year, being inscribed for
good in the book of life, and *gut yontiff* and nice things. But
the service for *Yom Kippur* acts so certain of itself and is so
demanding, almost like an old-fashioned schoolteacher, who
says to us, "You did wrong, and we all know it, and now stand
up and tell us you're sorry," with no chance for one to plead
that he didn't understand it was wrong, or to argue how what
he did might have been right after all if you only understood the
situation, or had a chance to ask for some flexibility.

Cantor Cory Winter: One of the most cherished relationships I've had in my life is the one I've had the great good fortune to share with Rabbi Mark Shapiro. We were colleagues on the *bimah* for many years and our friendship has remained to this day.

The *Yom Kippur Machzor* service is tough. "ALL READ TOGETHER," it says. "We have sinned, we have transgressed, we have done perversely." There's no asterisk indicating that if you think you haven't done so badly this year, don't say it. "READ TOGETHER," it says, "For the sin which we have sinned against Thee by abuse of power," and all the rest—with no opportunity for someone to argue in the margin about "What is sin anyway?" Or "just when did I abuse power?"

Yom Kippur is so righteous and unapologetically certain of what it is saying, especially about right and wrong.

And we are so confused about right and wrong.

Oh, we have learned to be confused, that is true. At least parents of teenagers have learned. "But mother, why is it wrong? I mean if you can't even give me a good reason except that you think it's wrong." Or "Dad, if Chuck and I move in together who are we hurting? He's willing to and so am I."

Our kids seem to know all the college ethics texts by heart, far before they take the courses. You know, those books which always find circumstances in which a seemingly absolute principle is suddenly made to look absurd. For example, one text I was looking through was discussing whether or not there were any absolute obligations, and it suggested, for the sake of argument, this one: "We have special duties of gratitude toward those who have done us good." But then, it went on to say, would it not be equally logical to conclude that we have special duties of vengeance toward those who have wronged us? Why not?

Azoy geytes. So it goes. We are left feeling that nothing could be absolutely right or wrong. Our bright kids do the same to us, until we give up and say: "Go on, maybe they're right, it's a funny world...who am I to say that they're wrong and I'm right."

> Cory: I had been BJBE's Cantor for only a few weeks when we embarked on our first High Holy Day services together in 1975. I suspect that he supported my becoming Cantor for several reasons: I had a good voice, we had shared musical tastes, I was young and of the '60s generation, I was recommended by two of BJBE's founding members—pillars of the congregation, and he liked my personality and occasionally irreverent sense of humor. Or maybe no one else applied for the job.

And then along comes *Yom Kippur* with its overwhelming smugness, its sense of having some absolute standards to impose on us and judge us. And we, who have not gotten away with that with our kids, resent *Yom Kippur's* attempt to do it to us.

I would like to tell you today that I think *Yom Kippur* is right. I think it contains an old wisdom which many of us have lost, or are fighting—but losing—skirmishes to maintain. I think that there is some absolute right and absolute wrong, and I think that much of the time one must stand <u>absolutely</u> for what one believes to be absolutely right or absolutely wrong.

Now everyone—even the greatest of philosophers—has come a cropper when they tried to state this in an all-encompassing theory. I don't have a real theory, I'm afraid, with or without flaws. I just believe, as the *Yom Kippur* service believes, that there is a God who asks certain conduct of us, and that when we miss the mark we can be absolutely wrong and guilty, or vice versa.

And if, as someone told me this past year, if this shows that I am getting quite a bit more conservative in my middle years than I used to be, then move over and make room.

I guess I am saying this: You have a choice of being either a weather vane or a compass needle. Both are arrows. But the weather vane arrow moves to reflect the way the wind happens to be blowing at the moment. The compass needle decides which way north is, and proceeds to point that way no matter how one turns the compass dial. Rather that each of us be the compass needle, even at the risk of being wrong about where north is.

> Cory: We never discussed my personal life. The congregation needed someone to do a job, and Rabbi Shapiro believed I could do it. At that time, I was definitely not "in the closet;" Franz and I were already together seven years. I just didn't think that my personal life was relevant, and it didn't even dawn on me to mention it to him. I guess it was just another case of "Don't Ask, Don't Tell."
>
> The 1975 *Yom Kippur* morning sermon, "Returning to the Eternal" took a historical perspective on the idea that each of us is an arrow, choosing either to be affixed to a compass (moral, that is) or a weather vane (pragmatic, that is).

This may sound strange in a Reform synagogue. As a matter of fact, the traditional complaint is that we are weather vane Jews, not compass Jews—that we go with all the winds of change. We abrogate laws and customs because the modern wind blows a certain way. They say that we are the captives of convenience and that our only absolute principle is "Do it the easy way" or "Do it the Gentile way."

Of course that is not true. And if our traditional brethren learned as much about us as we try to learn about them, they would know it is not true. We both draw absolute lines. We just tend to draw them more sparingly, and more democratically. Reform Judaism stands for Israel, absolutely. Reform stands for *Shabbat* observance absolutely, though we try to draw lines which will include and encourage rather than exclude and alienate. We try to draw lines at reasonable minimums instead of at elitist maximums. And often it is the Reform synagogue which we find setting and straining toward higher standards in both Jewish education and Jewish self-respect. Witness the fact that Reform synagogues require at least four years of Hebrew for *Bar Mitzvah*, while many traditional synagogues will sell a *Bar Mitzvah* for a sizable donation and six months basic training in that time-honored scholarly custom of memorizing a record. Witness also that the Israel Bonds Organization knows by this time that only Reform synagogues give them a hard time and refuse to make an appeal for bonds in the *Yom Kippur* service, as we at BJBE refuse.

Cory: I think we need to remember what it was like to live in 1975. One of the moral issues at the time, he said, was government secrecy. President Nixon had resigned in disgrace the previous year, and a few short months later, our then-President Ford (read weather vane) granted him a full pardon for his multiple crimes, pragmatically. Few could argue—then or now—that government secrecy was acceptable except in very rare and exigent circumstances.

We, as a movement, do not stand for absolutely everything—but we do stand, ABSOLUTELY for some things.

I think that you and I as individuals must do the same, must do more imitating of the compass than the weather vane.

And I want to illustrate it further by talking about two rather different areas, homosexuality and censorship.

Cory: Let me turn now to the other issue—homosexuality—better known as the juicy part of the sermon.

Most Jews in Chicago (then and now) prefer to live in fairly separate insular communities of like-minded people. In the not-so-distant 1960s, Malvina Reynolds had written the song "Little Boxes" to describe this phenomenon. Many members of BJBE had fled neighborhoods in Chicago, notably Rabbi Shapiro's beloved South Shore, as black families moved in. Rabbi Shapiro was a dedicated and enthusiastic leader in the U.S. Civil Rights movement of the '60s, but synagogues in his old neighborhood disappeared as Jews feared living amongst others. BJBE appeared to be a monolithic community in the safe suburbs.

I was going to say that one area was a broad one—censorship—and that one was a fairly narrow one—homosexuality. But if *Time* magazine is right about the number of homosexuals in the country—as they probably are in counting the number of gay bars—then the area is not a narrow one at all.

I think that there is a difference between understanding the situation of a homosexual and thus being concerned with his or her rights—a difference between that and outright admission that it is, after all, a matter of taste and no one can judge it right or wrong.

After all, it is much more than a matter of taste and personal preference. One test of the morality of an individual's action is to ask: "What would be the result of your action if everyone did it?" That is a fair test that can be applied to the man who cheats on his income tax or fails to vote or who waters his lawn when the town has a water emergency. And applying that test to the gay choice has a clear result: homosexuality, if universal, would be not only the end of the family unit as we know it, but the end of most reproduction. That is not just a matter of taste or personal preference.

Cory: Homosexuality may have seemed to be an insidious threat of an unknown enemy from within. At that time, the widely held belief in the medical establishment was that sexuality was <u>environmentally</u> determined, and therefore, a matter of human choice.

Homosexuality clearly challenges another value which I, for one, consider absolute. It effectively separates human love from the act of reproduction. The person one loves, in gay society, is ipso facto not one with whom you can create new life. I believe that the best parents are people who love one another and are willing to extend that covenant and love to a child. And that is impossible, given gay society.

Cory: Using that reasoning, then, it might be relatively easy for a homosexual to entice others to engage in homosexual behavior. So, now at *Yom Kippur*, knowing that one had the power to choose his or her sexuality, perhaps a man or woman could decide to repent and change sexual orientation <u>on that very day</u> after hearing those very words from their Rabbi!

I know that some of what I am saying is just the obvious, but it appears to me that the obvious is just what is being overlooked in most discussions about gay liberation. And maybe the most obvious thing needs also to be said—*Time* only hinted at it. The fact is that homosexuality is anti-biology and anti-nature. Like it or not, biology sometimes dictates destiny and always limits destiny. No matter how much science advances in rocketry, I can never plan to live on a world 90 light years away, for I will not live long enough to get there. Or maybe another example. If a group of people decides that it will not eat and digest food in the normal fashion but will exist completely on I.V. for life, we might defend their right to live that way providing it does not harm others. But we must also say that it is unnatural, and neurotic, for it indicates rejection of our bodies the way they are—as neurotic as an inability to accept my father as he is or my child as he is.

Cory: Imagine Rabbi Shapiro's surprise when immediately after the service, I asked (urgently) to speak with him in his office. My recollection is that there, in his office between services, I revealed my sexual orientation to him and offered to resign that minute (and not even finish out the day). He appeared stunned to me. How could there possibly be a gay person at

his <u>homogeneous</u> congregation? His immediate
response was that I should stay for a while and
that we'd see how things worked out. For my
(outraged) part, I insisted that he invite someone
to speak to rebut his views.

And I think it is for these reasons that traditional Judaism
has been dead set against all forms of the gay life. Not because
the males who said so were so afraid of their own homosexual
impulses that they projected the fear into hostility, but rather
because God's creation, including human physiology, was good,
and should be used as clearly intended.

This is not to say that gays should not have every legal right
to equal opportunity, access to public benefits and freedom from
harassment. It is to say only, but clearly, that homosexuality runs
counter to some very important absolute values.

Cory: What neither of us knew was that there
was a family in our congregation dealing with
homosexuality at that very moment. One of
the children in that family had come out to the
parents just the night before (*Kol Nidre*). Shell-
shocked, they came to services the next day for
spiritual solace and were confronted with that
sermon.

As the years progressed, and as medical
research advanced, it was scientifically proven
and generally acknowledged that homosexuality
is <u>genetically</u> determined; it is not a choice.

> Therefore, it couldn't be a contagious disease; in
> fact, it ceased to be considered a disease at all.

Liberalism does not mean being a weather vane, or giving up absolutes in search for liberty.

Are you ready for a less sensational, but much more important area? I am. In my list of absolute principles, to be defended until they come in conflict with another equally absolute principle, is the public's right to all the truth about its government, and the individual's right to all the truth about himself.

Those are important absolutes to enunciate, because they are so often walked upon.

It is hard to believe for example, that the Senate of our nation is presently considering legislation called S-1, which would actually impair the power of the public to find out what is happening, legislation which would have made Daniel Ellsberg clearly criminal for having told us the hidden truth. Provisions of S-1 would weave an even tighter net of secrecy around documents which the CIA, FBI, and those other Lancelots of principle and truth determine to be "top secret." Can you believe that such legislation could be passed in the wake of Nixon? But it could, and might. Government, even good government, likes operating in secrecy. It is not as messy. If you care about the bill, please join many of us in writing our Senators.

This issue was very well illustrated in the reactions of both Israelis and Egyptians to their new interim agreement. Israel has not been consistently the world's best model of civil liberties; she has used artistic censorship and news blackout a bit too freely. But on balance, Israel is an open society, where the great issues are subject to open debate. Citizens of Israel knew just what was going on in the bargaining. They knew what their negotiators were willing to give up. And, because a sizable minority was set against giving up that much, or even anything, Israeli society has been a frenzy of demonstrations, charges, counter-charges, violent Knesset debate, and even small riots. Public debate made it all happen.

> Cory: Rabbi Shapiro's views evolved also. Hanna and he and Franz and I socialized occasionally and we enjoyed each other's company. What was previously unknown and unfathomable to him became real and, I surmise, a lot more comfortable. Also, I suspect, he got over the procreation hurdle when he considered with alarm the possibility of my foisting offspring on an unsuspecting world.
>
> Ultimately, Rabbi Shapiro altered his views on homosexuality 180 degrees. Perhaps as a gesture of repentance (staying with the *Yom Kippur* theme) toward the above-mentioned family, he supported the establishment of a PFLAG (Parents and Friends of Lesbians and Gays) chapter at BJBE, which exists to this day. This guy has really walked the walk.

But what was going on in Egypt, a land whose negotiators were also making concessions which some Egyptians might have found too great? The streets were quiet and peaceful, for the public didn't know what was happening. Debate the issues? They weren't even allowed to understand the issues! And even now that the accord has been signed, the Egyptian public is told only the things they got, and not the compromises they made.

Government, given its druthers, might well choose the Egyptian way—unless people demand, as an absolute right, all the information.

And I would press that concept into personal areas, too. People have a right to know the truth about themselves. A doctor has an obligation to tell the patient what he knows about the patient's body, for the body is the patient's and not the doctor's. A person has a right to know if he is terminally ill, and I think that almost every time we keep that knowledge from a person— almost every time—we do the wrong thing. A child has a right to know about sex, a right we usually implement—but he also has a right to know about death and dying and cemeteries, a right we would rather keep from him, but must not. In my list of absolutes, these rank high—a person's right to know about himself and his destiny, as well as to know about the government which he established by social contract.

> Cory: A couple of times in the recent past, when Rabbi Shapiro and I have been sharing a table with others at an event, and the word "sermon" comes up in a conversation, he'll begin, (unsolicited), "I remember a sermon I gave a few years ago," referencing that *Yom Kippur* morning, and apologize to me publicly (and unnecessarily).

I do not know if my absolutes coincide with yours. But that isn't the issue. That you be inspired by the directness of *Yom Kippur*, inspired to take an absolute stand when you really feel it, not just when you can prove it. That is the issue. If you think that cheating is wrong, stand by that. If you think that promises must be kept, if you believe that parents are as entitled to respect as children are to space to grow, stand up for it.

> Cory: Very few people (let alone we clergy) atone
> so honestly and completely in word and deed. This
> quality that he possesses is only one reason why
> I consider Rabbi Mark Shapiro a *lamed-vavnik*—
> one of only 36 truly righteous people who walk
> the earth at any one time. I look forward to his
> next book, when I can give more reasons for his
> membership in "Club 36."
>
> Rabbi Mark Shapiro—believe me—is no
> weather vane. He just happened to buy a bum
> compass. I've bought a couple of them myself,
> and I'm sure that he and I are not the only ones.

You know, I really only look at the stars in the summer time. Maybe you're the same way. It takes the open fields of Union Institute to get me to examine the evening sky. And as the constellations move across the summer sky, as the Great Bear dips slowly toward the horizon in late August, and Draco twists his dragon tail, and the chair of Cassiopeia begins to fall over backward—on seeing this, one is all the more grateful to find Polaris, the North Star, around which everything turns. It is good to see the constellations move. It is exciting to know that we too, in our galaxy, are moving through space. But it is comforting to know that the North Star always shows north.

It is not so bad to be, at least some of the time, like that star. Better I think, than the weather vane, which can only tell us which way the hot air is blowing today.

Getting Out of Egypt

Erev Yom Kippur 5736/1975

---

*Though most were quite familiar with the story of the
Exodus of the Jews from Egypt, MSS reminded us of a part
of the story sometimes forgotten—the part about how Jews
had settled somewhat into their role as slaves, to the point
of even becoming comfortable with their lives there. That
made their journey into Israel and the great unknown much
more difficult, so much so that many believed they would be
better off remaining enslaved in Egypt. On this Kol Nidre, he
challenges us to consider our own personal Egypts, and the
fears, habits, and insecurities that continue to enslave us.*

WHEN JEWS HAVE REALLY WANTED to explain
something to one another, they have told stories...
stories of what really happened, should have happened,
might have happened. Some stories have died with the storyteller,
but others were preserved.

Why have some of these stories lived on? Why are certain
stories incorporated into the yearly reading of scripture while
others have vanished? I think we know why. The story that
survives is the story that has something to tell which each new
generation must learn. The story that survives is the one which
tells the truth about all human life... the one which, like a road
sign, tells us how soon to turn, how we can manage to get there.
And once in a while a story has our names on it.

Tonight I am thinking of a most common Jewish story, one associated more with *Pesach* than with *Yom Kippur*. I am thinking about the story of the Israelites and Egypt, and their escape through the waters of the Red Sea. A Saturday night prime time story.

It has its well-known parts, the ones everyone could tell by heart; 400 years of slavery in Egypt; the emergence of Moses as liberating hero; his confrontations with the court of Egypt, the plagues, the final escape, the first real step toward freedom in the crossing of the Red Sea.

And then there are parts that are remembered only on second thought—the fact that the Jews were really afraid to leave Egypt—had made their peace with it. The fact that they initially resisted Moses and thereby resisted liberation. We easily forget that at almost every stage of the Exodus and wandering, before, during, and after the Red Sea crossing, they wanted to go back to the comforts or at least the familiarity of slavery.

We like that story. The story of the escape from Egypt we think of as just a TV hair-raiser, dramatic, yes, an epic, yes, but concerned with the masses and not with me.

Tonight I feel different about it. Tonight I feel that the Exodus story is very personal, concerned with our feelings about ourselves on *Yom Kippur*, concerned with our feelings of "not being there yet," and not knowing how to start to get there.

The rabbi of Kotzk really understood the story of Israel and Egypt in the way I intend it. For he said, "Hard as it was to get the Jews out of Egypt, it was even harder to get Egypt out of the Jews." I like that so much that I have to say it to you again. "Hard as it was to get the Jews out of Egypt, it was even harder to get Egypt out of the Jews."

He meant that the fleshpots had seduced them. He meant that the pagan gods of Egypt and their ways had gotten deep into the bones of the slaves during those 400 years. He meant that going out of the house of bondage did not ensure that slaves would act like free men. And he was right.

But his understanding of the story opens it up, like a flower in sunlight, and displays the hidden and personal truth. Egypt is in us. All the things which enslave us, they are Egypt. All of the things which keep us from growing or repenting or being proud of ourselves... all these are Egypt. And everybody's job is therefore an echo of Exodus, to get out of Egypt, one Egypt at a time, one step at a time. The first step our people took was to cross the Red Sea. It was terrifying and they trembled in fear. But they had to cross, and somehow God helped them. Our job is to get out of the Egypts that bind us, to admit that we are still there, and then try to get out, and pray that God helps us.

I was with some youngsters this past summer who were able to grasp this idea and thus prove to me how accurate it is as a description of all of us and our situation and our task. At OSRUI we were teaching a unit on the section of the service called *Geulah*, "Redemption," which includes the prayer *Mi Kamocha*, "Who is like unto Thee," which is what Moses said when the people had crossed the Red Sea. We wanted the kids to understand what Egypt was like, and what redemption must have meant. So we gathered them on the *Tzofim* hillside, and explained just this much—that Egypt can stand for all the things that enslave you, that you wish you were free of but are not, and that crossing the Red Sea stands for taking the first step to get yourself out of that slavery.

To help them understand, four of us (three counselors and I), stood up and shared with those kids a personal Egypt of our own. One of us expressed an old fear that still haunted him; another talked about continual anxiety about going into new situations; another told of a habit that seemed to be unbreakable.

Then we asked the kids if they were willing to gather in small groups and share with us and just a few others what their Egypts were.

And they all understood it right away. Yes, it turned out, they all had their Egypts. Many, it turned out, were afraid of the dark, many were afraid of other people, many, many were afraid of being thought of as different, and these fears held them in real bondage.

During this exercise, I was sitting with a group of three youngsters. The first to speak was a very pretty girl of 12 or so.

She said that one of her Egypts was her fear to go into a new group for fear of being thought ugly, and as she said that another equally attractive girl opened her eyes in wonder and said, "You, too?" It was a magic moment for both of them... *satori*, awakening.

But that is not just a child's exercise. It could be right here, right now, if you and I trusted each other enough. It might be right in the spirit of *Yom Kippur* if we just cut out a lot of the prayers ahead of us and if instead we simply sit down with one another and talk about how we were enslaved, and then helped one another figure out how to cross the Red Sea. Maybe we should take advantage of the fact that everyone is here on these days for some hours and do just that kind of small group work. Hang the logistics: we could do it! Maybe our great slavery is that we probably never will interrupt a High Holy Day service for something like that.

But you could simulate it and at least get something worthwhile. Think of your Egypt now. Go on. If you were going to enter a supportive group of two or three others in just a moment, a group where you would feel comfortable enough to tell the real truth, what would you say? What is one of the Egypts still in you that enslaves you even though you look to be untroubled and free?

And were we really to do it, right now, divide up into threes and share our Egypts, how many times do you think that you would confess your slavery and another, listening to you, would burst out with, "You, too?" For though everyone has his Egypts and they all seem different, some cut across the midsection of middle-class American Jews.

You know what many of the confessed slaveries would be, do you not? You know ahead of time that many honest people would confess that they are in bondage to possessing things, having things, envying what others have that they do not have. That is such a common slavery, that when we meet someone who is not in bondage to envy, we feel we have met a saint.

People who know better sacrifice their families and their health for the sake of amassing just a bit more gelt. In Saul

Bellow's great new novel, *Humboldt's Gift*, older brother Julius has everything, money, homes all over the world, expensive knit slacks which he cannot squeeze into anymore. And Julius is overwhelmed with the need to make more and more. And on the very day before he is to have open heart surgery, when he stares death in the face, he can take comfort only in arranging another condominium deal, another scheme to let his dollars make more dollars. We all understand Julius because his slavery enslaves so many of us too, though we have less to show for it.

We want to have things. Not that Jews ever thought that the things of life are so bad, but we WANT them so much! Hearing the ninth commandment, "Thou shalt not covet," throws us into shock! We're even money to keep some of the commandments, a long shot on some of the others, but not coveting, envying, wanting things. THAT we can't even fake. Wanting more and more things is everybody's dirty little secret. And that is really why we spend more than we should have spent or could have spent on the *Bar Mitzvah* bash which is too much and too silly and sometimes absurd—because we need to say that we HAD IT... not experienced it, but HAD IT, the way one has a thing. And thus we induct our kids at an early age into our Egypt. They could probably not have escaped it forever anyway. They start talking about how much and how big and how expensive, and how much this one made, and that one made, until the final obscenity is played out in synagogues all over the land, including this one, in which youngsters stick five or ten bucks or maybe even more into an envelope and lay it on one another as the most clearly acceptable *Bar Mitzvah* offering, because cash can be turned into anything.

Yet once in a while we realize that people do get free from most every Egypt, even that one, and that we could too. Occasionally we meet someone who has escaped that scene. I heard someone say, not too long ago, "I have the feeling that we're rich," only I knew that they weren't, but she seriously meant a different kind of wealth.

I had that feeling recently when I spoke with a man who could have just as well stayed in slavery to envy for the rest of his life.

He had sold out his half of a business to his partner. Four months after he sold out, the business took an upswing, and the partner, now full owner, was a millionaire. But that partner, even with his new status, was having trouble with his wife and kids. And the first man, the one who sold out just too soon said, "I used to envy him. For three years that's all I thought about. But I don't anymore. I've got enough, my family is good and solid. He should envy me." And I think he meant it. I hope he did.

If only on this *Yom Kippur* we could take one step, just cross one Red Sea away from that Egypt of envy, of desire for things....

Maybe your Egypt is different. Maybe you share with some of those youngsters I mentioned another common slavery. You are afraid to try something new for fear that you will look silly, feel inadequate. Everyone knows how that feels. What agony some of us go through because of that Egypt—we fail to take positions of responsibility that are offered to us for fear that we won't make good. We don't go to meetings we should go to for fear of saying things that will bring smirks from everyone. We don't ask the questions we want to ask, thereby forfeiting the knowledge we need, because we are in bondage to what other people will think of us. Is that your Egypt? Do we share that one?

Sometimes the Egypt that enslaves us is just a habit. We have done something the same way so long that we do not know how to stop doing it that way. We respond to others as if we were computers, taped, and programmed. A child does something and we give him a programmed response, such as: 1) "I'm never going to buy you another thing if you break that." 2) "I always tell you not to do that." 3) "If all the kids in your class jumped into the middle of the lake would you do it too?"

We are slaves to the way we have always done things.

And often the habitual way of doing it is destructive. I'm thinking about human relationships, friendships, especially among us Jewish people. There is a sharp edge to our camaraderie sometimes. Listen to friends speak to one another, and from the content of what they say, you might doubt that they are friends. The conversation has a little too much knife edge, a bit too heavy on the put-down side. Oh, we pass it off as the *kibitzing* of old pals, but sometimes it seems more like sword play with not always blunted weapons. We just fall into that habit of having to make a smart comeback instead of just listening. We want people in a group to know that we're there, and are just as hip, just as cool, just as savvy as they are. Out of sheer habit it seems, some of us stick pins in one another, instead of just being supporting friends.

Habits are Egypt for many of us. Henry Kissinger bites his nails, maybe with good reason, and the kid next door or even closer is more and more of a pothead... and we stay in the same job, doing it the same way, with the same recreations and keep replaying the same fruitless arguments with our husbands, wives, and kids, because we are enslaved and yet are as afraid as our fathers of crossing a Red Sea to freedom.

If only we could sit down together, and tell each other what our Egypt is like, what it feels like from the inside out... if we could only help one another figure out where the Red Sea is.

The Bible story has just one bit of help for us, beyond telling us that we are in Egypt. When the Jews came to the Red Sea they were terrified. Going forward was as impossible, it seemed, as going back. It was the crisis, what Gestalt calls "the impasse." They called out to Moses, "Save us!" Moses too was at an impasse. He cried out, "God will do it for you, just watch and see." But God sets things in perspective as He says, "Moses, tell the children of Israel to go forward." And they do. And somehow they cross the sea.

That story is so true in its beginning that I cannot believe it is lying at the end. It is so accurate when it tells about Egypt, and how we are all there, and how we sometimes don't even want to get out, it must have some truth at the end.

The story says that God helps us cross the Red Sea. He does not cross it for us—Moses was wrong if he thought that. But He helps us. If we go forward, He somehow gives us the strength to keep going and survive without Egypt.

If we want to get out of Egypt, really want it, we can. Our people did. Others do. Yes, hard as it was to get the Jews out of Egypt, it is harder to get Egypt out of the Jews. But we can. *Yom Kippur's* message is that God cares. And somehow helps.

This year, you and I could get out of Egypt, could get Egypt out of us.

God help us, we could.

Shulayim: Rabbi-Cantor Nancy Landsman

I have learned so much from Rabbi Mark Shapiro. This viewpoint is from someone who has the unique perspective of being a congregant since age four, as well as a cantorial soloist who sat across the *bimah* leading services with him. As a child attending family services, I found Rabbi Shapiro's sermons to be engaging and, coupled with the Oneg *Shabbat*, they were the highlights of *Shabbat* for me. Rabbi Shapiro inspired me to be a camper at OSRUI, to become involved in the youth group, to pay close attention to his teachings in confirmation class, and then as a senior-year high school student, to attend the *Ma'ayan* program at OSRUI.

Both the content and the delivery of Mark Shapiro's sermons influenced me to choose the career path I did. My love of singing led me to the cantorial path, and to the honor of beginning my career at BJBE and then, several years later, returning.

There are two readings that stand out which Rabbi Shapiro read often over the years, and which I have incorporated into my repertoire. Every year during the *Yamim Noraim*, I would look forward to hearing him read the poem, "Lord, I

Have Time" by Father Michael Quoist. Not only has the poem made a great impression on me, but the way in which he read it has left an indelible mark. Every time I read this poem and deliver sermons about its powerful meaning, I think of Rabbi Mark Shapiro and I hear his voice in my head. Similarly, when I officiate at funerals and read, "Birth is a Beginning" by Rabbi Alvin Fine, I find that I am reciting the words in the comforting way I have heard Rabbi Shapiro read them. Now as a newly ordained Rabbi, I am humbled to follow in the footsteps of a truly remarkable man, my rabbi, Mark Shapiro.

Nancy Landsman is spiritual leader at Congregation Ahavat Shalom in Deerfield, Illinois. She was ordained by Jewish Spiritual Leaders Institute in 2016. She served as Cantorial Soloist at BJBE from 1986–1989, and was confirmed at BJBE in 1974.

I LOVE YOU

Rosh Hashanah 5737, 1976

What feelings live behind the words that we use to communicate with each other, and are we really transparent or authentic when we share them? On this Rosh Hashanah, MSS explored love between family members as it relates to other emotions and yes, expectations, as he examined all the things that we might be saying to our loved ones when we say—perhaps not so simply—the phrase, "I love you."

IN THE LATE 1940s, University of Chicago students were considered the typical egghead intellectuals. One story about them featured two university students who passed one another on the Quadrangles.

"Hello," said one. "How are you?" said the other. And as they walked away, each one muttered under his breath, "I wonder what he meant by that?"

Sometimes an ordinary word or greeting is just that— ordinary. But sometimes, even off the college campus, an ordinary word can have many shades of meaning.

In the Broadway play, with the long title *For Colored Girls Who Have Considered Suicide/When the Rainbow is Enuf*, the cast discusses the different things a man may really mean when he apologizes to his wife or girlfriend by saying, "I'm sorry."

He may say, "I'm sorry, but I mean it. Of course you know that, honey."

"I'm sorry, but you know I can't stand it when you do that."

"I'm sorry I did it, but that's the way I am."

"I'm sorry—there, I said it—what more do you want?"

And the girl concludes by saying to husbands and men in general, "Stop it! I don't need any more of your 'Sorry!'"

I'm sorry doesn't always mean what it says.

There are a number of phrases like that, which find their way into a family's life. Some are common: "What's for dinner? Where's the paper?" Some are deeper, like "I'm sorry" or maybe *I love you.*

I hope that *I love you* is a phrase that gets used around your house at least occasionally, spoken by almost everybody to almost everybody else.

But *I love you* can mean so many different things.

I think of that *Rosh Hashanah* story of Abraham and Isaac, going to Mt. Moriah together—Abraham knowing only that God has asked for his son; Isaac not even knowing that. We know they travelled for almost three days to the mountain and three days coming home, and hardly any of their conversation is recorded in the *Torah.*

But I can imagine Abraham saying to Isaac on the way to the mountain, "I love you, Isaac," and saying the same thing on the way home, "I love you, Isaac." Yet what a difference in the meaning! On the way to the mountain, Abraham's meaning was "I love you, Isaac, even though it isn't going to seem that way. I love you. Don't hold this against me."

And on the way home, with Isaac safe, God's larger purpose now revealed, Abraham's *I love you* would have been different. "I love you Isaac. How could I have ever thought to give you up? I love you Isaac, and I never knew how much until just now."

When we say *I love you* to others in our family, our kids, our parents, grandparents, grandchildren, we say it with different shades of meaning. In many of our families, I love you is only the beginning of a sentence.

In some families, *I love you* is almost always *I love you*, but…. "I love you, but why in the devil don't you start to…." "I love you, but I can't stand it when you…."

In some families I love you is used as a hunting license, as permission to demolish the ones you say you love.

Yes, it happens in all families sometime. But in some families it happens most all the time.

Have you ever seen that gross All-American event called the Demolition Derby? The one in which drivers of old stock cars try to put other cars out of commission by crashing into them? The last car to be able to move is declared the winner. Victory is achieved by annihilating the opposition.

Some families are miniature demolition derbies, week after week. Arguments don't get settled in such families. What happens is that the one who can keep yelling the longest and strongest winds up the winner because everyone else quits. You know how such scenes end; with a child saying the same thing over and over, and the parent finally saying in exasperation, "Go off and do as you please. I can't argue with you anymore," leaving the child not exactly the winner, but at least the survivor. Or maybe it's a discussion which slowly turns into a battle and which ends with the parent screaming, "You'll do it because I said so, period!" The adult wins not by maturity but simply by ordering the other players off the field.

Some homes are daily scenes of demolition derby. *I love you, but....*

The Demolition Derby game isn't the worst one that some families play. At least in that family game, your hostilities are expressed and sometimes exhausted. Some families play the game called, "I'll save my anger card until you give me an opening, and then, Pow!" You know how to play that game, and how it feels when it's played against you. You were furious when your daughter messed up the room, or when your husband came home late without calling. But there was no time to be angry then. So you stored it up and when they asked you for something two or three weeks later and they seemed vulnerable, then you played the anger card with a flourish. "*I love you too,* but how come you did that to me two weeks ago Thursday and now you have the nerve to ask me for a favor?"

Of course it's natural to play the demolition game and the anger-card game some of the time in all families. But is your family the one that by definition is a constant battleground between generations? Many are.

Somewhere, some of us have lost sight of a basic truth: We're all in it together. You, your parents, your kids—we have had, do have, and will all have the same problems and joys. Our inner feelings are really the same at the same life stages, our needs for appreciation, for recognition are the same. Other family members do not have to be demolished because they are not opponents in the game of life, but partners.

Example—we are planning a tri-generation weekend retreat. Bring the kids, but bring grandma and grandpa or other representatives of that generation in your family. Now how do you respond to that event? Do you say, as some have, "You mean spend a weekend with my parents and my kids? Forget it!" Or, perhaps you see the great possibilities for intergenerational communication and learning and sharing that could open up?

We really can comfort one another and even teach one another in our families once we stop demolishing. A man told me that he visited his elderly grandmother after she had come through a prolonged illness. The grandmother reflected on life and death and shared a deep thought with the grandson. "I wasn't afraid of dying," she said. "I've had a good life. When God wants me I'll go happily." They shared a tear or two. And the grandson's vision about life and death was thereby enlarged.

What comfort and learning can take place once we stop demolishing!

Once "I love you" stops being a hunting license.

There's another common way of saying *I love you* and meaning something more. Sometimes we say *I love you* and mean *I love you and therefore….* Therefore you really ought to be doing it my way, or thinking my way, or being what I always hoped you would be at this age. In other words, for some people, "I love you" is an IOU to be collected or at least requested regularly.

This *I love you*, which turns the speaker into a collection agency, has many forms. But the worst form is the one that says, "I love you and therefore you ought to be a mirror image of me, or at least an image of the things I always wanted you to be."

We use it that way to our mates sometimes. "*I love you,* so why don't you start making a better living?" We use it that way to our parents. "*I love you* so why can't you come out and sit with the kids like grandmothers are supposed to do?" We use it that way most often with our kids, though. "*I love you* and therefore... be a delight, get into college, be the perfect student, have a status position in the world, give me my *nachas* because *I love you* and therefore it will prove that all my wishes for you are only for your good."

That attitude, always a source of potential family problems, has become even more dangerous in our day. Some years back, parental expectations were more easily fulfilled. You want your kid to go to a good college because he's bright enough? You think he should be a CPA or a dentist or a lawyer? You want him to get his education out of the way first, and then look around. You want him to settle down with a Jewish girl after a marriage ceremony and provide you with grandchildren? Your chances used to be good that all of it would happen that way, and very good that at least some of it would happen that way. Because what our parents wanted from us we generally did. All these were available and society agreed that they were good.

But the world has turned a bit, and saying *I love you, so do it my way,* to your children is doomed to even more failure and more frustration than ever before.

The old growing up grooves are changing. Many Jewish kids, like many other kids, may not go to traditional colleges and will not get the scholarships, for most of them are reserved for children of other minorities, and that's just a fact of life now. Many Jewish kids, like others, will take significant intermissions in their college educations, and that is hard for some of us to accept, though it may not be a bad idea.

I know one father who has told me year after year that he is upset with his son because the boy has never quite finished college and has worked at so many different jobs in between. If only he would finish school and get on with his life, says the father. But to tell the truth, that young man is growing up just fine, getting practical experience in the fields of his interest. And when he puts the finishing touches on his education, he is going to be prepared for the real world. By all standards the boy is doing fine in his growing up, but the father cannot see beyond the fact that the diploma is not yet in the son's hand.

Our children's jobs will not necessarily be traditional high-status Jewish girl and boy jobs. Their social and sexual styles may be very different. They may not want to live in homes like our homes. Chances are that they will not grow up and become affiliated with the synagogue in which they grew up.

So we can only hope that our love will help them be their best selves. Not because they owe it to us, but because it will make their lives richer.

We all draw up ordinary wills.

Jews used to leave ethical wills to their children, final instructions on how to act. I read three of those wills recently.

A 12th-century scholar instructed his kids on how and what to study, how to raise their kids, and how to arrange their library. Pretty specific. A 19th-century scholar warned his children not to speculate with the small estate he would leave them, and told them to be friendly to all men... not so specific.

And when Rabbi Jacob Weinstein, *alav hashalom*, died in 1974, the will he left for his children said, in part, "I know I cannot impose my values and judgments on you, but I can and do request that you not let your Jewish heritage go by default. Make your decisions on the basis of knowledge as well as sentiment. It may be a real help in holding you all together." He knew that love is not a "You-owe-me."

Love is our wish that they be their best selves, emulate some shared values, and carry on a tradition—not because they owe it to us, but because it will probably make them whole and happy. Examples we can be. But collection agencies—never.

But too often *I love you* means *I love you and therefore...* or *I love you as long as....* And that kind of love is not a hunting license, not an IOU. That is a time bomb, a package that will self-destruct.

I love you as long as...as long as we have good times together, as long as it fits into my plans, as long as I feel the way I do now.

I know that husbands and wives and lovers are guilty of using it that way to one another. But I am even more concerned about families in which that *I love you* has already blown up. Families living with estrangement between brother and sister, between in-law and child, families in which others have been written off.

I'm thinking of a woman I know, with one son, one son who was the darling of her life as he grew up. But the woman had some difficulty with her new daughter-in-law and the *machetenisten*. And when her son sided with his in-laws instead of with her on a dispute, she decided that this was the end, and has not seen him since nor taken notice of her newest grandchild.

If this were a once-in-a-million horror story, it would not be significant. But seeing people at times of important family events, I know that these stories are becoming more and more common in Jewish families and, yes, maybe even in your family.

And what a tragedy it is that sometimes these problems are solved only when someone dies. I've seen it, you've seen it. This last year I saw seven brothers who came together for the first time in years at their mother's funeral. They had split into armed camps in prior years because of slights, real and imagined. But because they had to, they sat together to tell me what their mother was like. And they cried together too and held one another, and because grief is such a great catalyst and also a glue, they revived some good old feelings, and I think they are a bit more together now.

What it might have done for that mother could she have seen it! A week, two weeks before she died, one day before. In death she did what she could not do in life. She ended their estrangement.

Not *I love you as long as* but rather *I love you without reservations or hidden messages.* That is what many of our families need to be saying and living by. Maybe that is what yours needs.

Not every family can be saved, nor every relationship.

But if we could start to say *I love you*, not as hunting license or IOU or time bomb, but as a free gift of ourselves, then 5737 could be a good year for those you say you love.

And for you, too. For the overpowering truth is that if things go well with the family, life is worth living under almost any conditions. And when the family falters, no matter what other success we have, life seems to fall apart.

God... help us to find new ways to love the same old loved ones.

M'yuchedet
—Unique

Rosh Hashanah 5738/1977

---

*MSS and family took off to Israel for five months in 1977
as part of his first sabbatical. He returned with a better
knowledge of Hebrew, a slew of real-world experiences, a
new perspective on the land of milk and honey, and much to
share with the congregation that granted him the extended
time away. Just weeks after he returned, he shared some of
what he learned on that journey.*

SOME RABBIS HOPE THAT THEIR CONGREGANTS, at least a
few, will be led to Jewish scholarship. Some hope that their
congregants, at least a few, will become philanthropists.
Some want to make them Zionists, some want them to become
more Jewish in daily life, some just want their congregants to
come to Temple a bit more.

Okay. I lust in my heart after all those things. But on
examination, I conclude that my goal has been and still remains
this: to make Jews excited about their Jewishness. It's a simple
way to say it, but it's right. To make you prize the Jewish part of
yourself more than you may at the moment so that if you used to
think of your Jewishness as less important a part of your identity
than your golf handicap, or your football loyalty, you might move
it up, and do it out of a new excitement in your Jewishness. To
make Jews excited about their Jewishness—that's what I have

been trying to do from this spot for some years.

So I went to Israel, looking for fuel, for a personal transfusion of excitement for me, hoping to find that our people have built something especially good in that land—something out of the ordinary, something which can excite me and touch me about my Jewishness as I want to do for you.

I thought Israel should be the place. You know the way most people talk when they come back. "Israel!" You know the way the fund raisers talk—"Israel, ISRAEL!!!!" I went to find some of that excitement in depth, which one can only do in a more extensive stay. I wanted the Hebrew, the knowledge, yes, the change... but I needed some of that Jewish excitement.

I went hoping to find Israel a uniquely good and Jewishly exciting land, and among my discoveries was the fact that many ordinary Israelis are looking for the same thing. At least that's the way I interpret some very common, recurring reactions from people in many strata of life.

A lady from Kurdistan, who came to clean our apartment once a week and to teach us Hebrew on the side, would say, "Mordechai, Chana, *Tov, ba'aretz, ken?* It's good here, isn't it? It's better than America for a Jew, right? You are coming back for good some day, aren't you?"

An elderly lady from Iraq, without any teeth, was selling little amulets on the Jerusalem streets, and asked us, "Only tourists? But isn't it wonderful here, how can you leave?"

And a soldier we picked up on the highway in our last week, on hearing that we were returning to America in a few days, said sympathetically yet quizzically, "It must be hard for you to go back. isn't it?"

Quite a switch. I came to find the Jewish excitement, the Jewish uniqueness of the land of Israel. And ordinary Israelis looked to me, the visitor, for confirmation of the excitement, the uniqueness, the ultimate worth of living in the Jewish land if one is Jewish. "Hey tourist! Tell us that it's really true—that it's worth all the sacrifices to be here. We need to hear it from you."

They needed reassurance. World Jewry, American Jewry, in particular, is not storming the ports of Israel to make aliyah or even to try it out.

There is increase in *y'ridah*, the opposite of aliyah. Israelis are leaving Israel for other lands, with little intent of returning. Half of the decreasing number of Jews allowed to leave Russia decide in Vienna to go to America if they can. And they say that there are more Israelis driving cabs on the streets of New York than there are driving cabs in all of Israel.

They want reassurance. Also, because so many of them are overwhelmed by daily difficulties, and because subconsciously or even consciously so many of them have thought of whether it would be easier somewhere else. But they want reassurance that Israel is special. "It's better here than in America, isn't it?" They wanted me to help them see the forest, not the trees.

After a few months in Israel, we could empathize better. They live a hard life… more anxious than exciting. They live a tiring life. When we think of the Israeli we think usually of the archetypal strong young soldier, sleek and handsome, ready to join his comrades in the tank brigade, forget sleep and receive the thanks of a grateful country. After our stay there I also know that the face of Israel is that of the middle-aged woman going home after work, trudging uphill with heavy baskets, exhaustion etched on that face, too tired to smile or say *shalom*. Her face is also the face of the land.

They live a hard life, and financial hardship is well up on the list of difficulties. We hear about inflation and devaluation, but maybe the human side of the story tells it better. For example: For our family, a ride on the bus in Jerusalem was cheap. When we came, it was 11 cents for adults, when we left in August it cost us 14 cents, and much cheaper for school kids. A bargain. I said so one day to an Israeli and he reminded me of the facts of Israeli life. A good salary in Israel is considered 5,000 *lirot* a month; some make a bit more, lots make less. That is presently worth less than $500 a month. And that simply means, in relative terms, that the Israeli used to pay the equivalent of 75 cents each bus ride and now he pays a dollar—no bargain even for a middle-class-income family and much money for lower-income families. Israeli families just don't go out to eat. That's for tourists. You will take your family to Hackney's for $15 or $20, but if it cost $125 or more, the equivalent for the Israelis, you would stay home, and so do they.

They live a hard life, by our standards anyway. We take a telephone for granted. It is one of our recreations, the hub of our social life. Most of them still have no phone or are still waiting. When they must make a call they have to find a public phone which works—no small order—and then they must have tokens for the phone, called *asimonim*. And where can you buy them? Go try! A counter at the post office has a sign posted over it... "*Ein Asimonim*—No *asimonim* today." And why not? Because people have heard the price of tokens is going up and many are hoarding them and the tokens are manufactured somewhere in Europe and the factory can't keep up with demand.

They have a hard life. The middle class, even the upper-middle class, lives in large apartment buildings, small apartments, which were built rapidly and not very well. But even harder to bear is the layout of some new neighborhoods. The government hurried to build middle-class housing and somehow forgot that a neighborhood must have play areas and room for stores. And those with no cars, which is most, have no way to take kids to faraway play areas or take themselves to faraway stores. Daily *tzorres*.

Now maybe you think that these things sound like hardships to you only because you know something better. They do too. Movies and TV, which are their mass entertainment, too, are filled with American culture and American assumptions about the things which make the good life. So Israelis don't just have to look at American tourists to know what the good life can be. Their media folklore is filled with expensive jeans and stereo sets and cars and calculators and washers. "Visions of sugarplums" dance before them too. And they would like some of that action too.

They live a hard life. And maybe that is why they want others to confirm for them that it is an exciting country, a good country, a uniquely worthwhile country, hoping we could see the Jerusalem of Gold which hardship often obscures for them. And we could!

And to you I want to say that in the midst of the hardships

of daily life, there are hints of the Messianic, things that make a Jewish State special and exciting.

Here is one. Israel today is filled with South African Jews. There are many in absorption centers, many in new settlements, many joining *kibbutzim* and *moshavim* in large groups.

Now most of them have left behind quite a lot. In South Africa the Jews, like most all whites, had big houses with cheap domestic help and lots of leisure time. They had businesses and cars and positions and lots of money. And they left most of it behind, just in order to leave South Africa, left the house with the upstairs maid and the downstairs maid for a crowded few rooms in an absorption center.

They are running from trouble, but here is the point—from future trouble. As yet there has been no drastic change in South African life, no chaos yet, no wide-scale race rioting yet. But the signs are all around them, and many of them know history very well, and know that when chaos comes to a land Jews are often caught in the crossfire.

Now here is the exciting fact. Because we live in the time of the existence of an Israel, South African Jews have an early choice. If South Africa were on the edge of racial chaos 100 years ago or even 35 years ago Jews would not be getting out quickly because there would be no obvious alternative refuge. The very existence of Israel makes the situation different. Today they can ask themselves not, "Should we try to leave this homeland?" but rather…"How soon can we leave for Israel?" Today, foresight enables them to save themselves. In past years when disaster was on the horizon even a Jew who saw it coming could do very little. So Israel, built as a place of refuge for those who had survived a catastrophe, becomes a haven for Jews who want to avoid a catastrophe. Today Jews can save themselves.

For the South African Jews pouring into Israel, Israel is the miracle of safety.

And here is another—an event we lived through from the Israeli side. And if you heard it before, I hope you will listen again and try to understand what it meant.

A small ship set sail from South Vietnam in late spring,

filled with South Vietnamese who were escaping from the North
Vietnamese regime. They were dentists and college students and
housewives and they hired an old ship and a captain and a few
sailors and got on the boat, hoping to escape to somewhere. Very
naive, you might say.

Nobody really cared about them. Who are so forgotten as
the South Vietnamese? We fought for years to save them from
something, and then we decided that we were wrong and have
forgotten them and so has the rest of the world.

The rest of the world surely wanted no part of those 70-odd
men women and children in a boat... a boat which soon lost its
engine, had hardly any food or water left, was rationing water
out a few tablespoons a day and that only for the children. Other
ships came by, close enough to be hailed for help, but when they
saw that only South Vietnamese were on board, they closed their
eyes and sailed away.

And who came along and saved them? The third world or the
PLO? The U.S. Navy or the Red Cross? No! It was the good ship
Yuvali, a small plodding Israeli cargo ship with hardly enough
room for its own crew. It saved 70 bedraggled South Vietnamese
from the edge of death and eventually brought them home and
settled them in a new town amid the kind of welcome usually
reserved for returning heroes.

I wanted to know about the ship's captain. He was
interviewed by Israeli reporters. They asked him why he did it,
and he said, "What else could I do?"

Great heroes often speak simply!

"What else could I do?"

Let that statement, in context, be written on the blackboards
of all the Jewish schools and the non-Jewish schools all over the
world. Let it be graffiti all over the chambers of justice, and let us
memorize it in context, and let us repeat it with the respect that
we reserve for the *Sh'ma* or the *Kaddish*, or "give me liberty or
give me death."

What else could I do but save them? Oh JEWISH SHIP
CAPTAIN! You could have sailed away like the Panamanians did,
like the Nicaraguans did, and like the Japanese did. You could

have looked the other way. The rest did! You could have decided that you had no room. You didn't. Or, Jewish ship captain, did you look at the ship and see instead the ships of 35 years ago, filled with Jews who could find no port or captain in the world who would save them from sailing back into hell? Was it the universal principles of the prophets which directed you that day or was it just accumulated Jewish *menschlikeit* which made you stop to save lives and then simply say, "What else could I do?"

To me, it was as great a moment as Entebbe—no, greater. It seemed to me then that all of Jewish history and experience and teaching were just a way of producing a people which could produce a simple man who would later say, "What else could I do?" And if it only produced a land which could produce such a man, who saves others in his country's name... *Dayenu*.

Israelis live a hard life. They stand in too many endless lines and work too hard and lack the common courtesies. Recreation is a sometime thing for them. When they open the morning papers they read of strikes and hostile Arab speeches. They find it hard to see the forest for the trees.

But they—with our help—and with the help of centuries of tradition have created something unique and exciting. They have created a nation which is presently saving other Jews, and which produces simple and heroic Jews who can still care about others.

I owe them something for that. I owe them reassurance that we are with them. I owe them a gratitude which is willing to share some of the burdens as well as the victories.

You and I owe them a debt for reminding us that we Jews can be extraordinary *menschen*.

Yachdav:
Together

---

*In the story of Akeidat Yitzchak, the binding of Isaac, the
text frequently repeats the word Yachdav—together. Since the
story makes clear that Abraham and Isaac traveled together
to Mount Moriah to make a sacrifice, why was that word—
yachdav—repeated so often in the telling? MSS believed in
the power of relationships, he told us—family relationships
most of all. Amid concerns that people were choosing careers
and lifestyles over deciding to raise families, he taught that
the recurring message from the Torah meant that life was
meant to be lived Yachdav—together with loved ones.*

IF YOU REALLY WANT TO FIND OUT what people are thinking
about, go to the movies. There in the great darkness, they
project on the giant screen what a generation is thinking about,
worrying about, hoping for.

You can't go to the movies in the '30s and '40s anymore. But
the magic of TV gets us back there. And late on a Saturday night,
or sometimes at 1:00 in the afternoon, or on Channel 11, you can
see the movies that told what people were hoping and believing
forty years ago. They believed that love was great and holy—that
love meant marriage and that meant children and grandchildren
and forever. If there were problems, Jimmy Stewart would simply
"lick them," and hug his family all together at the end of the
movie. These were movies that promised that "every day's a

holiday because you're married to me." They... we... believed it.

Go into that great darkness these days and things are different. I don't just mean the language, the love scenes, or the price. Today the great screen shows movies in which people leave one another at the end. Jill Clayburgh, the *Unmarried Woman*, ends her picture by walking away by herself, prepared to live without being together with anyone for a while. One of the generation's great Jews, Woody Allen, tells us between laughs, that it hurts to get involved with other people. He can wish *Annie Hall* well, and maybe it's all for the best, but still they had to split. The screen of the '70s, like a great crystal ball, sees us clearly. We do believe that relationships can hurt; that facing the world by myself might be the way to find happiness.

So there are two ways of thinking about myself and others. The great things people can do FOR one another versus the awful things people can do TO one another. You and I know that both are true at the same time. Building relationships is holy and profane—marvelous, yet sometimes awful and painful.

The story of Abraham and Isaac combines these truths. You might say it stars both Jimmy Stewart and Woody Allen together. Can that be why we're really never bored with the story, although we know its ending so well? Abraham loves that boy beyond all else, that child of his old age. His life and Sarah's life are wrapped up in Isaac. And then because he trusts God as much as he loves his boy, he walks with the boy to fulfill the incomprehensible yet inescapable command: offer him up.

The *Torah* uses one word again and again to tell the story: *Yachdav*—together. The command comes. "Take the boy, go, the two of you, together." Isaac takes wood on his back, Abraham takes the flint and the knife, and they walk on, *yachdav*, together. Isaac stops on the way. "Papa, we don't have the material for the burnt offering, what does it mean?" And Abraham replies, "God will take care of it." And they went the two of them "together."

At the very end, the *Torah* says, "And they rose up, and they went home, together."

Yachdav, together. It is the drum-beat refrain. It is the word of triumph and relief at the end, as it was the very word which tore at one's heartstrings during the earlier narration.

The story tells it well—the things we can do for one another, versus the things we can do to one another. Is being together worth it? The *Torah* says yes. The movies used to say yes.

But I'm afraid that we, like our movies, are saying no too often. That it's not worth it.

Some of us, in a belief that a lack of human relationships and commitments will really make us happy, or keep us from being hurt, take aim at the family.

Family, among some people, is today's new dirty word. And I don't just mean our over-eager willingness to move away from extended family, or the fact that divorce, which never should have been a scandal, has become a "well, why not" thing. Beyond that, some people are just against the idea of having a family. Some young couples are saying, "We don't want kids. We don't want the responsibilities. They will take time away from what we really want to do." And then they say, "Besides, who wants to bring kids into this kind of world?"

Thank God that our ancestors never considered that question seriously. Because I like it here—right now. I like it much better than any conceivable alternative. And if one considers Jewish history and the epochs into which other Jews were born, the '70s in America seems like the Garden of Eden.

Yet people bad-mouth the family and having children. I hear it in pre-marital interviews with couples. Children? Maybe later, maybe one, maybe not. They have other agendas. If you're modern, you're off learning to row a kayak or climb a mountain or scuba in Aruba, not home raising a family.

And they point to our supposedly bad family experience, as if our experience were their reason for not wanting a family. They quote that frightening Ann Landers column of a year or so ago, in which she asked how many people would do it all over again, would marry and raise kids. Over half of the respondents said they wouldn't. Which shows either something about people who write to the paper or that some of us have been brainwashed and have bought the huckster line about the good life being the unencumbered life of the "handsome man, lovely girl, off doing their own thing, both with careers," and certainly without kids to mess up the schedule or freedom.

Aren't they having fun! But tune in on them later, 25 years down the road, when you can't scuba in Aruba because your back is bad; when you haven't become president of anything, not even the bowling league, when you look for something in your life that has meaning, then what will this childless existence look like? What meaning will it have had? What will you have given back to the world for all the things it gave you? What kind of immortality can you possibly have?

I think of people who have told me in pre-marital interviews that they weren't planning to have children. One couple especially—bright, sensitive, kind. They had decided not to have children because it would hold back their careers. Usually I try to listen and ask pointed questions instead of giving lots of advice, but I remember giving a mini-sermon, something like this: "If good, kind people like you decide not to have children, where are the good and kind and talented people of tomorrow going to come from? Some of the least responsible people in the world are going to have children. Those who have something to give to their kids had better have kids, just to keep it balanced, or the world will be like *Animal House*."

So today, some Jews are telling other Jews to have more children. It's because we care about the survival of our people, especially in the shadow of the Holocaust, but also because we believe that life and relationships are good and holy, and that searching for lifelong happiness by following just our own star is humanoid, not human, and ultimately a blind alley.

Yes, togetherness is often hard. But isolation is deadly.

That is true all over. It happens to be true in this building and true of this congregation and of the religious schools we have created.

We're blessed with some insightful educators who think about kids as people and not just as bodies, so we've embarked on a new major effort in all our schools. We call it "Building Community." We hope it will solve a problem, and also meet a need we are just now recognizing.

What's the problem? The problem is really that of "student

A and student B." Student A comes from a good Jewish family, his parents are somewhat observant, think positively about the Temple and attend frequently. Student A has reasonably good teachers, some great ones, and a course of study that is challenging. Student A feels good about religious school, not every day, but often. He likes coming to Temple, cares to get involved in groups, smiles a lot when he's here.

Student B comes from a good Jewish family, his parents are somewhat observant, think positively about the Temple, and attend frequently. He has reasonably good teachers, some great ones, and a course of study that's challenging. Student B feels totally hostile to the Temple and religious school. He doesn't like to come or get involved, he keeps his coat on because he wants to imagine he's not here, he frowns a lot while he's here and hardly says hello.

What happened to Student A that didn't happen to Student B? If it's not teachers or texts or classwork, it must be something else. Maybe you guessed it before we did. Student A feels comfortable here because he knows other kids, is known by them, feels that he really is a part of the world here, not just an unwilling consumer. And clearly, Student B feels the opposite. Transpose the issue into adult terms, and you will see that all the same things hold true. So we knew we had to reconstruct the school somewhat in an attempt to turn B's into A's and A's into A pluses.

But while we were doing that, we recognized something else. Those of us who didn't grow up in the suburbs, which means almost all of us, will understand it. Whether you attended a synagogue or not as a child, you probably knew something like the Jewish Community, because eighty percent of the kids in public school with you were Jewish, or there were Jewish stores and synagogues right around the corner, with billboards announcing the coming of Jewish holidays. Even without the synagogue, you knew you were part of the Jewish people just from living where you did.

That's gone for our kids. We all know that the world of our children is not the world of our fathers or grandfathers, but we tend to forget that it's not even like our world was when we were growing up. For the Jewish kids growing up in the areas this Temple reaches, the synagogue, and most particularly its school, constitute the only real Jewish community that a youngster knows. This means we'd better realize it and try to be a community as well as a school for kids, a community which lets them know other Jewish kids, makes them feel a part of a whole by helping him set goals for the larger and smaller community of the classroom. Because the Jewish world of our children is so much more narrow than ours was, the Temple has an extra task.

The principals and I thought hard about what we would do to change things. We started last winter. We brought in the best Reform educational consultant we could find to brainstorm with us. Then we brought her back for a weekend to train and help our teachers in techniques for building community and trust among kids.

That new emphasis in all our schools is going to need parents more than ever before, for no real Jewish community is all children, and kids know it.

What is true of us in general is also true of us as students. Isolation is disaster; relationships, a sense of community, being a part of something larger saves us, gives us the power to learn and love and be whole.

Abraham and Isaac walked toward disaster, but they walked together, and that helped. Eventually, they left the mountain together, saved from death.

If relationships can save, is the opposite true? Can lack of relationships or loss of relationships kill? The answer appears to be yes.

This last year, I attended a seminar on "Death and Dying" and heard Dr. James Lynch speak. Lynch is a professor of psychology, director of the psychosomatic clinic at the University of Maryland Medical School. He wrote a book entitled *The Broken Heart*, and his talk that day was entitled "Loneliness Kills." "Loneliness kills! I really believe it. We have just completed studies on possible causes of arteriosclerosis, cardiac disease, and strokes. There is an undeniable link between loss of relationships, separation from others, and actual bodily health. We've known for a long time the beneficial effect of someone holding the hand of a cardiac patient. It is documentable—it can even stop an arrhythmia. Now we know even more. Men who are divorced and do not remarry die younger than those who remain married or remarry. Single people have the highest incidence of coronary, stroke, and suicide."

And then he added, "We believe this pathology can begin in childhood, that people from broken homes, with backgrounds of family displacement and isolation in formative years have a much higher incidence of early coronary, early strokes, and early death." And Dr. Lynch concluded, "When I say that loneliness kills, I am speaking as a scientist, not a philosopher."

Lynch concludes, "Human companionship is quite literally a form of life insurance. We must either live together, or face the possibility of prematurely dying alone."

That's enough to make you forgive your wife or your husband for the sometime anguish they give you, enough to make you cherish your family, friends, and your children and your parents, enough to make you work at building Jewish community for kids, enough to say that Woody Allen may be telling it the way it looks today, but that Jimmy Stewart had a better answer.

Relationships can be enriching or difficult. But isolation destroys. And loneliness kills. The love of Abraham and Isaac, walking together, was good medicine. Not always sweet or painless medicine, but the way God made us, it is the only medicine that really works.

Shulayim: Rabbi Irwin Zeplowitz

One of the first times I came to Chicago to meet with Mark after I was hired as BJBE's first assistant rabbi, we stopped at Lutheran General Hospital on the way back. It was a Friday afternoon, with all the pressure of an approaching Shabbat. Mark insisted, however, that we go up to visit someone who was ill. He said something that has stayed with me ever since: "They will like your sermon, and may remember it, though they likely won't. But if they are sick and you don't visit, they will never forget it." In that brief moment Mark taught me that what matters most for people is not the intellectual acumen of the rabbi (though that is important), but the compassion, caring and *presence* of the rabbi in the lives of others.

Mark (or MSS as he always wrote) was an incredible speaker and spoke powerful, important, and thoughtful words on a regular basis, but it was that two-sentence "sermon" walking toward a hospital room that I recall the most. It was a teaching that reminded me that, in the end, it is our relationship with others that matters the most. Being present, showing up and having a caring heart—that's what makes a rabbi. And it's what makes us human.

That's the sermon of Mark Shapiro I carry with me every day.

Irwin Zeplowitz is senior rabbi at The Community Synagogue in Port Washington, New York. He served as rabbi at BJBE from 1984–1989.

The Unexpected

Rosh Hashanah 1978

*Why is it that Jews choose the most solemn of all holidays—
Rosh Hashanah and Yom Kippur—to show up en masse at
the synagogue? Wouldn't it make more sense to gather for
happier occasions, or for more festive holidays like Purim or
Simchat Torah? MSS spoke in this sermon about the cultural
irony of showing up at shul on the days that make us feel
most uncomfortable. Clearly we gather for a good reason,
and the result is both holy and wondrous, even if it's not
unexpected.*

SOMETHING VERY FUNNY AND STRANGE happened right in
this room last May. It happened about where some of you in
the middle and right rear are sitting. Some of you may have
been here when it happened, and maybe you remember.

Through the valiant efforts of Gene Schklair and his family,
Vladimir Lazaris appeared right here, speaking to about 200 BJBE
adults and kids. I'm sure you remember—Lazaris was the Soviet
Jew whom this congregation had adopted three years ago, and we
had written letters to him and about him, and through our efforts
and those of others, Lazaris was somehow allowed to leave and be
reunited with his family in Israel.

And then he was here, in the flesh—the person whose picture
we had on the bimah, whose name we had used like a slogan who
symbolized our concern about captive Soviet Jews—was really
here, thanking us, smiling at our kids, lifting them up and putting

them on his shoulders.

The strange incident occurred before most people had arrived. Someone had brought in a small TV set, it was sitting in the corner, tuned to a channel on which an earlier taped interview with Vladimir would appear. A group of us were standing around him, talking, wide-eyed, and suddenly someone yelled, "Here's Vladimir, on TV," and we ran to the TV set, leaving Lazaris standing almost by himself. We watched him on TV, as if that were more real than the real man actually standing next to us. As if we needed the TV coverage to confirm to us that he was really here and that it was therefore really important.

We are strange people often, more impressed with shadows than reality.

Something else important is happening in this room right now. In a way it is as unexpected as Vladimir Lazaris having been here.

It is that you are here. All of you, coming in shift after shift, to be assured of tickets, anxious to get here, not to miss it. Jews flood the synagogue on the High Holy Days—you being here is the big message.

And that is so unexpected that it is very significant.

Now I don't mean that we weren't expecting you. Otherwise we wouldn't have rented the extra chairs. We knew you were coming. But the fact that Jews have somehow chosen to flock back to synagogues on these holidays is unexpected. If you didn't just know this happens year after year you would bet against it.

Because—because these days are not "good-time" days. And many of us think that's all people want. *Rosh Hashanah* and *Yom Kippur* are not a good time.

They aren't smiling joyous days, like some other Jewish holidays in the synagogue. They're not celebrated with the informal abandon of a *Simchat Torah* or a *Purim*, or even a *Shabbat*, all holidays which seem more in keeping with modern informal lifestyles. Yet people flock here for the High Holy Days. The basic music of the Holy Days is the blast of the *Shofar*, a strange kind of non-music, not beautiful by any standard, but like a shriek from a long lost world that jars the ear. Yet people flock to listen.

There's no food served here on *Rosh Hashanah*, hardly any traditional edibles associated beyond the simple apples and honey. *Rosh Hashanah* is short on edibles and *Yom Kippur* is anti-eating which makes it a very strange Jewish day indeed, and yet everyone comes to celebrate it here.

Rosh Hashanah and *Yom Kippur* are not the fun times of the Jewish year, they don't meet any ethnic or gastronomic needs. As a matter of fact, their theme is one that should make us uncomfortable, and that is the theme of judging—God judging us, we judging ourselves. We flock to synagogues on the very days which we know will make us feel guilty of not being good enough as Jews or people and with all that lack of appeal, those very negative overtones, Jews fill the synagogue not on happy *Chanukah* or *Purim*, not on fragrant *Sukkot* or warm fuzzy *Shabbat*, but on these solemn Days of Awe whose message is Judgment, Penitence, and Atonement.

That is unexpected. As unexpected as Vladimir Lazaris getting here in the flesh—your being here, in the flesh these days, is more unexpected.

When the unexpected happens, it shows that we didn't understand the world as well as we thought. When Sadat went to Jerusalem it showed us that we didn't understand the Arab world as well as we thought. Your being here on these solemn days shows a lot about you, about all of us. And though your being here is the message, it may be that like some messengers, you don't know what message you're carrying.

I think that being here on these Days of Awe is your declaration that you still believe in the old Jewish truths. Not all of them, but some of them that are becoming more clear and true to you the older you get. And coming to the synagogue on serious days instead of just fun days shows that you at least pledge allegiance to those truths, and at best want to start guiding your life by them.

One of the truths we really do believe in is that life is holy. Being alive has a meaning far beyond the biological. You know as our faith has always said, that there is a meaning to life beyond what the laboratory can discover. You know that life is holy, and that any system which says that it is all right to take away someone's life when it will bring society greater good is already corrupt because there is no greater good or sanctity than life.

And we've seen that belief in life's holiness surface this past year among people who aren't philosophers or even pious people. It has surfaced in the great concern over the birth of the first child conceived in a dish instead of within her mother.

We're worried about that. Impressed, surely, happy for the woman and the baby, but worried. It's the beginning of something. That little Louise will be loved and valued like any other child, maybe more. We're not worried about her. But conception in a dish can lead to the possibility of one person carrying a child for another who hasn't the time and the genetic manipulation that might go on, and the awful possibilities of the *Brave New World* kind of breeding, where the elite and the workers were produced on demand. We're troubled deeply about that "desanctification" of life, and are rightly getting troubled at signs of this new trend, demanding that the world, both scientific and legal, discuss the ethical and religious dilemmas that this whole giant step has raised. Neil Armstrong said when he stepped on the moon, "One small step for man, one giant leap for mankind." Maybe he was right about the moon trip, maybe it will yet turn out to be a gain for humanity as well as for science, but we know too much now to believe that any scientific advance is necessarily a gain for humanity. You and I believe somehow that life is holy and our flocking to a synagogue on the most holy days, not on the most enjoyable days, shows that as clearly as our worry about what will become of conceiving babies in a dish.

There's another old truth that we believe. And you show you believe it by flocking to the synagogue on days when we don't serve *Challah* or anything else. You show that you believe deep down that man does not live by bread alone.

Well, you couldn't prove that by the newspapers. What are hotter items than food processors? Or courses on bread baking or creative cooking? In the newspapers I read, there is more food news than most other news!

Gourmet cooks, don't get upset. Food is good. Cooking is an art. But the overwhelming emphasis on it symbolizes our culture's real obsession—our passion for pleasure, for having things more beautiful, more lovely, more expensive. There is no one here I imagine, wealthy or not, who is not touched by that obsession for having pleasure through things.

Coming here today on these days of awe which have no connection with things or fun or food shows us what you really know, deep down. What you and I wish we could remember the rest of the year: That none of it brings real fulfillment or happiness.

Not long ago I sat with a family who had just sustained a traumatic loss of a parent. We sat within their lovely new house trying to grasp the extent of the tragedy, and as we looked at each other the message was clear—the new house gave no joy or adequate comfort. It could neither bring happiness by itself nor sustain us through pain.

All our lives are too thing-oriented, but being here today is your attempt to declare independence, to attach yourselves to values that can sustain.

We knew you were coming. Yet it is still unexpected that of all the days in the Jewish calendar, Jews would pick the personally challenging ones on which to show up in synagogue en masse.

I get another message from that. I sense people saying that they really want to be better Jews. Otherwise, why come to be challenged by the messages of these Holy Days.

I believe that Jews in 5739 want to be better Jews, wiser, more responsible, more proud. And part of the evidence is the success of the *chavurot* all over the country and the beginnings of success in *chavurot* right here, right now.

Everyone got a letter not too long ago signed by eight nice people. It invited you to try something very new—to become part of a small group within the Temple, a *chavurah*. What was the stated purpose? To do Jewish things together, to discuss Jewish things, to teach one another and learn from one another, study together with one's kids, or without one's kids. To be part of a group whose avowed purpose is to somehow grow into more

Jewishness at one's own pace, with one's own priorities, without ever having to feel left out or put down and through that, to build some new lasting relationships, to have another small family within the big Temple family which you can call your own. Rabbi Harold Schulweis, spiritual father of the *Chavurah* movement in American Jewry said, "The motto of the *Chavurah* will be the obverse of the *Haggadah's* instruction. The *Haggadah* says, "Even if all of us were well-versed in Judaism, it would still be our duty to retell the story of the Exodus." The motto of the *Chavurah* he says must be, "We are not all wise and do not know and do not understand much of the *Torah*, and so it is our mitzvah to start learning."

If I am right, if your presence on these challenging days is somehow your way of saying that you want to be better Jews, there is a special way to do it now—by joining a *chavurah* within this Temple.

We knew you were coming. And yet the fact that Jews like us gather in synagogues on these days tells me one more thing. That Jews still do believe... in God.

Rabbi Gene Borowitz, who really understands us, says it this way: the death-of-God movement in the '60s did most of us an unexpected good turn. It tried to announce that God was dead—but then it could not tell us where a compelling sense of humanity's dignity was to come from. It seemed to say that our goals and standards for human behavior were merely our own idea and nothing more. But most of us cannot even stay on a diet because we know we made its rules. So Borowitz concludes, "Having come face to face with people who really believe nothing, some Jews among them, we have discovered, often to our amazement, that we believe something. We do not understand very much about what we mean when we say there is a God who commands us, but after all the terrifying experiences of recent decades, that is what we know we believe and probably have believed all along."

To put it more simply, even the Jewish atheists among us are like the one who once locked the door to his room, closed the windows, turned out the light, and then said, "God, now that we are alone and nobody sees us, and there are no witnesses, why don't You admit that You don't exist?" At worst, we are nonbelievers who still talk to God.

So here you are again. I expected you, but it's still wondrous. As overwhelming as finally seeing Vladimir Lazaris standing here, when it was so unlikely that he would ever get out of Moscow. No, you didn't all come to see the pretty *Sukkah*, or light beautiful candles at *Chanukah* or have a bash at *Purim*, or drink wine and eat *Challah* and feel good on *Shabbat*. But tonight, on the Day of Judgment, and next week on the Day of Atonement, everyone is here. You, and we, are the unpredictable surprising Jews. You will keep the old truths alive… you will work at being better Jews. You will, we will, keep faith with God. I'll bet on you.

With God's help, we will.

Shulayim: Eric Schor

"I knew you were coming."
It was that line from a sermon of my youth, remember?
It stayed with me as a silent message to be present. How about you?
It was a calling of sorts, a purpose, a *l'dor vador* moment to show up.

Yes, the sweet sounds of that voice, his voice!
At times that voice had the velocity of a Chris Sale fastball
Demanding social justice, equality, questions that made us think.

Other times a softness to calm the turbulent
souls of his flock
With a look, a glance or gaze, those moments he
made stand still for us.
A pair of hands blessing above so many of our
heads,

A touch on a shoulder, a tap on a school boy's
desk, a word of reassurance,
A smile, a push of his glasses or the sound of a
throat clearing,
That tilt of his head, that ever-so-slight grin or his
subtle sound of laughter.

All unique, all his! No, wait...all OURS!

He was speaking to you! He was speaking to me!
He was speaking to us.
A seat in his study, or a romp with the Rabbi in
the backyard on Harrison.
He was that safe place for so many of us, lost at
times, searching or wondering,
A door always open, for he knew we were
coming.

Every life cycle event, he was there!
He was that constant, he was present without
question.
At times we strayed, for faith needs to be tested,
so he taught.

He never gave up on us and we never gave up on him.
How could we? He brought us through so much.

We all have our own moments with him and we all yearn for more.
Close your eyes, search your own memory and cherish those moments.

Smile. After all, he knew you were coming!

Hineini.

Eric Schor grew up at BJBE and was confirmed in 1978. His family has been part of the congregation for many years.

We Are
Your Jews

Erev Rosh Hashanah 5740/1979

---

*What does it mean to be Jewish—at this particular place in
time, in this particular space in the universe, when people
gather as a community to hear the Shofar and find deeper
meaning in their religion and in their relationships with God?
MSS taught that this generation of the Jewish People is here
for a unique purpose in God's great plan, and that we will
come to understand that purpose if we let ourselves receive
the message.*

I WANT TO REMIND YOU OF WHAT HAPPENED at the end of
the final *Ne'ilah* service on *Yom Kippur* last year, 5739. I
don't mean to imply that you haven't been around since then.
But what happened is worth recalling.

We approached the last page of the book, on which the final
Shofar blast is called. As we stood, facing the ark, four young
men and women of our congregation came to stand with us on
the *bimah*, each one with a *Shofar*. The note was called, *T'kiah
G'dolah*, and all four put their energy into the note and made a
joyful sound unto the Lord.

But it was more than just loud. People listening were stirred,
even moved to tears. Some said later that it was the most beautiful
moment of the Holy Days, though they could not exactly say why.

Some beautiful moments need no explaining. Explain them

and they can even lose their beauty. But this one called out for explanation. Yes, the fact that it was young people fulfilling the *mitzvah* made it memorable. But it also was like a proclamation of a truth on our behalf. It was a declaration of age-old music, expressed in the ram's-horn notes.

I think I found the words to describe what I felt in that proclamation. This new *Machzor* of ours gives us the words. We said them at the beginning of the service. We said: "We are Your Jews."

I think that the meaning of the *Shofar* blast at the end of Yom Kippur is captured in the opening words of *Rosh Hashanah*. WE ARE YOUR JEWS.

God, we have been, are, will be Your Jews.

And as each *Shofar* call has its own sound adding to the total effect, each word of this truth adds to the meaning. I want to find that meaning with you, now.

Let's begin. We are your Jews. WE.

That covers so much territory these days. Hardly any past generation of Jews could see how large it is. WE can. You and your family are in that WE, along with almost 600 families that make up this congregation. There are a lot of differences, even between us. It's still true that when there are two Jews there are three opinions, even when they've been brought up in the same neighborhood. It's still true that if most any one of you were put on that desert island you would build two *shuls*—the one you go to and the one you wouldn't be caught dead in. But you're all in the WE of WE are Your Jews.

Reform, Conservative, Orthodox, Traditional, Reconstructionist...organizational and philosophical loyalties abound within the Jewish community. Within a few miles of here you can find them all.

And there are real conflicts at those levels too. For there are real issues which are divisive—Who is really a Jew? What does God really want? Is our main job to educate Jews or defend them against anti-Semitism or aid the poor ones or help Israel or get the Russians out? And all those well-defended positions and the people who defend them are in that WE. WE are Your Jews.

We mean the old and the young and the unborn. So we tremble a little bit when we say WE, because we're not so sure of the young, just as our parents weren't so sure of us when we were the young. Will they grow up Jewish, stay Jewish, have kids who will stay Jewish, have kids at all to keep Judaism and the family alive? That concern helped make last year's *Shofar* blasts such a symbol: Young people declaring out loud with the blasts that they were and would continue to be part of that proclamation—WE are your Jews!

And when you go to Israel you see most clearly what it means to say, "WE are Your Jews," how broad is that WE. Again and again that struck people who travelled there with us in early July. We found Jews who didn't fit our model, Eastern Jews—and that doesn't mean New Jersey—Eastern Jews from the real East— Morocco, Bukhara—who didn't know about chicken soup or any other *mitzvah* of American Jewish life. Jews who looked different, spoke different, were part of cultures we knew so little of, yet were our brothers and sisters. They had found our old land, and we had found them there.

I doubt that a generation of Jews has ever lived which understood how much variety there is within that We which signifies world Jewry and historic Jewry, and few generations which knew quite how important it was to say and mean WE.

WE are your Jews, God.

But also, we are Your JEWS. Jews. Do you know that we're not used to that word in the prayer book? Past prayer books somehow avoided the word, leaning more toward Israel or Children of Israel, or House of Jacob or some other less direct phrase. But today the book opens up straight and simple. We are Your Jews.

Do you hear the overtones in "Jews" that aren't in "Children of Israel?" I hear some. People haven't liked us that much. It hasn't been easy. But we make no excuses about it. We are Jews. *Yidden.*

If you hear some such overtones too, then we've come a long way. If your parents were second generation American Jews, they wouldn't have written a prayer book that said Jews quite so clearly… and they didn't. Part of their dream, part of the time, was to appear to be a Jewish version of American Protestants, with no ethnic look about them. That dream was appropriate to their day, but we're beyond that.

We say we're Jews. And proudly accept all the accretions of meaning that cling to the term… that we're not just a different religion in a land of different faiths—that we're an old and unusual and unique group. We take the very title that has often been and still is used as insult, Jew—*Yid*… we take it with pride. The fact that it has those accretions makes it more precious.

You could hear some of that in the *Shofar* blasts last year I think.

For at times in our past, just sounding the *Shofar* was dangerous.

During the years before 1948, when the British controlled Palestine, Jews were allowed to visit and pray at the "Wailing Wall" under certain conditions and restrictions. One of the restrictions was that they not sound the *Shofar* or sing *Hatikvah* there. Both might be heard as a signal for battle or Jewish nationalism. So at every *Rosh Hashanah* and the end of every *Yom Kippur*, the mandatory police would be stationed at the Wall to try to enforce the prohibition. An eyewitness tells what happened one year:

> "The British police were there, on top of the houses and walls, joined by an armed squad of Arab Legionnaires. The *Yom Kippur Ne'ilah* service was ending. And the final words, "*Adonai Hu Ha-Elohim*—the Lord He is God" were spoken. There was silence. But everyone stood expecting the sensational to happen. And it did.
> From somewhere in the crowd the sound of a *Shofar* rent the silence. With that sound the Jews there gathered cried out, 'Next year in Jerusalem rebuilt.' The police jumped at them from rooftops, running to block the exits, striking out indiscriminately at Jewish young and old alike. They combed the area, found the *Shofar* and arrested several young suspects. Even the old people were not allowed to stay longer.

It wasn't so dangerous for those who blew the *Shofar* at the end of *Yom Kippur* here last year. But being a Jew anywhere is still to walk near the edge of danger, and something in the *Shofar* blast seems to remind us of that.

Even when it seems that being a Jew in America is worry-free, we round a corner and find ourselves at the edge of danger. Inevitably, it seems.

Maybe that is the only obvious thing we can learn from the *Alice in Wonderland* happenings involving Ambassador Andrew Young and the fallout of past weeks. During these Holy Days I want to address that whole question more comprehensively. But just the issue's surface makes the point here. There was a real controversy—what exactly we don't know yet—involving Young, Carter, Israel, our UN ambassador, our State Department PLO observer. That was the cast. But the story takes on an O. Henry ending in which American Jews, not even in the original cast of characters, emerge as enemy of the American Black community, which was also not in the original cast. There are real enemies in the world. Now who are the real enemies of Blacks, Carter and Israel? And how do we get cast as the racist heavy? It is the non sequitur which makes sense only to students of anti-Semitism and racism, and to us, who have experienced it before. So we are angry, but not altogether surprised.

There is no way we could have foreseen such an attack, unless we were prepared to start at every shadow—no real way we could have prepared. And now the prospect of having to refute the charges of being communally anti-Black seems as unfair as the charges themselves.

One lesson of the incident and the fallout: Being a Jew has always been to walk the edge of danger. It is yet. God, WE Are Your Jews.

God, we are Your Jews. YOUR Jews. That's the word that sounds at home in the prayer book. We understand and accept all the meanings and overtones of the word "Jews," but in that word "YOUR" the *Machzor* reminds us that, somewhere in our lives, God's purpose is being worked out, and that being Jewish is not just being part of this great family, and not just being proudly on the cutting edge of society's dangers, but also being witnesses to an absolute meaning and purpose in the world that our people believes is God's purpose.

We said it last year, before the final *Shofar* blasts: *Adonai Hu Ha'Elohim*. We said it today. We are YOUR Jews, God. And I think we believe it, even when it is hard to say the words. Testifying to belief, like evangelicals do, so freely, too freely, that's not our style. Deep down it seems that God's name used so easily is in vain, or even idolatrous. And talking about believing is also hard for us, and sometimes we itch to get rid of God talk and the whole problem is not worth much.

But watch us and listen to us. Watch what we do, translate some of our words accurately, sensitively, and I think it is clear that you and I today are saying that We are GOD'S Jews, that He lives as we live, and that we care so deeply about being WE, about being Jews, because He commands both.

I think of something that happened to a part of this congregation in Israel. This summer's trip was planned for a first-time experience. And so everything was new to almost everyone. And we did all the things that most tour groups have to do—saw Masada, walked Jerusalem, met Israelis, visited museums, and toured sight after sight.

One part of the itinerary was different from what other groups might do. We prayed together. (They went with the rabbi, what could they expect?) So we held our own services on four different occasions... on a lawn in Haifa (the same lawn where Begin and Sadat met a few weeks ago), in front of the Western Wall, at the back of a school, on a balcony in Jerusalem. We had our own prayer books and the prayers were the regular prayers. We gave some Hebrew names to people who didn't have them, asked an anniversary blessing for a husband and wife... we had services. Four services in two weeks, more than most people have back home.

And when we came back home, when people had thought about the trip and developed their pictures, we asked them to come to Temple on an August night and show some pictures and tell what the highlights were. Lots of highlights... and what was mentioned more often than any other? Praying in Israel. The services. I didn't force them to say it. I really didn't expect them to say it. (Well, I was hoping.) But they meant it, uncoached. Yes, they said, seeing the country was great: the sabra girls, the guide, the excitement and culture and learning... all important— but praying together in Israel, in our Reform way, that was the highlight for many.

Now these weren't *Chasidim* who went over there, nor were they necessarily the fervent and pious of the synagogue. They were like us, of us, people who touched Israel and found in Israel that they were touched by something higher... and were amazed and pleased that this something was an experience of God, which can take place here as well as there.

It was not just WE JEWS in Israel. We were His Jews, there.

God, we are Your Jews.

Eugene Borowitz, who will be here in November for a weekend of sharing and thought, said it this way: "We care about the Jews because—quietly to be sure, we care about God. When we worry about the Jews and the future... we quite naturally ask where God is. But this is not some childish remnant in our psyche, not some infantile hope that Daddy will save us. It is our deep bedrock sense that—odd as it may seem to say it so plainly—the Jews are involved with God."

And we know it all. Whether sounding in *Shofar* blast or simple words.

God. We are Your Jews.

Under the *Chuppah*

Rosh Hashanah morning, 5741/1980

The marriage is more important than the wedding, MSS often told couples preparing to become married. He officiated at hundreds of weddings over the years, sharing many sacred moments under the chuppah with those about to declare their marriage vows. What exactly was the covenant that he was helping brides and grooms enter into? In this sermon, he shared with engaged young couples, newlyweds, and those who have celebrated many anniversaries his thoughts on the love, commitment, intimacy, and adversity that are part of every marriage.

A NEW YEAR IS A GOOD TIME to correct oversights. So let me correct one this morning.

There are things I should have told couples during their wedding ceremony that I never told them. Of course, I had what seemed like good reason for not telling them everything. They weren't listening with all their attention anyway, I knew that. And I don't like long weddings.

But there were important things that probably weren't said by any rabbi or officiant who made you legally the spouse of your spouse. So I want to say to them on this morning of a New Year to all those of you at whose weddings I officiated, to all those married by someone else who also decided to keep it short, to all those who can use the reminding, and to all those who aren't yet married, but may be married by a rabbi who won't feel compelled to say it all during the ceremony.

So, you two... come on. Come under the *chuppah*. Step right up, we're going to enjoy this. Let me talk to you.

I know you've got a lot of hopes and prayers right now. You're hoping your mother will stop crying. You're hoping this ring will fit on the finger. You're hoping the wine won't spill down the front of that white dress, and, young man, I know you're saying a few prayers about that glass, very intense ones. "Lord, give me accuracy, give me strength, let me cream it the first time, please."

Those seem like big things. They aren't. If this marriage of yours is a good one, then no mistake in a wedding ceremony will hurt a bit. If it's not a good one, then all the fancy rented suits and well-timed processions and *chuppahs* with chandeliers won't help a bit.

Just before you walked down the aisle I heard what your friends, those who are standing up here with you, were asking. They asked, "How do you feel?" And you both said, "Okay, I feel okay." And then while some of the wedding party walked down the aisle, the band over there played "Feelings." Very appropriate, because feelings brought you to this moment.

That special feeling finally happened with this special person. You fell in love. You feel in love. And it feels as if it will feel that way forever.

I hope the feeling is there much of the time.

But this ceremony isn't about feelings, no matter what the band played. This ceremony is about your covenant, which means a decision and a promise. And Jewishly, feelings are nice, but decisions and promises are more crucial.

You're ready to say, "I do." That's the right answer. But do you know the question to which that's the right answer? The question isn't going to be, "Do you love each other?" We know the answer to that already. The question is going to be:

"Do you take this special one to be your mate, and do you promise to protect and cherish that one, in good fortune and adversity, and seek together with that one a life hallowed by the faith of Israel?

If so, answer I do."

Your "I do" is a public promise—a decision.

Any guest sitting out there who has been married for even a little while knows that the words of that question are realistic. Both good fortune and adversity are coming. Believe us.

Adversity is coming, big and little. Big mixed with little. The job goes sour. The washer falls apart the day after the extended warranty runs out. The dryer goes the next day. Adversity. Emergency rooms with your kids. The extra weight that doesn't want to come off. Chest pains and fear at night. Nothing to wear. Scared about how freely you use those little plastic cards. Homesick letters from your kids at camp. A death in the family... grief, maybe guilt. The question is, "Will you protect and cherish in adversity?" Promise hard now, and mean it! Adversity is coming.

But promise, just as hard, to cherish and protect in days of good fortune. It's coming too, God willing. And good fortune can be as dangerous to marriage as adversity. Maybe more. When things are too good, people forget that a relationship needs nourishing too. And buying things isn't nourishment. Everyone prays for the day when money isn't a problem, but when money isn't a problem, people get to thinking a lot about how they can enjoy it all. And if the enjoyment isn't regularly first-rate (and it never is), they start to wonder if they might not be enjoying it the way they should with somebody else.

So promise hard for times of good fortune, too.

They say that these are hard times for marriages and families. I've heard that. If that means that more people are getting divorced than ever before, it's true. Everyone knows it just from daily conversations with friends. I know about it from Temple lists. More and more single names with kids come into the Temple. I know it from sitting down this past summer with groups of 8–10 kids at camp, talking about family and finding that almost half of them have gone through divorce.

Why? Why is it happening? People like to blame society when they say that it's a hard time for marriages and families. Don't be so quick to put the blame on society. It's the same society for all, yet some build good marriages today.

More people seem willing to give up on the promise to "cherish and protect always" today. But I don't believe it's because society makes it so, and I don't believe that there are more bad marriages than there used to be. I have to believe that people don't try as hard as they used to. And the more divorce there is, the more it seems okay. If half the block is getting a divorce, why not us? Last year we got a pool table; this year we'll get a divorce.

Don't misunderstand. Many people come to divorce after they have tried almost everything. And many people come to divorce not because they want it, but because their mate will not work on it. We know that.

And don't think Judaism is Catholicism. Judaism makes provisions for divorce, knows it happened, happens, will happen. And nothing in our tradition justifies thinking of divorce as a blemish on a family's reputation or a person's reputation or as a skeleton in the closet.

Divorce is not a black mark. But is it most always a personal scar? Is it most always a terrible hurt? Is it very often a tragedy? Yes, yes, and yes. It can be all these things for the adults involved and I think it is always all of those things for the children.

Judaism never said that a person who divorces his or her mate is a bad person. But it did say, with meaningful hyperbole, that when one divorces the mate of one's youth even the altar weeps.

So, you two... stand here and hold hands, and know today that your feelings of love must become a promise, a decision, a judgment.

You've got to go beyond feelings, even today, because there will be times in the future when the good feelings disappear, hidden under some of the adversity of personal problems. And on those days you'll have to sustain your marriage by the memory of the promise and decision you make today, that you will live out the bad, even the dry times, with that special person.

The thought that if it doesn't work, we can split, both start over is like a crack in the foundation. Because it will be too easy to ask, regularly, how is it working? And the answer to that is never consistently "wonderful," not for anybody.

We all ask the wrong question. "Will this marriage work?" is the wrong question. Ask "will it work" about machines. The question to ask about marriage is, "Will they make it work?" The greatest strength a marriage can have is the decision, made ahead of time, that the goal is forever.

Let's talk about kids.

I'm glad you want children. Some don't. You said you didn't know how many. Tell you what. Have X plus one. X stands for how many you think you want, plus one. It's not just that rabbis need Jews in order to keep being rabbis, though that's true. Part of it is that we lost too many Jews in this century. Part of it is that in reasonable, stable loving homes, big families are better families. No, I can't prove it, but I think it's true anyway. There is a little more chance to learn to share, a little less intensity directed at any one child for too long. It ensures more uncles and aunts and cousins for the next generation, and we need that. And if you're worried about how to afford college for three or four kids, not every Jewish kid has to go college. *"Shteyt geschrieben,"* it isn't. Hand-me-downs and shared bedrooms can really be O.K. Let one go to a trade school or hang around mechanics, and let that one support you in your old age.

But no matter how many you have, there will be good moments and some hard ones. You may disagree on how to raise your kids. You may have a child who is especially difficult to raise. And the way you deal with your kids is so closely tied up with how good your marriage is. So now is the time to start thinking about it.

Do you remember the *Torah* and *Haftarah* readings on *Rosh Hashanah* morning? Each one is about a parent and a child. The *Torah* portion is about Abraham and his son Isaac, the *Haftarah* is about Hannah and her son Samuel. One kid, I think, turns out better than the other. And the portions hint at the reason why.

Hannah wants a child so much, that she says that having him will be enough, that he can serve in the Temple of Eli the priest when he is old enough. She conceives Samuel, in effect knowing that she will soon let him go, give him up to another life, his own.

Isaac is weak because he lives in Abraham's shadow. Samuel is set on a path, and left to walk it by himself.

And so the hardest part of raising your children will be letting go. And that should start early. Yes, you'll give them all the love and attention and advantages like every Jewish kid. And then both of you will have to let go. And maybe you will get *nachas von kinder*, and maybe you won't. They don't come into the world with a warranty card that says, "*Nachas* guaranteed."

Rabbi Richard Israel said it very well—

"No guarantees, not even that they will act grateful.
They probably won't, at least as often as you'd like. The
Midrash tells us that children do not love their parents
the way parents love their children. The most we can
hope for is that they will someday give to others the love
that we give to them. And having done our best, we must
eventually refuse to take credit for the things in them that
turned out well, and equally not take blame for the things
that don't. Well, a little, but no more."

So—don't give love to your children thinking that it's a gift meant to be returned to you. Think of it as a gift in trust for others. Maybe a gift for your grandchildren which your children will give on your behalf, because you showed them how to give it.

What a time to get married—in the midst of the sexual explosion. I don't mean the changing roles of men and women, I mean the explosion of explicit sexual information, and discussion which starts on the adult movie houses of Times Square only to wind up as the lead article in the *Family Home Life* pull-out supplement in the newspaper. It hardly raises eyebrows anymore. But unfortunately, it raises expectations about how crucial it must be to experience everything. The new goal is *Gan Eros*, not *Gan Eiden*. And average folks, meaning most of us, feel that we're missing something if our love life is not Mount St. Helen's.

Don't let the erotica brainwash you. Most people haven't experienced everything. Most <u>happy</u> people haven't experienced everything.

There is, however, an experience within marriage, sharable by two, which is exquisite, satisfying, renewable daily and at any age, and it includes sexuality. They call it intimacy.

Intimacy. To have found someone to whom you entrust your thoughts and your dreams, knowing that the other will treat them gently, will love you and not judge you for any of them. To have found one who listens in the dark, who gives you attention when you really need it. Intimacy. Knowing when the other needs a touch, a word, knowing what the other will say before it is said, and sharing the wonder of that simultaneous knowing. Achieving intimacy… being known by another. The Bible's way of saying sexual intercourse is "knowing and being known." There ought to be marriage manuals written about how to achieve that ecstasy. For when you have it, you have the best. The *Torah* knew how important it was when it said, "It is not good for one to be alone." And unless you work toward intimacy in your marriage, you might be married but yet alone.

What you begin to build now, your marriage and your family, is the most crucial factor in your personal happiness from this day forth. If it produces mainly heartaches, no success in the outer world, no name on the door or money in the bank can ever make up for it. But if this marriage and its family life are fulfilling, then life will feel worthwhile even if the world outside is rocky.

May God bless you and help you as you turn the feelings of love into promises, to cherish and protect in good fortune and adversity, and to seek together a life hallowed by the faith of Israel.

Amen.

Shulayim: Rabbi Alan D. Rabishaw

When it comes to teaching *Torah* (and giving a sermon), Rabbi Mark Shapiro taught me that it's got to be real, and baseball references are ok, too. Straight and honest talk, from the heart. These are the skills I watched him use to build our BJBE community.

The *Talmud* teaches: "One who doesn't build the *Beit HaMikdash* in their own time, it's as though they themselves had destroyed it." A bit harsh? Yes. However, Hasidic rabbi *B'nai Yissachar* teaches that the *Talmud* is really teaching that we must discover the *Torah* that we are uniquely meant to learn and to teach in our lifetime. If we do not, it is as though we, ourselves, destroyed the Temple in Jerusalem.

Growing up, Rabbi Shapiro inspired me to discover the *Torah* that touches my life. He taught me that building Temples is not about brick and mortar, but rather, about heart and soul.

Words are fleeting. What we say and what we do are much more important. Rabbi Shapiro's inspiration has taken root. His words, and even more important, his deeds, have guided me on my journey. I am a better husband, father, brother, and son because of what he taught me. And all this has led me to be a better rabbi—bringing my *Torah*, and my heart and soul to my Temple community. My life's work is a testament to the fact that Rabbi Shapiro's inspiration has had more influence than he would ever know.

Thank you MSS, for helping me discover my *Torah*.

Alan Rabishaw is Rabbi at Temple Or Rishon in Orangevale, California. He was ordained by HUC-JIR in 1991, and was confirmed at BJBE in 1979.

By Choice

Erev Rosh Hashanah 5742/1981

Around 1980, the Reform Jewish community began to refer to those who had converted to Judaism as "Jews by choice," instead of the term formerly used, "converts." In this Rosh Hashanah sermon, MSS wondered what it would be like if everyone in the congregation had to decide whether they were simply Jews who were born into the faith, or whether, given the option, they would choose to be Jewish—to become Jews by Choice.

WITHIN A FEW WEEKS THERE WILL BE a seminar on the North Shore entitled, "Jewish Spirituality: Worship, Gerontology, and Jews by Choice."

Everyone knows what worship is, and most know gerontology has to do with the elderly, but many people don't know what Jews by Choice means.

Jews by Choice is a fairly recently coined term which refers to those who have become Jewish by converting to Judaism.

We needed a new term. The traditional term for a convert to Judaism is *ger tzedek*, but using that makes them sound eternally different. And calling them "converts" isn't accurate for long, because they wanted to be identified as Jews, not "converts." So the new phrase—Jews by Choice. Not by birth, but by choice.

The Reform Jewish community is getting more interested in helping Jews by Choice become integrated in the Jewish community. We here have been trying harder too, and we've created a support group of and for Jews by Choice which has been meeting for over a year now.

But the message tonight isn't that we born Jews haven't done a good job of welcoming Jews by Choice, though we haven't. The message isn't that we have to start doing better by them, though we should.

The message for *Rosh Hashanah*—to all of us born Jews—is to become a Jew by Choice. Not "by chance" as many of us are, but a Jew by Choice.

Rosh Hashanah is called *Yom Hadin*, a Day of Judgment, a good time to think about making a personal judgment, a choice.

Now many people have known for some time that this *Rosh Hashanah* would be for them a day of heavy, difficult decision and choice.

Apples and honey or the Honey Bears? The football game or *Rosh Hashanah*? Who will have more no-shows, the Bears or the Rabbi?

You could tell the way people were making choices by the way they stated the dilemma. Some said, "What a shame that the Bears' Monday night game at home has to fall on *Rosh Hashanah*," while others made their priorities clear by saying, "What a shame for *Rosh Hashanah* to fall on the Bears' Monday night game at home."

I don't dismiss the conflict as a childish problem. There are those whose loyalties to sporting teams are much like religious loyalties or inherited obligations. I really do understand that, and I don't put it down as childish, having similar loyalties myself to an entity somewhat south of Soldier Field. And people know that if they wanted to put a Yiddish-style curse on me they could say: "May the White Sox be playing for the pennant on *Erev Yom Kippur*."

So being here tonight—for some people—is like making a personal statement that they are Jews by Choice.

But the phrase goes deeper, too. I asked a bright, nice lady in the congregation to help me start a group of Jews by Choice. And after she began to meet with the group she came back to me and said, "I'm very comfortable in that group because, you know, that I'm a Jew by Choice, too."

I knew what she meant. I know that she was born a Jew, thus originally a Jew, born so by chance, but that she had become a Jew by Choice, had discovered her own Jewishness. So the only difference between her and the others in the group was that she could utilize her past memories and childhood upbringing in her chosen Jewishness, whereas other Jews by Choice were starting from scratch.

But the lady was right. She was a Jew by Choice, too.

Some of us are Jews by Choice and some by chance.

There are some kids who love to tell us that the only reason they come to Religious School is because their parents want them to. Such *schlimazels!* They had to have parents like that!

And there are adults who still feel the same way. They're still coming and being a little Jewish because their parents want them to. The adults in question may be 50 or 60 years old, their parents may be long gone, but they're a little Jewish because their parents wanted them to be. That's Jewish by chance. By chance you got those parents.

Do you know that some people say they began to feel like more of an adult when their parents died—that finally they were the older generation? Wouldn't it be nice to become a Jew by personal choice before bereavement?

And there are people here who are ready to be Jews by Choice.

I really believe in moments of decision. Not the revival kind where the teacher tells them to make a decision for Jesus and come down to the front to say so, not that kind because that treats people like sheep. But I believe in the power of moments of decision. Like the moment you decided you were in love and this was the person. And today, on the world's birthday, our Jewish Day of Decision, you could make a decision to no longer be a Jew by chance but rather by choice.

What does that mean? It's easier to give examples than to define, so let me try...

Every year we try to make the Confirmation experience for our high school sophomores an opportunity for them to become Jews by Choice. It has to do with the individual blessings. And though the blessings are all private, the procedure can be shared.

The 10th graders are told toward the middle of the school year that the blessings at Confirmation aren't automatic. They have to decide whether to be blessed or not. They have the responsibility of saying yes or no.

Then we talk about how they can decide to say yes or no. I usually put it this way: "If there is something within Judaism or being Jewish, that is very important to you, something about which you can say: "Yes, I believe that, I care about that," then you should say yes, you want to be blessed, to confirm that personal choice. And if you can't find anything in being Jewish that is now important to you, you should probably say no."

And they have to tell me privately, either yes or no. I don't want to tell you the cumulative scores over the years, but we're doing okay.

And what if we did the same thing now? What if we adopted the image of the *Un'taneh Tokef* in which every person passes under the shepherd's staff, and asked everybody to walk up to the ark and say their "Yes" or their "No"—meaning, yes, there is something for me here, or no, I'm still just a Jew by chance. What if one year we didn't sing the songs and say the prayers and give sermons but instead asked you to say out loud a "Yes, by choice," or "No, by chance."

Let's do it without facing the logistic problem. Imagine that you're doing it. What would you say?

I foresee some problems. Here's one: Many who really feel that the answer for them is yes would be afraid to declare it because they might be called called Orthodox. They're not prepared for *kashrut* or traditional *Shabbat* or any of the minutiae that they always have assumed is expected of those who are actively Jews by Choice.

Being a Jew by Choice does not necessarily mean moving closer to Orthodoxy. If only... if only we could burn out that voice of ours which whispers, "BJBE is Jewish. *Beth Sholom* is more Jewish, Skokie Valley Traditional is most and Devon Avenue is even more so."

I know it's hard not to think that way. Because our

grandfathers surely would have seen it that way, and deep down we still consider them the religious experts.

It's hard not to think that way because Jewish life in Israel so clearly proclaims that being a religious Jew means Orthodoxy.

There is a wonderful Hebrew phrase—*Ba'al T'shuvah*—which identifies one who has come back to Judaism after a period of alienation. I think that there are many *ba'alei t'shuvah* here and in other Reform congregations this evening, because those who come back generally want to bring their liberalism with them. Yet in Israel they use that wonderful term only to mean one who has come back to *Yeshivah*-style Orthodoxy. And that's wrong. Even the Israeli distinction between *dati* and *lo dati*—between religious and not religious—that divides the Jewish world into Orthodoxy and everyone else, is not a traditional distinction. So you can choose to be Jewish without changing synagogues.

Stay with the make-believe for a moment, in which everyone walks up to the *bimah* to say whether he is a Jew by choice or by chance. Imagine that Dan Rather is interviewing selected congregants as they come off the *bimah*, asking them exactly what they meant by declaring that yes, Judaism was important to them, they were Jews by Choice.

I can imagine some of the answers. "I stick up for my religion. I've never let anyone get away with saying a bad word about Jews. I've never denied it, Mr. Rather, and I never will."

Would that do your heart good? It wouldn't do much for me.

Of course it's a kind of Jewish identity, and if you say it with the right touch of macho, it sounds heroic, shades of Iwo Jima and the Six-Day War. And of course it is something positive, given the right circumstances. If you're on the next plane hijacked by the PLO and if they ask you if you're Jewish and if you think you could fool them because the name on your passport or the look of your face doesn't give it away. Then—if in those circumstances you stand up and say nevertheless, "I am Jewish"—that is certainly a positive heroic act of a Jew by Choice.

Except that situation doesn't come up regularly. Being a Jew by Choice, whose choice means that he will never deny it is the lowest common denominator. It's just too easy, and we know it.

If being Jewish is worth risking your life for the sake of not denying it, then it has to be worth a lot. If it's worth guarding with your life it must have good stuff inside.

The message tonight is simple. Choosing to be Jewish doesn't mean you choose to be Orthodox, but it must mean more than just standing up for it when anti-Semites spit.

I just heard about a young man, early 30s, with career and family, who determined that never having had a Jewish education was a personal loss to him. He lived in a university town, so he started to get that education at an adult level, and he got so interested in a course on Yiddish that it has become his avocation.

That is one of the hundreds of similar stories these days. There are Jews by chance who have become Jews by Choice who are studying or doing *mitzvot* or pursuing *Tz'dakah* or singing or reading or subscribing, who are living out one or a dozen or more pages of *The Jewish Catalogue*.

And what's the difference between us and the Billy Graham Crusade? Billy winds up asking you to make your decision for Jesus, to come down front and confess that you believe it.

Whereas our tradition asks you to make a decision to be what you are—a Jew—and to make it choice and not chance, and decide to do something about it.

Billy Graham's appeal for his people to make that choice is very powerful. "You need it!" he thunders.

Jews like to have some insurance. So we say not only, "You need it," but we sprinkle in just enough Jewish guilt—"We need you!"—to keep it going. "Grampa," we say, "would be so proud."

A fact that sometimes overwhelms me is that in 90 years all the people you and I know as Jews will be dead. And the people who will then be the Jews then are the as yet unborn and unplanned. Those who are not yet a gleam in anybody's eye will have to be the teachers the scholars, the leaders—the Jews. We can leave them the books and a note in the *Mezuzah*, but beyond that Judaism is in their hands.

And then I realize that it's the same way today. The old Jews, no matter how good they were, are gone. There's just us. Oh, and a few good people joining us, some very fine Jews by Choice who didn't start out life as Jews. We need them very much, too. Whether we're terrific or awful, we're the only Jews God has right now.

Maybe the best thing you could do is to make a decision for 5742—to be a Jew by Choice.

Shulayim: Rabbi Deborah Gardner Helbraun

As a kid, I always looked forward to the "sermonette" when Rabbi Shapiro told a story. Whether it was the one about the crack in the diamond or some other tale, I waited for the signal to close my book and to hear him tell a tale in his special way.

From the sermonette, I graduated to the sermon. At first I was known for falling asleep in the front row before it ever began, but as I grew and took interest in what MSS had to say, his words, his mannerisms, and his general presence in my life are what helped to shape my future and my decision to become a rabbi. As far as that is concerned, a few ideas always stick out in my mind. First, Rabbi Shapiro said that a Jew was a person who ate corned beef on rye with mustard. I didn't like rye or mustard, so I was unsure where that left me, but I most certainly did not eat it on white bread with mayonnaise.

The second was the sermon where Rabbi Shapiro spoke about how heredity made us "Jews by chance" and how we had to work to become "Jews by Choice." I've always focused on this to inform my rabbinate and to help me guide others on their Jewish path.

The last thing was that MSS told me that to be a rabbi, I would have to believe in God "a lot" (his words). Although like most people, there are times when I struggle with this idea, I always think about it and how his words are so influential in my life.

Deborah Gardner Helbraun, Hebrew School Principal at Temple Jeremiah in Northfield, served in that role at BJBE from 1999–2003. She was ordained by HUC-JIR in 1993, and was confirmed at BJBE in 1982.

M'chayeh

Yom Kippur 5743/1982

What are the things that are truly life-giving in our lives?
Gourmet food may give us pleasure, but what really fills us
up? MSS spoke about the wonders of study and service—
study of Torah, study of books and commentary, engaging
in prayer, combined with the richness of g'milut chasadim—
deeds of lovingkindness, in helping us to unpack the real
meaning behind the magical word "M'chayeh."

I WONDER IF SOME OF THE MOST POWERFUL statements from the *Torah* don't sound at times so obvious that they don't need to be said. I'm thinking of the climactic sentence of the *Torah* reading this morning, when Moses quotes God saying to the people: "I have set before you this day life or death, the blessing or the curse—therefore choose life, that you may live."

And I can half imagine a wise guy type, sitting far enough away from the *bimah* to whisper to his pal, "What did He expect? That we'd choose death and curses 'cause we don't want to live?"

It does seem obvious. All, except those who really need help, want to live. In a way the statement is no more profound than those found in bubble gum or fortune cookies.

Everybody wants to choose life. But MOST of us are confused SOME of the time about what really gives life, and SOME of us are confused MOST of the time.

Let's take the word *M'chayeh*. It started out as Hebrew *M'cha-YEH* which means one who gives life, which meant God. It became Yiddish *M'CHA-yeh*, which means something that adds a little spice to life—usually a food. And then it came into Yinglish as *Am'chayeh.* or *Tsam'chayeh*, which meant anything terrific. *Tsam'chayeh!* Except that many of the things about which we might say *Tsam'chayeh!* are not so life-giving. To lie down and soak up the sun for a week, tsam'chayeh, except that too much sun's going to make you prematurely wrinkled and maybe give you skin cancer. Haagen-Dazs regularly, if you can afford it, *Tsam'chayeh*, but probably not for the arteries. What nutritionists are finding is that the foods of the rather wealthy and the very poor are equally bad for them, with the health nod going to the wealthy only because they have access to better and quicker health care. The gastronomic m'chayehs we eat when we're successful enough to afford them, turn out to be anti-*m'chayehs*, things which shorten life. "I have set before you this day life and death," says the *Torah*... and we all want to choose life, but sometimes we guess wrong.

Someone shared with me a good way of thinking about it. The world is like a department store the morning after someone broke in and changed all the prices on all the items, mixed them all up, and our job is to try and figure out where the prices really belong, to get things back in the right order... to find out where the good stuff really is, the best buys, the *m'chayehs*, the things that are life-giving.

I want to share with you three areas in which I think we've mixed up the value signs. The first two I've talked about before, but maybe this is your year for being interested. And the third is such a priority of my own that I'm amazed I've never given it center stage equal time before at the High Holy Days. Let me therefore suggest *m'chayehs* for your mind, your conscience, and for your children or grandchildren.

Yidden, what's a *m'chayeh* for your mind and soul too? *Torah*. Don't tune out! Given the right atmosphere, a little loosening up and feeling comfortable with the others around us, I'm convinced that just about everyone here would enjoy sitting and studying a Jewish text—reading it, arguing with it or for it, finding something new in it, or just something old which to them is new because they just found it.

Let me tell you why it would be for you a *m'chayeh*, different from a course in biofeedback, or how to talk to plants, or assertiveness. Because learning *Torah* makes you feel whole again, back home.

If you know even a little *Torah*, which really means Jewish learning of any kind, you at least know that learning was the mainstay of the Jew. Elie Wiesel spoke at the dedication of the HUC-JIR library in New York last year and recaptured some of that flavor in these words:

> "I never saw my grandfather without a book in his hands. My father had books in his grocery store. While waiting for customers, he would study. 'You have nothing to do?' a father would admonish his son—take a book, any book! You have a headache? Study and it'll feel better."

Wiesel continued, bringing his audience closer to his Holocaust days:

> "As a child I would spend my allowance buying books. I remember the bookstores and their owners. I would buy more books than I could afford, but my credit was good. Many books were left unpaid, but it was not my fault. A certain event occurred and our lives were interrupted. When I left for that faraway kingdom of hell, I had in my knapsack more books than food."

Get the picture? A Jewish kid going to face hell with a Jewish survival pack—books.

All of us know that tradition. Have heard it. Have internalized it by now. We know Jews should be learned, even if we never quite got started.

That's why Jewish study is for us Jews a *m'chayeh*, life-giving. We touch hands with Elie Wiesel's grandfather, who was never without a book in his hands, and with all the unknown branches of our family tree. We are not just learning a skill but reawakening a whole mental circuit.

Something magical has been happening in synagogues, Jewish homes, retreats, *chavurot*. People are studying Jewish text, usually Bible, and a not-so-learned Jew will pose a question or make a comment or attempt to explain a difficulty in the text, and what he is saying will be so close to what one of the ancient rabbis said about that verse. Rabbi Akiba's insight rolls off the tongue of an accountant or a broker or a pharmacist or a hotshot salesman. And then when you point that out, they're really impressed: "This is good stuff and I can do it. *Tsam'chayeh!*"

I know you all have respect for *Torah*. I think many of you would run into a burning building to save a *Torah*. God willing, you'll not be tested on that. You don't have to rescue it or even defend it. You just have to make its acquaintance.

Can we help you? Can we help you! The Reform movement has now come out with a marvelous aid, the new *Torah Commentary*. The Temple has some for services, and you can get one of your own. If you have a *Bar* or *Bat Mitzvah* coming up, your youngster will be buying one that the family can use.

If you're really at the beginning of Jewish learning and thinking that's where you want to start, we're offering a new Saturday morning class taught by Barbara Irlen, the teacher all the adults want, coinciding with Saturday morning school hours. If you're ready for deeper waters, a little more formal, we've helped Spertus College of Judaica bring Jewish learning to Glenbrook South High School Monday nights, for adults. And there are other good Spertus courses not much farther away.

Torah is life-giving. Somehow it got mis-marked or mis-priced or mis-shelved in our generation, but *Tsam'chayeh*—life-giving.

Next *m'chayeh: G'milut Chasadim*. Deeds of Lovingkindness.

A lot of good things started here last year. Some people volunteered to go visit residents in nursing homes. Others volunteered to conduct services for them on a fairly regular basis. Our volunteers got to be fairly well known to the residents, even to those who are mentally handicapped. And because the people giving were getting more than they ever thought they could, they wanted to do more. So they held a *Seder* for the residents. Which turned to be not only for the residents, but for their families who also came. A son and daughter had a chance to be with their father at *Seder* even though Papa was institutionalized. The pictures of the event and the letters we have on a bulletin board downstairs told the story.

And just a few days ago one of our groups did a *Rosh Hashana* service at the nursing home. And our people told me that there was something spiritual in the room that day, thanks to the Cantor and the way he reached the people, thanks to the inherent possibilities and sometimes even the magic in *G'milut Chasadim*, deeds of lovingkindness. And a resident came to those services, a young man still a Temple member too, with unique difficulties. He came to a service on his own for the first time and was touched and maybe given a path back to life. Magic, life-giving, *m'chayehs*.

Some of you have done other things. Some of you were willing to join Hanna and me in caring about some of the Soviet refuseniks we visited in Russia last April. You wrote letters, adopted families, collected money for and joined Chicago Action for Soviet Jewry... and we need more. One couple decided to visit the Soviet Union also, to bring their own skills and selves and Jewish warmth to the Refuseniks. And I have to tell you what is resulting from that trip because it will be such a *m'chayeh*. Lynn and Scott Kane met the Bubes family in Leningrad, became quick friends.

The Kanes met Edward Bubes through another Refusenik, Boris Kelman, whose son Chayim will be symbolically *Bar Mitzvah* with the Kanes' oldest son Evan, this coming Saturday, right here.

But in the meantime it turns out that the Bubes family somehow got a release from Russia, and they have just arrived in Massachusetts, and they are coming here this weekend to share in the *simchah* with the Kanes, to represent the Kelmans, to celebrate *Sukkot* and Consecration with BJBE. This Friday night, in the midst of all the little kids flocking to the *bimah* for Consecration, a scholarly looking middle-aged, balding gentleman will be called to his first *aliyah* ever, "consecrated" in a way. That will be Edward Bubes.

At first I wondered if it wouldn't be a shame for a Soviet

family to come to their first Reform service here and see the chaotic atmosphere of Consecration. And then I remembered a poem by Danny Siegel which might have been written for this moment. It says:

> "A recent immigrant comes from the Soviet Union to his family in the U.S.A. and asks three questions in *shul*. 'Where are the children? Where are the children? Where are the children? Did I pass through Auschwitz to see a synagogue too dignified to tolerate five-year-olds playing on the *bimah*? Did I live in Leningrad for 30 years at *minyans* of feeble *zaydes* to find a freedom empty of the noise of unadulterated childhood?'"

So when Edward and Irma and Alla Bubes come here this weekend they will not have to ask: Where are the children?

Some of you are part of this, you who have written to Refuseniks and on their behalf... others can begin. And maybe there are a few of you to pick up the chain we've begun, who might go to the USSR to do it, too. That is double *m'chayeh*.

There is now a group here which visits the ill. There is a group here working to comfort the bereaved. There are *Tz'dakah* cans to take home and fill.

And there is still my low-profile people-to-people project, where all of you who might help others through a specific difficult experience because you have been there and survived. If you want to be on that private list of potential helpers, hand-holders, healers, *m'chayehs*, call me. Some of you have helped already. And if you need such help, call me, too. I'm looking especially for helping people who have lived through a *Bar/Bat Mitzvah* of a child with the extreme trauma of family breaking up or already broken.

None of these are new. Deeds of lovingkindness are life-giving.

And finally I have to tell you what was *m'chayeh* for me, that gave me new life and is still giving it to Jewish youngsters. The best creation of the Reform movement, Olin Sang Ruby Union Institute, the camp outside of Oconomowoc, Wisconsin, is now in desperate need of people to give it life. It's where I first learned to be a Jew, and a place that has done much the same thing for 60–70 BJBE kids every summer.

Every rabbi has a priority Jewish project outside his own Temple. For some it's scholarly writing, for some it's outside speaking, for some it's involvement in one of the many Jewish organizations that needs leadership. For me, that overriding outside Temple commitment has been that camp. I give it my time during the year and every summer, usually three and sometimes four weeks. I have walked around the Temple collaring and *schmoozing* both parents and kids to spend a summer session there. And some of you have been on the receiving end of that and more of you will be. Sometimes I get so carried away that I push too hard and I have to apologize.

But here's why it's so important. The place just brings Judaism to life. It lets kids be with rabbis and other Jewish role models with no barrier in between. It teaches kids to sing Jewish songs with the spirit they usually reserve for rocking along with The Who or The What or The Where. It makes services seem like the normal thing to do.

It makes Hebrew come to life because you play games with it at the dinner table. It gives high school kids a chance to be fluent in Hebrew beyond the wildest dreams of parents or long-lost ancestors. And in that sense BJBE has the best Hebrew program anywhere because we so encourage kids by urging and by scholarships, to keep going on to *Chalutzim* at camp, the all-Hebrew seven-week session… and I have to tell you with just a little modesty that this seven-week program is better than the ones our Conservative friends rave about at Camp *Ramah*, and theirs is pretty good. Any kid who has ever been there, even for one session, will never forget that *Shabbat* can be a blast, holy, exciting, a *m'chayeh*.

I used to say that I never met a kid who didn't love that camp. That's not quite right. Some do feel that the all-Indian or all-sports camps are better for some kids during most of the camp years. Okay. But even for such kids, one year at OSRUI can open their eyes to Jewish possibilities, can give them a comfort level with Judaism that many adults never attained.

Yes, there's a danger. One mother of a first-year *Chalutzim* camper called and said that her daughter is dragging her to services all the time now. What a nice girl. *Tsam'chayeh!*

If you've never sent a child there, and if you're entering that stage of your life, or if your child might take a year off from someplace else and go there for a summer... you will be giving them a *m'chayeh*.

And this year the camp needs help. More than ever before. And because we send more kids there than any other synagogue and because I'm so deeply committed to the camp, my priority this year will be urging us to contribute to the fund-raising effort being made on behalf of the camp. When I realize how much we do for kids up there with a physical plant which could use so much renewal I think God must really be on our side. But God won't build the new cabins or make the *Bayit* habitable again or enlarge the kitchen or build the arts center or outfit the new library learning center or develop the waterfront into what it could be for kids. And fees from campers just buy food and hire staff.

Will you, this year—because you were there yourself; or have sent kids there, or are going to; or just because you believe that if your rabbi makes it his first priority you are willing to help—will you make at least a contribution to that camp drive, and if you can, a substantial one to keep that *m'chayeh* going?

Three *m'chayehs*: *Torah* for mind and soul, *G'milut Chasadim* for conscience and soul, OSRUI for Jewish survival.

In his great opus *Gulag Archipelago*, Solzhenitsyn tells of a scene inside the main Leningrad prison for political dissenters during the World War II siege of the city. A woman prisoner was being taken to interrogation by an impassive silent woman guard with unseeing eyes. Suddenly bombs began to explode right next to their building, sounding as if at any moment they would fall directly on them.

The terrified guard threw her arms around the prisoner and embraced her, desperate for human companionship and sympathy. Then the bombing stopped and the guard's eyes became unseeing again. "Hands behind your back; move along."

Solzhenitsyn adds, "There is no great merit in becoming a human being at the moment of death."

But you and I this *Yom Kippur*, with many more years left, God willing, could discover what really matters—could decide to choose life and blessing and <u>be</u> *m'chayehs*.

Breaking the Glass

Rosh Hashanah 5744/1983

What meanings lie behind many of the symbolic and traditional elements of our rituals and religious practices? MSS often helped us make sense of them, as he did in this sermon when he helped us find meaning in the ritual that marks the end of every Jewish wedding—the breaking of the glass.

W E'VE KNOWN ABOUT THE CUSTOM for so long, or seen it so often, that we take it for granted. Yet, it is a strange custom. Non-Jews find it fascinating. Ending a wedding by stepping on a glass and breaking it? Who ever thought that one up?

We're not so sure who first thought it up. But we think we know why that first person did it. And I'd like to tell why he did it, how tradition then gave it a different meaning... and then I want to tell you of a newer meaning that I find in it today. It all has to do with whether we live happily ever after, and it's also about our children. Stay with me.

Why did they start breaking a glass at weddings? Anthropologists tell us that it was common to believe that evil spirits hovered about the bride and groom on their wedding day, the same evil spirits who were around at every point of passage in life, against whom our ancestors said *kinnahora* or just spit.

But you wanted the bride and groom protected by more than just a spit or a curse. So the bridegroom would take the glass from which he had just sipped wine, and at the end of the ceremony, he would throw it back over his head and against a wall, shattering it and making enough noise to scare the devil out of the demons and send them back to an Isaac Bashevis Singer story.

That's the origin. Really. Somehow the custom caught on among our people, like the *kinnahora*, or the red ribbon. The rabbis of the middle ages didn't like the superstitious origin of the custom, and they tried to give it a more spiritualized meaning. They said (and this has become the traditional explanation) that breaking a glass reminds us of all the "breakings," the destructions that have taken place in Jewish life, especially the destruction of the Temples.

So the origin of the ceremony assumed there were evil spirits; the rabbis' explanation emphasized destruction. Isn't the mood of both of those very much the same? I think they both translate into the same message, namely, "Don't expect to live happily ever after."

"And they lived happily ever after." Even after we knew that the fairy tales were only tales, many of us let ourselves keep believing that last line, that they lived happily ever after. We stopped believing that the pumpkin turned into a chariot, and that the shoe could only fit Cinderella, but we wanted to believe that last line... they lived happily ever after.

But they probably didn't. It wasn't ever after because they both had to die and one had to die first, and that certainly wasn't happy.

Danny Siegel tells us what sounds to me like the real story in his poem called "Cinderella."

"And when she opened her eyes the next morning she rolled over and noticed a small unpleasant scar on the left side of the prince's nose. Then she turned back and closed her eyes and dreamed of days by the brooms and fireplaces."

It wasn't so bad, by the way, to find a scar. It certainly didn't mean that they would live unhappily ever after. Loving someone is finding out about them. The biblical word for the act of sexual love is *yada*, to know someone else. So the morning-after came, and they knew one another, and the knowledge contained recognition of scars, awareness that Prince Charming wouldn't always be charming.

Kids out there, you listen, too! This is not just a message for adults. We don't live happily ever after. You live a long time if you're blessed, or with difficulties if you've got strength, but not ever and not always happily. And almost all of what's really good you've got to earn. And that's what breaking the glass should mean.

But some people missed that message. Maybe they thought the groom was stamping out a fire in the carpet.

Because a lot of us expect an awful lot of marriage, of family life, of work life. So much. Too much. As if it had been promised to us.

Who promised all that happiness ever after? Did our parents? Did the rabbi promise you at your *Bar Mitzvah*? When he talks to you in a whisper at Confirmation, is that when you think he promised that you'll live happily ever after?

I know that our world does seem to promise people a lot. And sophisticated as we are, we let the promises of the ads, the jingles, the catalog people get by our more rational defenses. And inside, a part of us believes that there's a lot of gusto out there, or that a Porsche would really be happiness forever, or that each new vacation spot is just a bigger thrill and more like paradise. And we sort of forget the other side. We forget that the beer which promises a life of gusto really just makes you slow and sloppy. We forget that you can hardly drive the Porsche because where is it safe to leave it? We forget that even the nicest vacation has some arguments before, after, and during, and you always have to pack and stand at airport carousels and often really do need a rest after the vacation. And then, when it all falls short of the promoted promises, when work is just work and family life taxing, not relaxing, and even your spouse doesn't feel or act just as you wish they would, then we think... "Something is wrong with me or her or us or the job because I'm not so happy! How can I get at that happiness ever after?"

And the truth is that once you focus on being happy, you lose it. You know how you can see certain things more clearly in the dark only if you look a bit to the left or right? Well, you never see happy if that's all you're looking for.

Think of it this way: what do photographers say when they advertise for your wedding or *Bar Mitzvah* business? They say, "Preserve your happy moments." And that's what we do. We hire them to be there at only these right times. So if you're fortunate, you have a wall of pictures or albums capturing the happy moments: Jeffrey dancing with his *bubbe* at the party; you and Jeffrey, standing with his Jewish bride and all your friends at tables smiling. And maybe you're lucky enough, one day, to have a picture of a golden wedding anniversary and everyone is smiling again. Now all those pictures add up to what most Jewish people call happiness.

But... what it took to get there! I know, because I share such photographable experiences with families regularly, as well as some of the behind-the-scenes process. You know, too, what it takes to get there. You know that if there were a photographer hired to shoot the whole story as a documentary, there would be other pictures, pictures of tears and anxieties, pictures of late-night conversation and lost sleep, pictures of illness and hospitals, pictures of people practicing that old Jewish skill, hanging in, and not smiling.

You and I know that there is no one whose happy-day pictures are telling the whole story, or even most of the story. To get the happy pictures took endurance. Most of all it took standing for something, being responsible to and for others. I found the best definition of love in Martin Buber's *I and Thou* this summer. Buber said, "Love is the responsibility of an I for a Thou." That has the promise of some happiness in it, I think.

You don't live happily ever after. You live <u>to</u> things and through things, both good and bad, and you have chances for real *nachas* here and there. That's plenty. And our tradition tries to tell it that way at the end of every wedding when the groom breaks a glass.

Lately I have also come upon a slightly different way of

interpreting the glass-breaking, one I also think you should know about: We break a glass to show that a family's former constellation of relationships has to break to allow the new family to form. It isn't just adding a son or a daughter. It means making room for them to be adults, not just your children anymore. It means realizing that a new good relationship can be built only when people let the old one change. That's also what breaking the glass today means. Let them be a family. Love them, but don't hang onto them.

And that is such good advice that I wish there were a ceremony of breaking the glass when kids are much younger to remind us of how wise it is, how necessary it is to let the cocoon we build for our kids part and break, so they can become someone.

Earlier this summer, I had a chance to think about this when I listened to a rabbi who has become a family therapist. Rabbi Ed Friedman told us: "Of this I am convinced about families: The worst thing one can do is to make a child into the salvation of the family."

And then he added, "Most suicides are people who were taught that the hopes of everyone in the family were riding on them. Then, when that person meets failure, he can't forgive himself for having dashed so many hopes." That's heavy. But my experience of Jewish families tells me that it's true. When kids are made to be the salvation of the family, the family is in trouble and so is the kid.

You may say that nobody does that anymore to their kids. You may think that only happened in the old days, in immigrant families where the parents couldn't make it because they were greenhorns without English, but wanted their kids to be Americans and to lead the family into the style of life America promised. You may think that only parents in poverty look to their children as the salvation of the family, but I think you're wrong. It happens in this generation and in our zip codes.

Aaron Stern, a psychiatrist who treats families says it this way: "When first I began to practice, I was frequently consulted by parents who were seeking an evaluation of the development of their children. They came to me to be reassured of the normalcy of their young, to be reassured that things were progressing within normal limits. At that time, if on the basis of my findings I reported to the parents that they had a nice, normal, average youngster, they were relieved and delighted. Today, when I describe a child as average, the parents leave my office depressed."

If you want your child to be normal, you want that for him and for you. But if you need your child to be special, I think you're only wanting that for you. The name of that game is narcissism, subtitled, "I'm really only thinking about me even when I say that I'm only thinking about you." And narcissism isn't really a game, it's a sickness, and one that hardly ever gets cured.

I'm talking about things we all recognize. Remember the cartoon showing the father and son walking on the college campus, the father looking with appreciation at a cute coed and the son saying, "Dad, this is my university!" Smart kid.

Yet, I hear parents talking about the project of choosing a college for their child as if it were the parents who were going off to school. I see people fighting all a kid's battles, being so intensely interested in how a kid feels, in every little up and down of school progress. I hear people saying, "I'm giving my child all my energy." Who can take that much attention? Better to have some benign neglect. When our tradition says not to look at a tree every day to see if it's growing because you can't see it happen, it speaks the truth about other growing things, namely us.

Sometimes parents call me to make arrangements for their child's wedding or their grandchild's naming. They are hurt when I tell them that if their child is old enough to be a mate or a parent, she's old enough to make those arrangements herself.

A child grows into an independent human being when parents are as committed to freeing their child as they once were to protecting that child. At a certain point, freeing is protecting. And so the broken glass is a symbol not just for becoming a husband or wife. It stands for breaking free.

That doesn't mean stop nurturing. Kids need just the kind of love that most of us know how to give in quantity. Hugging and tenderness and consoling is as good for boys as for girls. No one becomes a *mensch* without that. But saying, "you are loved" doesn't mean, "you are our life."

So from the glass breaking at weddings, I think you can learn two lessons. First, you don't live happily ever after. Second, you'd better let go of kids if you want the best for them.

Why do I tell you this at *Rosh Hashanah* instead of at a wedding? Because you listen better at *Rosh Hashanah*, and because it's too long for weddings. And because it's really about the *Torah* and *Haftarah* portions of today, though I haven't mentioned them. Abraham and Isaac learn that life isn't lived happily ever after. Hannah realizes that the son she wanted so desperately is one she must let go.

These two lessons could be the foundation for a good marriage, a fine family, and a reasonably sane, sweet New Year.

Learning from an Orthodox Jew

Yom Kippur Kol Nidre 5744/1983

How do we as Reform Jews measure up against our Orthodox brethren who typically practice a more traditional brand of Judaism? Do we—should we—feel less Jewish, or perhaps less holy? On this Yom Kippur, MSS helped us see the value in helping Judaism evolve, while at the same time reminding us what we can learn from the members of the Orthodox community.

I WANT TO TALK JEWISH TALK TONIGHT, but I want to start with a problem in psychology.

A man comes in to a psychiatrist and says that he has an inferiority complex, which centers around his twin brother. "Doctor," he says, "my twin brother is so much better than I am in everything; he does everything perfectly. No matter what I do, it's not as good. I feel like such a flop. Help me!"

What does the doctor try to do? If he can, he helps the patient become more realistic both about his twin brother and about himself, helps him see that the twin brother isn't infallible, that <u>he</u> is not a flop, and that each one has weaknesses and strengths.

How would you know that the man is really cured? How about this: The man is cured when he can be so objective about his twin brother that he can see a good quality in the brother and want to adopt it for himself without feeling in the least inferior while doing it.

This is the whole outline of what I want to tell you tonight. But please stay around to hear what goes between the lines.

I think that some of us have that inferiority complex. And the brother we feel inferior to is the traditional, Orthodox Jew.

Now that's not everybody's problem, I know. Some people have symptoms of the opposite—a hostility complex toward Orthodox Jews. But examine hostility closely and you may see fears of inferiority behind it.

So let me try a quick-cure. Let me try to neutralize that traditional Jew peeking over our shoulder. Let's see if there's anything at all we want to learn from him, even when he declares: "YOU'RE NOT A REAL JEW: YOU'RE A PHONY!" And then when you try to defend yourself with your membership in a Reform synagogue and a certain level of involvement there, he whispers, "You're only there because it's easier." And he rings the bell on some of our guilt-ometers again.

"You're not real Jews," the voice says. I can tell you not to believe that, tell you that we are just as authentic as they. And you'd like to believe me, I know. Except you also know that you can never win an argument with a traditional Jew about it.

One of our members, a bright, thinking person, started attending a discussion group led by an engaging young *Lubavitcher* rabbi. Though the group was billed for all branches of Judaism, the rabbi finally got around to discussing why Orthodoxy was the only real Judaism. Our member tried to present arguments against that, but was frustrated. Her words didn't sound so good. She called me for some advice—what should she say to that rabbi? Wouldn't I come and say it to that rabbi in one of the discussions?

I declined. I had a premonition of doom, of being destroyed on the *Lubavitcher's* home turf.

But had I been foolhardy enough to do it, here's what I would have had to say. Judaism has changed. It has reformed itself over the years. It had to. It changed as Jews moved from shepherding to farming to cities. It changed when they were no longer a nation governing themselves. It has gone through significant evolutions. As Ellis Rivkin describes it, Judaism survived not by holding on for dear life to what it was, but by creatively going through mutations. Evolution and mutation are as critical to Jewish survival as almost any belief or observance.

I hope you're not shocked to hear a good word for evolution coming from the *bimah*. I believe in it. I believe that life has evolved, and that Darwin was right, the story of creation in the Bible has a great deal of truth in it, but not scientific truth. I think God continues to create through evolution. And I think every Jew who is non-Orthodox also believes in evolution. You can be proud of it, not ashamed.

How can I prove that Judaism has evolved, and thereby survived? Simple. Read the *Torah*. And think about it. The *Torah* talks about a Judaism with priests, one main Temple and animal sacrifices. It doesn't say a thing about congregations, rabbis, services, community philanthropy, welcoming *Shabbat*, sitting *Shivah*. That all came later, replacing what had been.

Actually, more than a third of the commandments in the *Torah* can't be kept anymore because the conditions that they assume are gone. And if they can't be kept, they can't be broken either. Which has led Allan Gould, the humorist, to make a list of commandments in the *Torah* which Jews never transgress anymore, including, "The high priest may marry only a virgin," and "A Jewish woman may not marry an Ammonite or a Moabite."

When the *Torah* talks about this Judaism of priests and Ammonites and sacrifices it doesn't have an asterisk, referring you to the bottom of the scroll footnote which says, "But God wants all this to change in a few hundred years." As far as the ancients were concerned, that was the real Judaism.

How did this mammoth change come about? We say the Jewish people, with some divine guidance, made sure Judaism would survive by helping it to evolve. Traditional Jews say either that there are hints hidden in the *Torah* which said it should change, or that God gave a second private audience to just a few Jews at Mount Sinai, authorizing the changes.

An Orthodox rabbi would call that analysis *treif*, but I call it the truth, and I think you think it's the truth, too. Judaism has evolved. Moses wouldn't recognize our service in either a Reform, Conservative, or Orthodox synagogue; he would probably feel more comfortable in a mosque.

So when an Orthodox gremlin leans over your shoulder and says, "You're not a real Jew," remember that.

What about when he says, "You only go to a Reform temple because it's easier," how will you respond? Can't argue that point, because it is, actually, easier. We can say that the task of choosing what to observe instead of just doing it all as written makes it harder, but the truth is that most of us don't expend much energy in researching Jewish options and then choosing.

Yes, it is easier here. Only a masochist would say that's by definition bad. But that can't be why most of us are here. Because if we wanted easy, why not choose easiest, which is no Temple, no Holy Days, just Vienna Kosher-style Judaism. That's the easiest.

No, I think you and I are here because we have to be. We can't be one thing in Temple and something else outside. We can't be religiously schizophrenic. We have been brought up with Western values which include the following: Unprovable authority isn't always right. A mature person makes up his own mind. A person has free choice, called by some autonomy. In Jewish terms that means we all believe God somehow gave commandments to his people but He also gave each one of us the freedom to say yes or no to authority. And we believe that He wouldn't have given us that freedom if He didn't want us to use it. Those Western values happen to be Jewish too, I think. Jewish tradition is where we learn first about the individual's worth and dignity.

This is what we all believe deep down. And if you do, you literally cannot be Orthodox and give up that right to choose. We are not here because Orthodoxy is wrong or because we are shiftless... our Judaism just has to be the form which gives us our freedom of choice. We do not choose to tell lies or cross our fingers in the synagogue.

Does that help some with the inferiority problem? I hope so. I'd like you to feel better about it. So much better, in fact, that you can look objectively at what a traditional Jew might teach us which would still leave us our freedom of choice. Learning from a brother doesn't mean we're inferior.

And if you're willing to learn with me something from the traditional Jew, why not learn from their ability to draw a line and their discipline to make it stick.

They draw lines. Real traditional Jews are good at drawing lines about eating and praying and observing. We don't have to draw all those lines, and the lines we draw are ultimately ones we choose to draw. But if your Reform Judaism says that you don't have to draw any lines, and that even the ones you have already drawn are negotiable in a tight spot, then my Reform insides tell me something is wrong.

Gene Borowitz gives what I think is a classic example. Borowitz is a Reform Jew who prizes freedom of choice. So a Jewish couple in New York who liked his writings wrote him a fan letter. Eventually they became friends. The couple had no family in the area, so the Borowitzes invited the couple to their home for the first night of *Seder*. The couple accepted. And three nights before *Seder* they called. At that time the play *Deathtrap* was the big show on Broadway, and nobody could get tickets. The couple apologized and said that a wonderful opportunity had come their way to get seats for *Deathtrap*, but it just happened to be that first *Seder* night, and of course they couldn't turn down the tickets.

Now you substitute whatever would seem awfully attractive to you in order to understand the situation: Pavarotti? White Sox in Game Seven of the World Series? Borowitz says he believes in a Reform Judaism in which people have the right to make choices... but not when they wind up choosing *Deathtrap* over *Pesach*. That makes Reform Judaism an absurdity.

So what the Orthodox Jew has to teach us, I think, is that we also have to draw some lines.

I don't believe that's really so hard for us. Our Jewish sense of "ought to" helps us believe in drawing lines. What we could use the best Orthodox Jews as examples of—is discipline, the discipline to stay with something after we've decided it's meaningful, the discipline to stick to the Jewish obligations we accept.

That's hard for most of us. Liberal Jews in general get a C- in discipline.

Do you ever feel that some people get into Reform Judaism as a fad? Sometimes I do. I once called a youngster whose family had dropped out of Temple after *Bar Mitzvah* without staying on for Confirmation (that's one of the lines we try to draw very sharply), and I told him I felt badly that he wasn't coming back. Don't feel bad, Rabbi, said the youngster, my Mom said that this year we're going to join the Y instead. (Not even the J.)

Suppose you decide that keeping *Shabbat* in some way is really important to you... that you want it, need it, it'll be good for you, you think God expects it, any of the above reasons. That's pure Reform Judaism. But at that point you may borrow a bit of muscle from the traditional Jew to discipline yourself to <u>do</u> it, to keep doing it, the discipline to pick it up quickly again if you just have to miss it once or twice, without saying, "Oh, now that we've blown it we'll forget it."

A number of you have adopted Soviet Jewish families, by twinning a *Bar* or *Bat Mitzvah*, or just because you were moved by my appeal or Scott and Lynn Kane's. That adopting or twinning isn't just another party or one-time gimmick. It's an active commitment. It means writing letters regularly, even when you don't get answers back which you can show your friends. We have to find the discipline to keep doing it.

I even think that "marrying Jewish" may at bottom be a matter of self-discipline.

Finding discipline is harder than mentally drawing a line. I know it. I have trouble with some discipline, too. I have trouble asking that discipline of others, even in times of death and mourning. You know that Reform Judaism doesn't ask mourners to go to daily services to say *Kaddish*. But it does suggest that weekly attendance at worship, or as close as you can possibly get for the first year, would be appropriate. I know how hard that seems to many of us and empathizing too much, I fail in not suggesting it with some force. So most people don't do it. But the people who actually do it, and some here do, find it very meaningful. And as meaningful as is the choice of that weekly service attendance is the discipline it calls for and creates.

I have to use more courage in suggesting that people exercise a greater discipline.

There are opportunities to draw some positive Jewish lines here at Temple this year. You can study Bible with me on Sunday mornings, come hear a marvelous teacher like Jerry Bubis in a few weeks, study with Spertus teachers, study Hebrew, learn Jewish mysticism from Larry Kushner, and *chavurah* and doing *mitzvot* of love and kindness. The menu has nourishment, but it only nourishes if you can find the discipline to do it.

My teacher Arnold Wolf has his own description of what it is to be a liberal Jew. Wolf says, "I walk down Jew Street. Along the street are bundles of *mitzvot*, all the observances, the ceremonies, *Shabbat, tz'dakah, g'milut chasadim*, personal honesty, Jewish books, everything. I pick up what I can. Some are light. Some take effort to pick up. Some are so heavy that I cannot lift them and they must wait for someone else, or for me to get stronger."

It takes no effort to walk Jew Street. It takes courage to pick up a bundle of *mitzvot*, and it takes discipline to hang on to them.

That discipline we could learn from Orthodox Jews, at least the best of them. They aren't <u>real</u> Jews or even better Jews, and they honestly are not the ones who will enable Judaism to survive by evolving in an evolving world. That happens here. So get them out of your closet of anxieties, off your shoulder, and off your back. And once cured of that feeling of inferiority, God willing, draw a Jewish line this year, make a Jewish choice, and beg, borrow, or just find the discipline that will make it, this time, stick.

Shulayim: Rabbi David Fine

"Don't say *Torah*, be *Torah!*" Attributed to the *Maggid* of Mezeritch who lived 300 years ago in Poland, our own Rabbi Mark Shapiro has been living this way over the course of our lives right here in Chicago. As our teacher, rabbi, mentor, guide, and friend he has been our *Torah*.

How does one pay proper homage to Rabbi Mark Shapiro? By recounting the ways in which he has reminded us of how to be our best.

Are there stirring sermons in this collection? Absolutely. Timely and timeless bulletin articles? You bet. Each one of us recalls our favorites. Some made us smile. Others made us squirm. A good chunk of them referred to the White Sox. If you are like me then you find yourself quoting Mark and continuing to be impressed by his wisdom.

Mark delivered in his own inimitable way. The smile. The laugh. The lilt in his voice. The questions he would ask. Each was a dispatch to our soul. How are you? Who are you? Are you ready to face the Divine? Better yet, are you willing to face your deepest self and your tradition?

Details may get hazy over time, but the caring and the genuine love for his family and his congregation are as present today as they have been through decades of work and dedication. Each one of us is proud to declare that Rabbi Mark Shapiro has been our rabbi. And we know, by listening and observing, that he has been our *Torah* as well.

P.S. If I were to deliver this note in true Mark Shapiro fashion it would be in front of the congregation on a simple black music stand. The text itself would be drafted on a series of large cards or small stationery. We would know that it was Mark Shapiro genuine by the typewritten cross-outs and ellipses as well as the handwritten comments and assorted personal touches. His writing, his *Torah*, however, has never been about perfection. It has been about intellectual depth, integrity, honesty, and expressing his optimism in us, partnering with the Ultimate to create a better world.

David Fine is Director of Consulting and Transition Management for the Union of Reform Judaism. He served as rabbi at BJBE from 1989–1995.

Learning From Each Other

Yom Kippur Yizkor 5744/1983

---

*Of all the services over the High Holy Days, the Yizkor
memorial service on Yom Kippur afternoon might be the
most intimate—it's smaller, and many of those present came
thinking about loved ones they had lost. MSS often saved
special messages to share at Yizkor; in this sermon he
explores the grieving process, speaking about how
those in the community can help each other through
this shared experience.*

MOST OF THE TIME IT'S HARD TO TELL what brings a person to services, and it's hard to tell what the person brings with him to services. There's a reading in the prayer book which talks about how many different moods there may be in a congregation at a single time.

Except right now. Because your being here means that you're already thinking about those who died, or are ready to think about it. Some of you come with a recent grief, some with older grief, but so many of you have known grief.

There is a lot of wisdom under this roof right now about grieving and bereavement. Wisdom that other people need. There are things you should tell them about what you know. So I want to take these few minutes at *Yizkor* to focus on what I think you have learned about grief, to make it easier for you to share with others.

Every one of you who has been bereaved knows that grieving is work. They even call it "grief work." Part of the work you do consciously. Part of it just goes on inside of you. It usually begins with having to tell the story of the death of your loved one again and again to all the new people. It means crying with each new one as if you were telling the story for the first time. That's not being irrational, that's part of the work.

Part of the work is accepting what has happened, being able to use the right word: "dead." And you know that it's important to use that word, not any of the silly euphemisms like "passed away," "passed on," or "departed." Just as you know it's important for most people to watch a casket being lowered, to see beyond the artificial grass mats and flowers and recognize that it is a grave. That is part of the work of grieving.

Yes, people do grieve in different ways and heal in different ways, but so much is the same for so many that we can generalize.

Grief seems erratic. You will be all right for a while, and suddenly like an unexpected wave, it hits you again. That's true during the first week, the first month, and the first year. The late surges seem like surprises. As Earl Grollman says, "Just when you are making great strides forward you receive a startling setback. It may happen on a holiday, birthday, anniversary, it may be triggered by your favorite song being played on the radio, and in a moment you feel as if you are back to square one of grief."

The people around you during *shivah* are important. They get you through the nightmare time, they help you know that what has happened is real. But when the people aren't there anymore, the calls slack off and the letters too, you find that you feel worse, lower even than during the first few days.

Then you needed people, didn't you? We should all teach others how important it is to keep contact with people four months afterward, six months. Most people say the worst part of the depression that bereavement seems to bring to almost everyone takes place six to nine months after the death.

You really are a mourner for a year. The tradition is right. People may forget, but you don't forget. Each holiday without the loved one is a new painful hurdle to cross. The first *Pesach* without, the first Thanksgiving without—are very painful. That's why you're a mourner for a year. The second *Yontiff* without is also hard, but not quite like the first. And some people have said that their body does not actually feel good again, quite as it did, for two years.

Grief does psychosomatic things to almost everyone. Grief isn't only emotional or mental upset. People do have nausea, dizziness, palpitations, tight throat, dry mouth, rashes, headaches, back pain, loss of appetite, weight loss or gain, insomnia, sighing, fatigue. Many people even have the certainty that they have the same fatal illness that killed their loved one. We can reassure one another that these are all our body's responses to bereavement, not more surprising than a body's response to a serious surgery.

People in grief can be driving a car and forget where they are. Phone numbers they've always known are suddenly gone, as are people's names. You can add your own personal examples. The thing to know is that you're not going crazy, that it happens this way to almost everyone.

Grieving is work. You have to make yourself do a lot of it. Your body and mind do some of it even without your approval.

We've learned a lot about children and grief in the past years. Children do mourn, usually not in an adult rhythm. We have to allow them to mourn. Thinking about how we deal with our children when death occurs is very appropriate because it is, in a way, how we must deal with adults, for in the very face of death, everyone becomes a child.

How good it is that people are learning that all the old attempts to shelter children from death are wrong. Keeping them away from funerals and cemeteries is the worst thing you can do for them. Jews used to say *"Sha—shtill!* He's only 14, he doesn't have to know about all that yet." But even kids of five or six should go to a funeral and mourn with the family. That experience is strengthening. As I've said to many of you individually, that lets children know that funerals and cemeteries may be sad but they're not scary. The fantasy of what happens there is so much worse than the reality. The reality is not so hard to cope with, especially if you're with your family, and feel important because you too can be a mourner. When I make a funeral or *shiva* call I always make it a point to say to the child as well as the adult, "I'm sorry that your grandfather died, you must be feeling very sad." The child is a mourner, too.

It turns out that it's fine for kids to see their parents and grandparents and family crying. Now we know that we don't have to keep a stiff upper lip for anybody, not even our kids. Your crying says to them that it's okay to cry. And that's a good lesson.

We've found through our experience at least all the things one shouldn't say to a child. One shouldn't say, "Grandpa is up in heaven," because we really don't mean that. We don't say, "Grandpa is on a long journey," because it's not true, and why teach a child to fear journeys. We don't say, "Grandpa is asleep." Why teach a child to fear sleep? We don't say, "Grandpa was so good that God took him," because taking him away from us doesn't seem at all like a reward for being good. We've learned not to say to a child what we don't believe about immortality. But if you believe that the one who died is "with God," that's good to communicate. My best answer to the question, "Where is Grandpa now?" is this: "His body is in the ground, but a part of him is somehow with God though I can't explain how or where, but if it's with God, it's got to be okay."

We've found out that the things we want to keep from children are really the things we don't want to think about ourselves. And because we're more free to share the experience of death with our children, I think there will be fewer adults in the next generation who just can't deal with death, than there are in our generation. Grief will be hard for them, and they'll have to do their grief work. But they will remember that it is work that can be done because they saw us doing it, and even did it themselves.

We have learned a lot. Our experience with grief has probably taught you something about the significance of the *mitzvot* of tradition that our people has preserved, to help us get through death, the funeral itself, the *k'riah* ribbon, *kaddish*, *shivah*, the stone. Some say that you can't understand how all this helps till you go through it. And of course, not every ceremony helps everyone. Some like covering mirrors or pouring out water—I find these meaningless and some of you may as well.

Sometimes it's hard for teenagers to understand the process that Jews set in motion when death comes. A grandfather died recently, and one of the grandsons saw his aunt begin to assemble the food responsibilities for the family for the period before the funeral, and the time of *shiva*. The grandson was a sensitive teenager who had loved Grandpa and couldn't see why the death had only started this food preparation chain. Was this the way to start mourning, he wondered?

I empathize with his feelings. At certain ages you want to show your deep feelings by forgetting about food, or by finding solitude. To him, these preparations sounded more like a party. Yet you and I know how important all those traditions have been. They give us something to do, a way to help with our hands when our minds and mouths can't think of or speak anything helpful. Even the food preparation provides the right backdrop for the whole grief experience. It says that life, though you may not feel this way right now, will go on.

It just works—the catharsis of a funeral, putting on shovels of earth—earth from Israel in the casket which ties our grief to that of all our people, the tearing of a ribbon, which is the outward symbol of how we feel "torn" inside, the *shivah* candle, the best symbol of what a memory can be, light giving and warmth giving.

Shivah itself works. I know that many of us like to shorten that period, but less than three days can hardly ever be enough. There is a rightness to seven days. After almost a week you're ready for it to be over, and sitting *shivah* has deposited you one week after the funeral. You've lived through the first week, and others have helped you.

Prayers at home help a lot of people. They remind us that the comforting words of the synagogue also belong at home. Saying *Kaddish* at home just feels right. Being at services all that month and maybe even all that year is a way of allowing ourselves to be in mourning. Who says that we have to be stronger than our ancestors? Who says that we have to end grief more quickly than they did? The traditional observances give us something to do at a time when by ourselves we don't know what to do. They work!

They help us do the work of grieving.

Occasionally someone's relative will die, and the deceased will have requested that there be no traditional observances, no funeral, not even sprinkling of ashes, no marking of the time. And I find, and maybe you have too, that this is the hardest thing for the family. No matter what the deceased wanted, you can't feel like going back to life as usual without some acts which officially express grief and say goodbye. The traditions work, at a time when we need them, even the chain of food preparation that the teenager found inappropriate.

And almost all of you know all of this from experience. You've got the wisdom, the understanding of what hard work mourning can be, how long it lasts, and the sureness that we do live through it.

All that wisdom we should share with others, as this afternoon we've shared it with one another.

Shulayim: David I. Jacobson

There are many ways in which I have been touched by Rabbi Shapiro's words, such as when I have been at a funeral conducted by him. When ready to begin, he says in a comforting-yet-clear voice: "We're going to begin the service for ..." In those simple words, Rabbi evokes comfort during an uncomfortable and emotional time.

I have heard many of his sermons and felt his genuine words, and until I met him, I wouldn't have believed that someone can speak to a crowd of 1,500 people and still make it feel like he's speaking directly to me.

I really admired how he talked openly about facing his own depression. To see someone who was a leader share his struggles encouraged me to think more about my own. I can picture him in his office at 901 Milwaukee—he was very approachable and always made time for me.

I also got to see Rabbi Shapiro work as a chaplain at Lutheran General and in hospice care after he retired. He was such a great hospice rabbi. He's a human being who has a big heart, and an ability to understand how other people are feeling. That's how he speaks to everyone, and that's why people can really connect to him.

That's the skill of his that I appreciate most. Connecting with us all while still connecting with each of us as individuals.

David Jacobson, a longtime member of BJBE, is Founder of Chicago Jewish Funerals.

To The Students of HUC-JIR

As Part of an Alumnus-In-Residence Visit
(Others May Listen In)
Cincinnati, Ohio, 1984

What wisdom would you share with a group of students
about to embark on a journey that you yourself had taken
some years earlier? In 1984, MSS returned to Cincinnati to
serve as an alumnus-in-residence at Hebrew Union College,
where he was ordained as a rabbi 25 years earlier.
He addressed students, staff, and colleagues alike in this
sermon, in which he tells the story of the Tower of Babel
to illustrate some of the wonders and some of the challenges
of the rabbinate.

I BEGAN MY *KOL NIDRE* SERMON this year by saying the following: "If you belong to this congregation you run the risk of getting put into sermons. Occasionally you and I will share an experience that just cries out to be used as an example. I change the names, I try not to identify you in any way, but you always know it's you. And you never know when that's going to happen, so stay alert."

To you I say much the same thing. If I happen to talk about you this morning, you'll know it's you.

I can talk personally about the you who is becoming a rabbi

because we share a lot, right now. This experience for me, right now, is qualitatively the exact same experience you have had fairly recently when you spoke to your first student congregation. You have so much to say and want to say it all, which promises a much-too-long sermon, and then you sit down to write it out and you find you have nothing at all to say, which makes you wonder how you'll fill even 15 minutes, and you, in that student pulpit, and I back here share something else—high anxiety. Speaking before the faculty, even if most of them are new to me, is intimidating even for this non-anxious tenured senior rabbi of a happy "E" congregation.

So let me find momentary refuge in the *parashah* of the week and bring to it some well-developed exegetical skills, which will let me suggest one of our goals, some of the ways things don't work, and a personal truth about being a rabbi.

The story of the Tower of Babel and the generation of the dispersion begins this way: "All the earth had the same language and the same words."

The same language, even the same words. So the words could be used for uniting, not dividing.

D'varim achadim, it says. The words were the same. *Achadim*, to me, implies a oneness, a pluralistic wholeness…a wholeness that was ancient and idyllic and a worthy goal of synagogues and rabbis.

I once heard a colleague of ours receive this great compliment. "He's the only rabbi I know who is the same person off and on the *bimah*."

Being the same person, on and off, in its narrow and widest sense, is a worthwhile goal. Buber calls it "all-of-a-piece." It makes one effective and keeps one sane.

Being all-of-a-piece isn't easy. Let me point to a failing I find in some colleagues and an ongoing difficulty of my own.

I am amazed by how many of our colleagues use a pulpit voice. I guess their congregants aren't amazed, they must think it's normal. Maybe the higher the *bimah*, the lower the voice. It must be compensation.

I'm pretty sure that they don't teach you, on any of the four campuses, to speak like that. Nor, I'm sure, do they teach you to make those grandiose hand motions for "please rise" and "please be seated," like directing a crane.

And I think I know why it happens to us. It's not only because we emulate older colleagues or the rabbis of our childhood, but because up front is scary, and if I can just be somebody else up here then I won't have to be scared because I'm not here!

Wholeness is worth a risk, even at the risk of terror.

It's hard to be "all-of-a-piece." Often, instead of being able to integrate the parts of my job, I would feel a pull in different directions which could immobilize me.

Example: I sit in my study at Temple and feel opposing force fields at work. Behind and beside me are all my books—the written record of Jewish wisdom and tradition. I rest among them.

They call to me with siren voices, which sounds like the HUC-JIR rabbinic faculty in chorus, and they say: "Shapiro, you were smart enough to be more learned than you are. Here in our pages lies your first rabbinic loyalty. Read! Study! Open up the books!"

And out there, walking in to my office, are the congregants— all those people to whom I am pledged to be accessible. And there is no end of things I could be doing with them and for them, and there is no end of untouched books, and no end of the things you're not doing which you are sure all of your colleagues are doing. Then, the rabbinate can feed that obsession and even paralyze you.

Of course I'm just talking about me.

D'varim Achadim. Safah Achat. All-of-a-piece, integrated, and whole. How can you be able to acknowledge and even blend into your rabbinate your frailties, your mishagass, even your childhood? To be able to integrate the faculty with the congregants and hold them both in a comfortable pluralistic suspension. Messianic? Yes, but worth working at it.

Yet, you can have achieved a nice integration of those items and yet not be so good at what you hope to accomplish with amcha. Even a unified person has to know how things work. And they don't all work the way we think they do. Babel teaches a lesson.

The whole scheme of the city and tower builders falls apart.

It seemed like such a natural way to achieve renown or at lease ensure survival: "Let's build us a town and a tower and thereby gain some fame and at least make sure we're not scattered abroad."

So they gained no fame, but infamy, and what they feared most happened anyway. Nothing worked.

What went wrong? The text says that God didn't want it that way, which might be another way of saying, "It doesn't work that way." It did seem sensible—others could see the tower and admire it and the builders would have a rallying point—but it doesn't work that way. Reputation is in the fickle hands of others, and working only for survival defeats itself. It just doesn't work that way.

Many of the ways in which rabbis imagine they will make their name and do their jobs well, don't work that way. Believing they do, programs are defeated.

Here's the scene: the year is 5762. It is a meeting of the Jewish principals and rabbis and teachers of your area. You are on a panel in a workshop called, "Putting Jewish Education Back On Course" or "The Tragedy of Minimal Jewish Education." No matter what the title or purpose, someone will before long set the level of the discussion by proclaiming, "What can we accomplish in so few hours of school?" or "If parents would only set their priorities straight," or "If only all the rabbis would preach about this on the same *Shabbat* and make a massive effort to…" You can feel swept up in either utter despair or with false heroism about your ability to slay those dragons.

You cannot believe how often that has happened over the years. The people and topics will change but the underground script will emerge: You've got to improve your people, teach your people, exhort your people, make them see the truth, come up with the great plan that will be the force to move them.

Except *amcha* doesn't really mean your people. It means God's people. And they can't be moved that way. It doesn't work that way, never has.

Let me suggest a better way of conceiving it. Judaism is not something we have that we must sell to *amcha*. They have it already. They own it as much as the rabbis and teachers do, and

if we all learned all the *Torah* from God and were all slapped
into post-partum forgetfulness, then I don't possess anything they
don't, I just spent time in "remembering-school" while they were
studying accountancy and law. When they are ready to explore
their forgetful selves, I think I can help them to rediscover. Until
they are ready, not much will happen. But I still have a present
task. Because they will not necessarily tell me when they are ready,
and because they may not even recognize it themselves, I have to
keep throwing out a variety of possibilities so that when they are
ready there is something attractive to grab.

If I view the task this way I can't get mad at them for not
being moved by what I teach, or flagellate myself for what I didn't
get them to do. *Amcha* means God's people, not mine.

I was once on a task force with lay people and rabbis called
"Jewish Spirituality and Religious Practice." My experience
with such groups had been that when the rabbis take over, the
lay people stop coming, but this one started out pretty well. We
shared early religious experiences and dilemmas openly. We
fell on our face, in my opinion, only when some of the rabbis
revealed their hidden agenda, which was to draw up the minimal
acceptable standards for a Reform Jew to practice and get them
accepted in all our congregations.

The real agenda, now revealed, was control. Who has the
authority? So the laypeople stopped coming which left the rabbis
to discuss this interesting issue of authority in the absence of those
who have to give it to you. It was rabbi-talk, and I stopped going,
too.

I wasn't so quick to learn another good message about how
things really work. I always wanted to have my successful adult
classes become ongoing self-directed groups, and as much as
it seemed to be a natural, it usually didn't happen, even with
prodding. They didn't know how to keep it going without me
because it was from the start "my group." I finally learned by
trial and error. A staff person can convene a group which is
supposed to continue as a *chavurah*, but the staff person can't
be at the second meeting or the group will never be autonomous.
And the rabbi can't convene it at all by herself, but can be at
the first meeting, to say hello, and leave early and say, "Good

luck." Yes, if no staff is at the second meeting the group may die anyway or decide to become the BJBE gin rummy *chavurah*. Isn't empowerment great? That's the way it works.

I had a great idea years ago, and I never understood why it wasn't working. Before *Rosh Hashanah* I sent the congregation a letter titled *Brit u'Mitzvot*, and a list of *mitzvot*, commandments they could consider taking on for the coming year. The accompanying letter (I thought) was good. It talked seriously and clearly and not demeaningly about God, covenant and *mitzvot*, and I suggested they actually sign up for new *mitzvot*. I did it three different years, to thunderous silence each time, maybe a trickle of response. I guess it showed them I was doing my job but it didn't even seem to have set a tone.

Because my telling them or exhorting them or even selling *mitzvot* in a wonderful letter isn't how it works. It works only if I let it belong to them, which happens only if the rabbi can practice *havlagah*, which might be translated as "stifle yourself."

I did better, years later, when I let people choose "One *Mitzvah* More" as an adult retreat theme, let them study *mitzvot* they cared about and used the last session to let them share with the group what *mitzvot* they might take on. There was a validating community, and a support group of friends who would help you "remember and do," and that group decided to have regular reunions to help them keep the promises of doing *Shabbes* better, visiting the cemetery more often, learning Hebrew, seeing that difficult aunt. Getting the message from a rabbi about *Mitzvot* and sitting down with his list is not the way it works.

Whether you like it or not, it all belongs to *amcha*. You can help them remember what they forgot, but if you really want to control your people they will lend you their bodies sometimes, but never their souls.

And the last thing I want to tell you is hard to find in the text—it comes from the text of my life, so far.

I have found being a rabbi wonderful. I thought I would. I did. I do.

On my first day on this campus in 1955 I took a walk down Clifton Avenue with my classmate Shelly Gordon *zichrono l'vrachah*, and he said, "This is great, isn't it? At college I was always trying to steal some time to do my HUC reading and now that's what we get to do, *full time*."

Though the rabbinate wasn't kind to Shelly, he never lost his delight in the study, but I thought he was right and I still do.

We get to deal with Judaism and values full time.

It's hard for me to imagine what it would be like to have success measured by selling lines of advertising or "x" carloads of gloves or billable hours of legal advice. Instead, no matter what I do it has some relationship to what I have decided is ultimately worthwhile. And they pay us for it.

Yes, the rabbinate produces stresses. And you can read all about it in the back issues of *Sh'ma* magazine and hear about them in the halls of the CCAR. But talk to some of the other professionals and businesspeople in the congregations: their stress is just as great, and what is more they have to produce in ways we don't, and some can't close their eyes at night and know for sure that what they tried to produce had real value, much less served a higher cause.

But we can. Even on bad days. The older I get, the more that is worth.

We have the luxury of doing every day what we know has worth and we have the gift of a sure-fire formula for doing it effectively—being a *mensch*.

No, I'm not sure how to define that. Arthur Green has a wonderful article in which he says there is a secret fifth section to the Code of Jewish Law, entitled *Hilchot Enoshut*: "How to be a *Mensch*." Green says the first section is called "Know the Other." Try to know how the other feels.

This is really the message from my congregation to you. I asked our oversized Board of Directors to write out individually advice from them that I should give to student rabbis while I'm here.

They gave me variations on this theme. Tell them to be a *mensch*—to be sensitive, to be a good listener, to be empathetic, to know what it feels like to be in their congregation. To know the other.

And one of them later reminded me of when he knew that our first assistant rabbi was really his rabbi.

"It was two weeks after we had put my father in the nursing home," he said. "And I ran into Irwin just before services. It was a busy time. He asked me how I was, and I said "Okay." "No," he said, "How are you really?"

"That" said the man, "is when he started being my rabbi."

This is a wonderful calling.

It will help you be sane. If you work at wholeness, at being the same person off *bimah* and on. And if you learn how *amcha* really works.

It is above all a wonderful calling because it is the only job I know where being a *mensch* ensures some success and being less than that ensures failure.

At *Kol Nidre* I told my congregation that they always run the risk of finding themselves in sermons.

I hope you will try to find yourself in this one.

Shulayim: Dr. Gary P. Zola

One of the many benefits that came to me as a camper and, years later, staff member at OSRUI was the opportunity to become acquainted with the many rabbinical leaders who served on the camp's faculty. This is where I first met Mark Shapiro and, as a result of our being together at camp over the course of many years, this is how he became one of my rabbis.

Mark Shapiro taught me many lessons through his exceptional teaching skills, his wonderful sermonic messages, and his truly remarkable listening skills. For all these reasons and more, Rabbi Shapiro's rabbinate has significantly influenced my own career. Yet of all the lessons I have learned there is one that deserves special mention for me.

After falling in love with my beautiful bride Stefi—shortly after the summer of 1974, when we met at OSRUI—I began to think about a topic that had not previously crossed my mind: what kind of a husband and, one day, a father I might like to be. Of the many rabbis I knew and admired, it was Mark Shapiro who first showed me how a talented and dedicated rabbi could concomitantly be a loving husband as well as a devoted parent (and, later, grandparent). It was for this reason, among others, that Stefi and I invited Rabbi Shapiro to officiate on the occasion of our marriage.

Four decades later, Stefi and I still recall Mark's delicious words, his sage wisdom, his competent guidance and, above all, the personal example he and Hanna have set. Together they remind us that our families—those whom we love and who love us—truly constitute life's most enduring and impressive legacy.

Gary Zola taught in the high school at BJBE in the 1970s. He is Executive Director of the Jacob Rader Marcus Center of the American Jewish Archives, and the Edward M. Ackerman Family Distinguished Professor of the American Jewish Experience and Reform Jewish History at HUC-JIR in Cincinnati.

Cemetery Tales

Yom Kippur Yizkor 1985/5746

A cemetery can be a moving, comforting, and even magical place, MSS taught. He looked forward to leading annual services at Mt. Jehoshua, the BJBE cemetery on the West Side, as well as to taking groups of students out there. He would introduce them to some of the people buried there, tell a few stories and explain some of the rituals associated with death and burial. He chose this Yizkor service to talk about the role that the cemetery plays in helping us make memory a natural part of our lives.

THE PRAYER BOOK HAS LOTS OF POETRY and philosophy about grief.

I'd like to tell you a story about a cemetery, and then talk a little bit about our own Temple cemetery.

The story is told by Rabbi Zalman Schacter, who will be at BJBE some time during the next year.

There was a man who was an idler, the kind who hung around street corners gabbing all day. One day he was walking in the forest and he sees the princess returning from a swim. She was very beautiful and he falls in love with her. So the next day he approaches her and says, "Lady, I love you. When will we be able to be together?" She takes one look at him and says, "In the cemetery."

Well, he wasn't too bright, so he goes to the cemetery to wait for her. When she doesn't come, one day, two days, he figures she's busy, a princess' life is busy, she'll come when she can. He stays in the cemetery begging for food and money from those who come by. He starts looking at gravestones, thinking about the people, pondering what their world was all about.

He sees funerals come to the cemetery, he watches people who visit graves saying things like, "She was so pretty when she was young," or "He was such a handsome man."

He thinks about why he loves the princess—is it her beauty? He has much time to think. He realizes that her outer form is only one phase of beauty, that the source of beauty must be without form. It must be God.

People saw him at the cemetery constantly. Word got around that he must be a holy man, or what was he doing there all the time? People began coming to him and saying, "You know, I've got such and such troubles. What do you advise?" He started giving opinions, even blessings. The advice worked and so did the blessings.

Meanwhile the princess was married, but childless. Doctors couldn't help. Someone suggests: "Go to the holy man in the cemetery." She goes to him and asks for his blessings to help her have children.

With one look he recognizes her. He said, "It was your beauty and your words that sent me to the cemetery in the first place, and since I've been here, I've become fairly wise. If there is good in anything I've learned or done for people, I want it to be transformed into a child for you." And that is how he blessed her. And soon after, he died.

The lesson that Zalman Schachter draws from that story is that one can learn from the love of a woman or a man how to come to the true love of God.

That's a good message, and I think, true. But one of the other messages of the story is that you can learn something in a cemetery, from a cemetery.

I'm thinking now of our own Temple cemetery, Mt. *Jehoshua*, and what I've learned there over the years. Since 1962, when I became rabbi of *B'nai Jehoshua* I've been there often. Twice each year we hold a memorial service there, on Memorial Day and on the Sunday between *Rosh Hashanah* and *Yom Kippur*, as we did a week ago Sunday. And this year the wisdom of the place seems even a bit more personal, for now a special loved one of mine is buried at Mt. *Jehoshua* too.

The cemetery association started even before the synagogue. Many of those who come out regularly for the memorial service have at least a few generations buried there. And many of them think of the cemetery as a part of themselves. Their attitude toward death and loss is one of acceptance.

I remember being out there on a Sunday years ago and heard a radio playing, with the football game on. And there were two older gentlemen of the congregation, in their old clothes, working away at a bench with paint and brushes. They waved to me, offered me an apple from their lunch. The area was the one in which their family was buried, the newest grave the grave of the wife of one of the men, the sister of the other. Yes, they said, the bench near these graves needed a painting and some repair. So they had come out to spend half the day doing it, and brought lunch and the radio. It was so appropriate, "just right."

They were so much at home with the cemetery. I'm sure it was a place that brought the sadness back to them, yet it was for them a good place. Good memories were there, and they could sit back, and rest in the lap of all those memories.

I thought then about cemeteries on *kibbutzim* in Israel. Each kibbutz has its own cemetery, right on its own land, not hidden away, and therefore one passes it all the time, both children and adults. You grow up used to the idea that people come and go. The cemetery becomes a part of daily wisdom, reminding you of mortality, reminding you of the heritage of the past, reminding you in a gentle daily way.

Every year, for some time now, we take 3rd grade youngsters on a field trip to the Temple cemetery. We think it's important for them to know what it looks like, to get used to it when it isn't a time of crisis for their families. So every year we descend on that cemetery on a spring Sunday, parents and kids, 50, 60, 70 of us.

I guide the tour, giving them questions to which certain marker stones have the answer. We stop at certain graves and I recall stories about the people buried there, humorous ones as well as serious ones. After a few minutes the kids lose inhibitions and the place becomes more friendly. They run around a bit looking for special graves and feel comfortable enough to yell to one another. "We found it."

One year, when 60 or 70 of us descended on the cemetery, a few veteran *B'nai Jehoshua*-ites were out there visiting their own family graves. Our 60 or 70 got very "comfortable," and I was a little worried that the youthful exuberance of our kids, which was fine with me, might offend them. I came over later ready to apologize. "Oh no," they said. They had loved it. They loved the idea of kids visiting the cemetery. They loved the enthusiasm. I shouldn't apologize for the kids. They were grateful they had been there to see the kids, and hear their questions, and their voices.

That attitude, displayed toward the cemetery regularly, seems to be a part of how they dealt with their grief. They didn't enshrine it. They made the memories an ongoing part of their lives. And eventually that cemetery became an important place, yes, even a good place, and not a shrine which you protect from the rest of life.

You keep living. You make the fish without your mother or grandmother.

Every time we have the official cemetery memorial service, I offer a short thought, a story, a quote and an interpretation, or very short sermonette. A week ago Sunday I had nothing specific ready. I was depending on inspiration at the moment, a dangerous thing—for if it doesn't come, one talks too long and uninspiredly.

But the day was beautiful and as we stood there, I knew what I wanted to say. I said that we had stood there over the years in all kinds of weather, rain and cold as well as gorgeous fall and spring days, days when the sun warmed and days when the wind bit deeply. Grief is like that. Sometimes it just bites like that stinging wind, and no overcoat and no comforter or comforting takes away the chill. And at other times that grief becomes a memory that warms like the sun. As the bereavement fades into the past, the memory is more often like a sunny day than a bitter one. But not always, and even at a distance of years, grief has the power to sting like that unexpected springtime chill. So the very rhythm of the natural world and the rhythm of our feelings go hand in hand. Going to the cemetery year after year, even the weather teaches us that.

Year after year we go back. The little kids, the very old people. We learn that people triumph over their grief by making memory a natural part of their lives.

God gives us the power to triumph over our grief. That is what the cemetery teaches me.

Shulayim: Rabbi Dan Rabishaw

I must admit that when I was growing up, I didn't always listen to the sermon at services. Even so, as I look back upon my own career as a rabbi, I realize that Rabbi Shapiro's sermons affected me greatly. I may not remember many of his exact words, but I do remember him speaking about trips to Israel, clandestine visits with Soviet refuseniks and his beloved White Sox. I also remember stories.

Rabbi Shapiro told stories to children in religious school, to youth groupers sitting around a campfire at OSRUI, and he used stories as examples during his sermons. It was his way of telling a story that I not only remember, but try to emulate. Rabbi Shapiro used his voice to create and define characters, set a mood, and even indicate intrigue or an ironic twist. Most importantly, though, Rabbi Shapiro used his voice to speak to each person as if he or she was the only one in the room. That ability is not just a talent, it's a gift. It is a gift that I will treasure and strive to pass along to others I meet along life's journey.

Dan Rabishaw is Associate Team Director at Seasons Hospice and Palliative Care in Chicago. He was ordained by HUC-JIR in 1997, and was confirmed at BJBE in 1982.

You Ought to Say Some Words

At the Dedication of the Renovated BJBE Sanctuary, 1986

When the new sanctuary was dedicated at 901 Milwaukee Avenue in 1986, MSS spoke about the congregation's roots and journey from the old B'nai Jehoshua building on Ashland Avenue to school gymnasiums to rented churches to a partially completed upstairs with bare bricks and a concrete floor. While sharing some of his favorite features of the new space, he remarked how good it felt to be home.

FREDERICK BUECHNER WRITES OF A TIME when he and a friend were walking in the woods, and the sap from the maple trees was running. The buckets were hung from every tree and if you listened you could hear the dripping from all over the forest. Buechner's friend asked what pure sap tasted like, and Buechner answered that it was pure like rainwater, with just the faintest touch of sweetness. So Buechner unhooked a bucket from a tree, gave it to his friend, who tipped it to his lips, ready to taste for the first time the lifeblood of a tree, and the friend stopped, looked at Buechner who is a pastor, and said to him, "I think you ought to be saying some words."

Saying some words to make sure both of them knew that what seemed like an ordinary moment might be a holy moment.

Some words should be said tonight to help us know that this moment is a little different too. That walking into the sanctuary tonight, just being here tasting for the first time the new personality of the sanctuary—this is a different moment, special, set aside from other moments, which is just what Hebrew means when it says something is *Kadosh*—Holy.

Some of the right words have been said already: Opening prayers and *Shehecheyanu*. And I want to say a few more about the way it looks in here, about what the new items say, and about what the danger is in here.

It looks good. That's not a pronouncement, it's just an opinion. Everyone's reaction to artistry is different and there's no accounting for tastes, but I think your opinion is in accord with mine. It looks very good.

The further back you go in BJBE history the better it looks. When I first came to BJBE in 1965 we were holding services in what is now the wrestling room at Gemini Junior High. Our portable ark, *Ner Tamid* and *Sefer Torah*, candlesticks, and all the *Oneg Shabbat* trays, were stored in a medium-sized closet just down the school corridor, and every Friday night they came out of the closet. And then they bumped us out of there to the east gym at Springman with its resident odor of boys' gyms. And then, bumped from there, we went to Niles Community Church on Oakton, a friendly place with a caring pastor, but you had to ignore the big blue curtain at the front which covered "you know what," and if your hand caressed the outside of a bench on the aisle, you were reminded that you were in the domain of the cross and not the Star of David.

The further back you go in BJBE history the better it looks tonight. Maybe you recall what it was like in here fourteen years ago, a roller rink, years ahead of the Axle. Lots of space, concrete block on all sides, concrete on the floor and card chairs for all, a little damp, not exactly a place that seemed to invite the still, small voice. Eleven years ago the sanctuary was completed. The ark was more open than was comfortable for some, too much like a cage for others.

But it looks fine now. It looks good because important words encircle us. It looks good because the very letters are alive, beginning with the *dalet* there, continuing through the letters standing for the Ten Commandments, each one alive and burning with an intensity that promises never to go out.

The ark doors, which to me do just what they should, shield the *Torah*, yet let us be aware of its presence. So that opening the ark is like a small explosion; and we rise to meet it. And of course the doors are alive too, even as the letters are alive on the sides. The closer you get to them the more life you see and in greater detail without beginning or end, because everything in the story of the doors is happening at once. And of course the *menorah* comes to life also echoing the images in the doors.

And the light—the *Ner Tamid*—not hidden back there anymore but out, closer to us, with a sense of also being alive, some bird in flight, yet it's also a picture caught in a moment after an explosion of light.

And outside, the lovely *Tree of Life* and the *Book of Appreciation*.

And the inside inscription "Know Before Whom You Stand."

I like what it teaches me. I like the message. I suggested it. So I like it. There are a lot of quotes that have been found in sanctuaries: "I have set the Lord before me always," or "This is the gate of the Lord." I like this one because it shakes me up a bit as I enter the sanctuary and tells me, "You're not the biggest thing around." A sanctuary should be warm and friendly and ours has always been like that, but it's not just another room. To get into the mood, we can sometimes use a little shaking up.

The inscription doesn't define God for you. It doesn't even say God—you have to insert what for you is the highest, before which or whom you stand, judged at your most serious moments. And therefore everyone's private response to that demand is somewhat different depending on how they see God. And all these different views of that *Whom* join together, letting us be individuals before that *Whom*, but uniting us before the *Whom* than whom none is greater.

Know Before Whom You Stand. That's why on the *bimah* we occasionally turn and face the ark, not the congregation; to remind ourselves and you that we do not just stand in front of one another as in a theater, but that we all stand before God.

The Ark doors. I can't really explain the doors because the artist Arthur Schneider didn't really have explanations for everything... and that's just as well because you'll feel even more free to use your imagination as you look at them. And if a sermon or whatnot gets a bit too long or wordy, there's something marvelous for your imagination to play with.

But I can tell you a little about the images within the doors. They point to real life—as simple as that. In the carvings you find birds and eggs and young herds of cattle, beasts of prey both nurturing and hunting. And these animals play out the drama of life in which we are as much involved as they: conception, birth, homebuilding, growing with the sun, hunting, and being hunted. The strength of the lions of Judah representing our people, and then an image of destruction towards the upper left; the lioness has trampled on a birds' nest and the young are gone. We Jews know that "all is lost" feeling. Yet the uppermost image on the left is the bird singing. And because the bird sings next to the *Menorah* I imagine she sings a song of hope.

I like the message. I believe in it. It's a Jewish message; As Eugene Borowitz said, "If the measure of one's hope is one's willingness to continue in the midst of adversity, then it is clear why Judaism is the religion of hope par excellence."

The *Ner Tamid*. The design is based on the Lurianic description of creation which says that God first sent His light into the space in which we live, enclosed that light within vessels, which then broke open and the sparks of God's light were scattered everywhere. And some lodge within us and others. The *Ner Tamid* reminds us that the beings around us may be carrying that spark and that therefore we had better treat the person next to us—and the one in the back row— just as if precious as sterling.

The Book of Appreciation outside. I like what it says too. It says, "People, you can't have your own names everywhere, for this is the house of God and the Jewish people and of *Torah*. But those who are blessed and share their blessings with us are together like a tree of life, like *shomrim*, guardians of that tree."

It looks good inside. I like all the messages.

The *Torah* portion quoted in our pamphlet of dedication says, "Don't have alternate weights or measures in your house; if you want to endure on your land, write honestly on your deeds as clearly as that inscription is written on the wall, because dishonesty makes even the beautiful abhorrent." We want to become a place where everyone is part of the get-well committee, the caring committee

We're not there yet. The message of the *Torah* is thus: We, like most others, haven't made it yet, and if we turn items into idols we are even farther from having it made as a congregation.

This evening, please stop and look at the glass case downstairs to see the exhibit of BJ and BE and BJBE memorabilia from the past. They are wonderful... what the presidents used to look like, how the kids used to dress for services, how the Men's Club dressed up for services. Even a receipt for the six dollars the Temple paid the Pilsen Clubhouse for a month's rental of a Sabbath school room.

And look at a program from 1953, a regathering of Confirmation classes. What would you call a regathering of former Confirmation Classes? I know what they called it: a Homecoming.

This is home for so many. It has always been good to come home. It is the people who make it "home." The surroundings help, but only we, knowing before Whom we stand, make it a home of *Torah*.

Scharansky, Hawkeye, and Abraham

Rosh Hashanah 5747/1986

There are so many things in life that are beyond our control. How do we live a life of sanity amidst all that cannot be changed? MSS shared some thoughts on how we, as Jews, might learn to navigate such a world by citing two somewhat predictable examples—Abraham the patriarch faced with God's command to sacrifice his son, and Anatoly Sharansky banished to Siberia—and one less likely one: Benjamin Franklin Pierce, the surgeon stuck in the Korean War and brought to life by Alan Alda on TV's M*A*S*H. (Sharansky has since changed the spelling of his last name, but in 1986, he still spelled it with a 'c' so we kept that original spelling intact.)

Y EARS AGO, WHEN WE HAD THOSE "little prayer books," that is, the old *Union Prayer Books*, I was looking for something more contemporary to add to the *Rosh Hashanah* service. I found a loose-leaf style "Modern High Holy Day Service," (in the '70s, that meant the *Sh'ma* played on a banjo, followed by "Blowin' in the Wind,") took a few interesting readings from it, and added them to our service by sharing them at various points.

Most of the readings were just novelties, and I dropped them after a year or two. When we got to our present *Gates of Repentance*, I dropped all but one: the one called "Lord, I Have Time," based on a poem by Abbé Michael Quoist, in which everybody is rushing to catch up with time, but they never do, no matter how frantic they get. It concludes by saying, "God, you do give us enough time, if only we could use it properly."

I keep doing that reading because people keep commenting on it, and asking for copies. Maybe it strikes home because so many of us are particularly troubled by the parts of our lives which seem to be out of control, and we like to be IN control. "Time" admits that we don't usually control our time very well, but at the end it sounds hopeful that we might learn to do it well. That's good to hear, for you and I know that there are lots of other important things that are and will always be OUT of our control: How Congress acts, how the market acts, how your firm acts, how your boss acts, how your parents act, how your children act.

OH! WE WOULD LIKE TO CONTROL SOME OF THOSE. AND WE TRY.

We try—like the mother who is leaving her child at school or at a friend's home for the first time, and who spends so much time describing to the teacher or counselor every nuance of the kid's psyche.

"Todd gets upset if you hurry him through meals, and he doesn't take his baseball cap off for dinner or even for a bath."

Such a mother once said in a rap group: "It dawned on me that I wasn't letting go. Wherever my kid went I'd be there first, trying to orchestrate his environment."

But the environment ultimately is not under our control and frankly, neither is the kid. Bill Cosby wrote a book called *Fatherhood*, in which he reminds us that we can't control them because *most* of the time we don't know what they're thinking *or* doing. He says:

> How can you control or even direct a kid when the kid's basic response is, 'I don't know'? The kid shows up with a skinhead haircut and papa says, 'Where did you get that crazy haircut?' and the kid says 'I don't know.' But when

your 15-year-old child does respond, he says one of two other things – either "OK," which as we all know means "I haven't murdered anybody," or the blood-chilling, "No problem."

But it's not all comedy. Judith Viorst says, "There will be times late at night when our children are out and the phone rings and reality will remind us, in that heart-stopping moment before we pick up the phone, that anything, any horror, is possible."

The world is out of our control. Bad things can happen. Your parents could get divorced; your kids could get divorced. Your kids could be on drugs; your parents could be on drugs. Go to the synagogue in Istanbul at the wrong time and become a statistic. Our everyday lives contain serious risks, with no immunity granted for those we love and none for us either. We've got to live with all the uncontrollable dangers of life.

How can you do it sanely?

I think there *are* some Jewish responses. I see them personified in two Jews and one who should have been Jewish. We can learn something about living without much control, from Anatoly Scharansky, from Benjamin Franklin Pierce, and from our father Abraham.

You can learn a lot from Scharansky. Scharansky faced the uncontrollable world by going within and finding and creating strength.

Oh, he did a lot of other things too, heroic things, the kind that get into stories and even into songs eventually. Like the story of his *Book of Psalms*, one of the few books allowed him. He lost it in a snowy exercise yard. A few days later when they came to tell him he was finally released, the little man stands up to his full 5'4" and says, "I'M NOT GOING WITHOUT MY *BOOK OF PSALMS*." And they had to send guards to search in the snow for the book, because they saw that the little man would not leave without it, and then they bring it and he says, "Okay, now I'll leave."

And what he did when they exchanged him on that bridge! He gets out of the black Russian sedan and they point across the bridge to the American car waiting for him on the other side. They say, "Walk straight over there," and he smiles at them, and with his big fur hat wobbling, he walks not a straight line, but zig-zag!

But the best lesson we can learn from Natan Scharansky is to live sanely as a Jew when you don't have control—by going within.

Is your life out of control? More than HIS was? They even controlled his eating when they chose to. He was force-fed when he wanted to starve.

But inside, he was his own master. He memorized *Psalms*.

He worked on his Hebrew. It's hard for me to imagine how a man, for whom Hebrew was a language he learned as an adult, could go without speaking it to anyone for eight years, and then emerge from prison and be able to speak it decently. Yet he did. Because INSIDE, he had worked on his Hebrew, even in jail.

He analyzed himself. He tried to understand his emotions, tried to think through the most ethical way to act toward his jailers and his fellow inmates. And in a recent interview he said that, since his release, he has had to do so much talking to groups and the media that he hasn't had his own time with himself as he did in prison. And not only does he miss it but he feels he is not as good a person now as he was then.

I don't know how he did all that. I don't have a way to tell you or myself how to do it. Yet Scharansky did it, and he is not so different from you or me. His parents didn't give him more love or strokes than yours did. He was originally an assimilated Jew without much Jewish knowledge or passion. So it can be done. One can go inside, to thoughts, books, study, prayer, dream analysis, self-discipline, *Torah* of some kind. One can live in the inner world freely. Scharansky did it to survive the totally out-of-his-control environment.

Scharansky's way is one way.

Benjamin Franklin Pierce's is another way.

That's Hawkeye Pierce, you know, the character that Alan Alda played and keeps playing on M*A*S*H.

Hawkeye's not Jewish. But leave his boozing out, and most of the rest of him—especially the way he copes with his world—is, I think, classically Jewish.

See, his world is *really* out of his control. He's in the army—stuck. He has to live with no-sense bureaucratic rules. He can't get the right equipment. He is the healer who keeps getting cases that defy healing skill. And the maimed and the wounded and the chopped keep coming on choppers, unscheduled and always.

That's *takeh*, uncontrolled.

So what are his classically Jewish responses?

He keeps doing what he can, as best as he can do it, and he uses black humor and playfulness to keep things in perspective.

He keeps on doing what he can. In his life, that means keeping them alive and hoping they'll be sent home instead of back to war, or hoping they'll last till they can get to the base hospital.

He does what he can. Even when the lights fail and the bombs fall and the carton labeled morphine turns out to have tongue depressors—he does what he can, even when that happens to be triage, deciding who might live and whom you will certainly have to let die.

You do what you can—for your unit, for your family, your friends, and for the world. Hawkeye couldn't stop the choppers from coming. And you can't keep some of your worst nightmares from walking to the very edge of your life, or closer. It's not just nuclear buildup you can't do much about—it's also AIDS and also the drug scene, and the world's casual acceptance of sex and its implications for your kids. You can't do much about that, or the growth of intermarriage, or your father's too-quick aging, or his too-slow dying, or finding that lump in the wrong place if that's your worst nightmare. We're not in control of any of that. And that powerlessness is for some of us the very worst part of all.

So, as Hawkeye does, you do what you can. You keep saying what you believe, at home. You write letters and make calls and hold your father's hand. You give an example of working at a marriage.

You *do* the Jewish things you can, you keep the *pushke* out and you use it, and you do *Shabbat* dinner no matter how crazy the schedule, and you read and you remember the sick and lonely. You do one *mitzvah* more even when it means visiting and trying to love your goofy uncle.

That's how Hawkeye survives, and he does some good, too.

And he gets his second wind from that classic Jewish source—the barbed and bitter jest. He plays Groucho Marx while re-sectioning a bowel. He tosses off one-liners that make absurdity livable.

I do think that Jewish humor has helped the Jew survive what we have survived.

I was teaching a sociology of religion class at Glenbrook South one day and was talking about some of the cultural aspects of Judaism—like food, dance, music, and humor. They didn't understand how a joke could be Jewish. Could I tell them a Jewish joke? I tried to think of one that was G or PG and also would be understandable at Glenbrook South.

One came to my mind. I told them the joke in which Hitler is out for a ride in the park on his horse when the horse hears a car backfire, and starts to run wildly. Hitler loses the reins, yells for someone, anyone, to save him, as he is almost falling off this wild horse. A young German sees him, runs alongside the path, grabs the bridle, gets the horse to stop. Hitler says "You saved my life, what's your name?"

"Israel Goldfarb."

"Goldfarb," says Hitler, "a *Jew!* Well Jew, you have just saved Adolf Hitler's life, (Goldfarb goes white as a sheet) and though it hurts me, tell me what I can do for you, anything and I'll do it."

"Please," says Goldfarb, "Here's what you can do for me. Keep this a secret!"

If you ever list the reasons why we lived during and after the Holocaust, do not leave out our ability to make up and tell one another, and laugh at, jokes like these.

Perspective helps. When up against those crises that sit immobile in our path, immobilizing us. And sometimes lightness, even playfulness, helps us gain perspective.

I sat once with a lady who was dying, and her mother and sister were there. There was nothing more to do but wait.

What do you say? Nobody gives a rabbi a script for those times either. Searching for *something*, I said to the mother with a raised eyebrow and a wink, "What was this one like as a kid?"

It almost seems, in the retelling, too playful, but the feeling in the room just changed, as the mother and both daughters started remembering funny stories of when the daughter was bratty. All three of them laughed and replayed those old scenes. "Do you remember when I came home late, ma, and you were...."

That did some good. It reminded them that there had been wonderful times too, which still could be remembered and replayed, which still gave pleasure. It brought perspective.

You do what you can, with as much sense of humor as you can muster. That's how Hawkeye survived out-of-control Korea. Maybe it will work in your Koreas too.

And sometimes you have to be this morning's Abraham, who trusted God enough to start walking and kept walking with Isaac, even though death seemed to be the destination.

Talk about not being in control. You see, if God really wanted Isaac dead, as he seemed to command Abraham, then what could Abraham do anyway? If Abraham had run away like Jonah will next week, God could have dispatched Isaac with a lightning bolt or smallpox.

Abraham was in control of *one thing only*—what to believe. See, in the chapter before, God had promised Abraham many children through Isaac. And today God seems to be saying that He wants Abraham to end Isaac's life. Both can't be true.

Abraham had a choice of believing that somehow God had a plan which was good for him and his son, or believing that God was a devil and the world and life were therefore bananas.

He decided to believe there was a good plan. He trusted the future to God, and he set out.

Okay, it doesn't sound like effective executive problem solving. The *One-Minute Manager* might give snappier advice.

But trusting that God somehow knows what He is doing is sometimes all we can do. And there is evidence that life itself, through God, or because of God, or because of itself, works things out and can be trusted to bring healing, to bring us what we need.

Like gray hair. Do you know that gray hair is the body's way of softening, not emphasizing so much the lines that come to our faces as we age?

Life carries its own right answers along with it. Isn't it amazing that today's best hopes for fighting cancer are in substances within us already, that we are our own best medicine?!

Abraham had no control. He went quietly on that walk with Isaac because he trusted that God wanted life and not death. He couldn't prove it and I can't, either. But just because I know that the best healer can be the body itself, because I know that most problems never really get solved, but just might get better in time, so I believe that life has built in healing, and that scrambling to control what will not be controlled is often not nearly so wise as just letting things be.

Dr. Ken Moses told this story this past year. If you heard him tell it, you're about to hear it again:

A grandfather was taking his grandson for a walk in the park. "Look there on the tree," said the grandfather, "in the cocoon, see it? A caterpillar is slowly becoming a butterfly. When he's ready, he will move about inside and with his new wings he'll rub a hole in the cocoon and squeeze out, and fly."

The boy was entranced and curious. He went back the next day to listen to the cocoon, to hear what he could hear. He wanted to see what that almost-butterfly looked like, so he decided to help the butterfly, and get a look at him, too.

With a little knife he cut a small opening in the cocoon. And there he saw the larva moving a bit. He came back the next day too, but it was clear by then that the butterfly would never emerge. The larva inside was dead.

The boy cried. He ran to his grandfather, told him what he had done. "Grandpa, could I have cut the butterfly with my knife when I made the opening?"

"No, " said his grandfather, "but that killed him anyway. You see, the butterfly has to work hard so that it strengthens its wings. When it has worked hard enough to make its own opening, its wings are strong enough to fly away. You didn't help it. You just kept it from being strong. But you didn't know."

I'm not sure either—and neither are you—when life will just makes something all right, and when we have to intervene to try to make it right.

But I know that life's inherent wisdom is often wiser than mine.

Does it hurt not to be in control? Welcome to the club.

Scharansky, Hawkeye, and Abraham weren't in control either. One went deep inside, one did what he could and laughed about the rest, and one just gave himself and his son to God and said, "I trust that it'll be okay."

Join *that* club.

Shulayim: Barbara Irlen

Mark Shapiro's sermons touched people. I was lucky enough to hear many of those sermons over 15 years, and I know that, almost all the time, almost all the people sitting in the congregation felt that the rabbi was speaking directly to them. While also connecting with Jewish sources and Jewish ideas, Mark was able to speak directly to people's inner thoughts, fears, hopes, and struggles by being willing to share his own.

Pirke Avot tells us to "raise up many disciples." Rabbi Shapiro's disciples are legion and stretch across the country. I am blessed that the wonders of social media have brought me into close contact with three of them: one an ordained Reform rabbi, one a lay rabbi with a regular position in a congregation, and one a gifted artist who is also often asked to give the *d'rash* at her congregation and who has begun to write these down for publication. They are all different and each very, very special. But they share with each other what they learned from their rabbi: to speak from the heart as well as from the tradition, to be willing to give a little of themselves away so that others will know that their hopes and fears are okay, too.

I told the ordained rabbi that her sermon I read was a "Mark Shapiro sermon." She replied that she could receive no greater compliment. For him, there can be no greater legacy.

Barbara Irlen served as Religious School teacher, principal and as educator at BJBE from 1971–1985.

What Do
I Owe You?

Yom Kippur Kol Nidre 5747/1986

What compels us to go to BJBE every year for Yom Kippur?
And what exactly do we expect to get from the experience?
In this sermon, MSS imagined the Day of Atonement as a
balance sheet, with a list of benefits received as well as a
corresponding list of obligations—to ourselves, to God, to our
community and to others in need.

LET'S IMAGINE YOU HAD NEVER HEARD of *Yom Kippur.* Can you imagine how you would react if your Temple tried to introduce something new to you that resembled *Yom Kippur*? There you are, opening the Temple bulletin, and the front page declares:

WE'RE STARTING A BRAND NEW *YONTIFF,* AND WE URGE YOU TO COME CELEBRATE AT TEMPLE. THERE'S NOTHING TO EAT, THE SERVICES WILL BE LONGER THAN USUAL, THEY'LL GO ON FOR HOURS. THE MUSIC WILL BE NICE, BUT KIND OF SOLEMN. IF YOU STAY UNTIL THE END, YOU'LL BE EXHAUSTED, AND THE PRAYERS WILL REMIND YOU OF EVERY ROTTEN THING YOU DID THIS PAST YEAR. PLEASE COME AND ENJOY!

Do you think we'd have trouble with people saving seats?

Yet *Yom Kippur* is rather like that, and you come, lots of you come to EVERYTHING on *Yom Kippur*. Something pulls you. The reading from *S'lichot* this year said, "Something is very gently, invisibly, silently pulling at me. I feel the tug of it."

SOMETHING pulls you here in great numbers on *Yom Kippur*.

Yet if you ask people their favorite holiday, *Yom Kippur* would be almost a non-starter. If you would ask the negative, "Which holiday do you like least?" *Yom Kippur* might do very well in that poll.

Not just because it's long and taxing. But, it seems to me, because it lays on the guilt. If the rabbis don't lay the guilt trip on you, the prayer book does a fine job by itself. And if it makes you feel defensive after a while, you're not alone. Lots of Jews are ready to say, "Hey, my parents and my kids do a fine job of making me feel guilty, I don't need more. *Yom Kippur* is overkill. It makes me tune out the prayers!"

Yes, *Yom Kippur* comes on strong. It makes us uncomfortable. If *Yom Kippur* were a person, it would be the one who says, "Why didn't you...?" and "You SHOULD have..." And we don't like to be SHOULD upon.

So let's re-imagine this *Yom Kippur* business. Forget the guilt part and just imagine that on *Yom Kippur* we receive the bill. Think of it as just you and God settling up.

God says: Shapiro, you again? Well, you showed up on time.

Shapiro says: Thank God, er, thank You. What do I owe you?

God: Your file hasn't come up on my screen yet, busy time of year, you know. Well, did you have a decent year? Did things go okay?

Shapiro: Some good, some not so good, but I'm still among the living.

God: So I see. Okay, I've got your bottom line now. Here it is, with services rendered and minimum charges very clear. Take your copy.

That re-imagining comes to my mind because we do owe for what we've received. No free lunch. And receiving an honest bill doesn't make us feel guilty. When you get an honest bill, you may not be happy about it, but you say, "Oh yeah. I knew this one was coming, okay, better get it paid." And you pay it—at least the minimum.

So change the image—think of you and me coming before God on *Yom Kippur* and saying, "Here we are. You let us show up again. What do we owe you?"

What will be listed as services rendered?

Granted, it will be a little different for each one. But you and I will have both a human tax and a Jewish tax that we owe.

What will the bill say for all of us here? Maybe this: SERVICE RENDERED: YOU HAVE BEEN ABLE TO BECOME—or more likely—YOU HAVE BEEN BORN INTO THE WORLD—A JEW.

Okay, a few Jews might consider that a liability, not a service. But I know you don't feel that way. You don't want out—your being here right now shows that.

And you know some of the benefits. Being Jewish just makes you somebody rather unique in the eyes of most others. Yes, sometimes we don't deserve credit when they say: "You people really have close family ties. You people practice religion in your homes, too. You're warm and open. You know moderation at all times. Your kids don't get into trouble." We don't deserve all that credit, especially when you read all the Jewish names coming out in New York and Chicago political scandals. But being Jewish does make you seem like a "somebody."

It gives you cousins everywhere. Is there another people under the sun which gets such *naches* from being halfway around the world and finding a *landsman*, a Jew, in a store, on the street, in a taxi, or one who will raise his eyebrow at you and say, *"Bist du a yid?"* and make old connections light up?

You can find Jews in County Cork; in Kishnev-Ukraine-U.S.S.R.; in Baghdad; and in Dumas, Arkansas. Moment magazine told the story of a couple traveling in Katmandu, Nepal, who were unexpectedly caught there for *Pesach*. In two days' time, they found 23 Jews, one *haggadah* and one bottle of real *Pesach* wine, and did *Seder* in the shadow of the Himalayas.

Yes, it gives you cousins and makes you somebody.

But it has this extra dimension too—SERVICE RENDERED: YOU HAVE BECOME, OR BEEN BORN A JEW AT A PRIME TIME IN HISTORY: WHEN ISRAEL IS NOT JUST A NAME BUT A REAL PLACE.

When Hanna and I take groups to Israel, entering Jerusalem on foot is a highlight. On one trip a lady seemed overcome with emotion as she gazed across the *Kidron* valley at the domes on the ancient Temple Mount. I stood next to her and said (with profundity), "It's something, isn't it?"

"Yes," she said, "but the tears are because I'm standing here for my grandfather as well as for me. He's holding my hand, and he's crying with me."

And when you went there or when you go, you will be experiencing it for others too—for ancestors you may not even know of.

So what do we owe for that service rendered? For the unbelievable luck of being or becoming a Jew in these days?

I think the bill will say: "MINIMUM CHARGE: PULLING YOUR WEIGHT AS A JEW!"

And you and I know what that means: no guilt trips but real trips. It means simply that you have to get to Israel if you haven't been. You have to make sure your children or grandchildren get there; you have to go back if you've gone already.

PULLING YOUR WEIGHT AS A JEW. That's the minimum charge. That's what we owe and the statement is specific. It says that if you're not giving some money to JUF or to Israel in some way, you're embarrassingly in arrears. It says that if you're a Reform Jew and proud of it and know that Israel needs our pluralistic vision that sees all types of Jews as worthy, then your minimum obligation also includes joining ARZA, the Association of Reform Zionists. The Temple agreed it was so important that they risked confusion and made it an add-on to the Temple billing. I hope you said yes! PULLING YOUR WEIGHT AS A JEW—it's got to mean giving *Tz'dakah* for the *landsleit*, for the poor Jews here and there, having a *pushke* and using it, letting *Tz'dakah* be a line item in your own budget.

The services have been, and are still being, rendered. You don't have to feel guilty. Just pay what you owe. Pull your own weight.

There's one more item that's going to be on everyone's bill— one you can especially appreciate on *Yom Kippur.*

SERVICES RENDERED: You have enough to eat. When you fast, it's by choice, not by necessity.

Millions of people are fasting this *Yom Kippur.* Only one out of five is Jewish. The others fast most of the day because they have to. Our fast will end tomorrow night with a wonderful meal. But neither their fast nor their hunger has an end in sight.

We know it. Hunger walks the land. Hunger walks the globe! A mother in Tennessee said: "When school started I was so happy because it meant that my boys were going to eat more than I was." A three-year-old in Alabama has only cereal with water for days, until the cereal runs out and then there is just water. A father in Texas breaks into sobs as he says that sometimes he can't feed his wife and three kids.

The last blast of the *Shofar* isn't going to bring a break-fast for them.

SERVICE RENDERED: WE HAVE ENOUGH, MORE THAN ENOUGH, ENOUGH FOR GUESTS, TOO.

MINIMUM CHARGE: Pulling your weight as a Jewish human being by doing something to feed those hungry.

You and I cannot control the thousands of children who die each week because of hunger, no more than M*A*S*H's Hawkeye Pierce could stop the choppers from coming with wounded. But like Hawkeye, you can do the best you can, and I want to tell you about a specific old-new way to do it. It's based on the old Jewish tradition that says you must invite the poor to your wedding feast, and that if you don't, you're a social outcast.

How this new tradition started: A Jewish magazine editor and a well-known rabbi were talking about hunger and what Jews could do. As they stood talking in the Temple parking lot, a caterer's van pulled up to the Temple door to drop off items for the *Bat Mitzvah* luncheon the next day.

They looked at one another and said, "Eureka!" For through channels like that caterer pass millions of Jewish dollars every year. What if just a percentage of that could go to feed the poor, Jew and non-Jew?

Leonard Fein, the editor, wrote in his magazine: "Let us launch a Jewish campaign against hunger. Let us set aside a portion of our joy to feed the hungry. Specifically—when we celebrate the joys of our lives with food, let us all add a 3% surcharge to our *simchah*, and contribute to a new Jewish pooled fund we will call *Mazon*, meaning food or sustenance."

Harold Schulweis, the rabbi, knew it was right. "It's personalized giving," he said. "When my daughter gets married, I know I've gotten something out of the world and I have to give something back."

And what a great thing for a kid to know that he or she is not the only one doing a *Mitzvah* project for *Bar/Bat Mitzvah*.

Let's talk dollars. What does an extra 3% mean? To a celebration that costs $3,000, add $90. To an $8,000 party add $240. To a $20,000 splash, add $600.

That won't control hunger or wipe it out, but it can make a dent. Listen to these figures: One conservative estimate is that the American Jewish community spends (gulp) $400 million every year on catered affairs. Three percent of that is $12 million. If only one-third of the Jews gave 3% to *Mazon* that would be $4 million. THAT'S NOT PEANUTS. It's almost equal to the total budget of OXFAM in America, one of the most effective agencies in combating hunger.

The trouble with most of our resolutions is that they're too vague. But *Mazon*, a Jewish response to hunger, is specific and organized. They even have cards for you to put on a luncheon or dinner table, saying, "A PORTION OF THE COST OF YOUR GUEST'S MEAL HAS BEEN GIVEN TO *Mazon*" to feed the poor. That card on the table makes all that food kosher in the best sense of what kosher means—fit and proper. That card guarantees you're serving Jewish soul food, chicken with a message.

I think *Mazon* could bring all of us satisfaction out of proportion to 3% of anything. And that's why I'm hoping that the Temple Social Action committee will continue to study *Mazon* and endorse it, and I'm hoping that the Board will discuss it and go on record as urging it for all our congregants. Nobody can make anybody else do it—there's no control, especially in liberal congregations. But just on its own merits, won't you consider this way of *kashering* a celebration? And if hearing that we spend $400 million just to feed one another fine food makes you feel a bit guilty, being part of *Mazon* can make you feel fine again.

SERVICE RENDERED: YOU FAST BY CHOICE AND BREAK FAST WHEN YOU CHOOSE!

MINIMUM CHARGE: FEEDING THE HUNGRY: PAYMENT BY *MAZON* ACCEPTED.

A lady in Wisconsin shows how the idea can broaden. She said, "I had a party. It was just social, at my home. I contributed 3% of the cost to *Mazon*. It felt comfortable. I don't know if I'll do it for every party, but…" So you see, *Mazon* can even be for those of you who thought this didn't mean you because you haven't got a *simchah* coming up.

I read a true story about a lady living an active life, who had a brain tumor diagnosed, surgery within a week, and came out able to see only the faintest bit of light. She went home, tried not to admit the loss, then realized that it wasn't helping, that she had to go to a rehabilitation center.

She did. She let others help her, and that community of the blind did it—they gave her a birthday party, they helped her see with the inner eye.

After she had turned the corner she became a helper of new patients instead of the recipient of help. A doctor began to notice how thoughtful she was being to everyone around her, and he said, "You've become the new angel of mercy around here, haven't you?"

She responded, "I just know how much I owe to the others here, it's always on my mind. But you've seen people like me before. Will I always feel this caring?"

"No" he said. "But you never completely forget—it comes back. And when it doesn't, you appreciate being reminded."

I don't know if you appreciate being reminded of what you may owe God and the world for services rendered, as a Jew and as a human being.

But they have been rendered. You're part of the Jewish people at possibly the most challenging time in Jewish history; you live in that part of the world which eats well and fasts by choice, not necessity.

So we owe it to them, and we owe it the final collector... The One with whom we want to have the best credit rating. *Farshtey?*

Necessary Losses

Yom Kippur Yizkor 5747/1986

---

*MSS was personally moved by Judith Viorst's book,
"Necessary Losses," and quoted from it liberally in this
sermon delivered at the Yom Kippur Yizkor service. Do we
cover up our pain with cheery optimism, as perhaps President
Ronald Reagan did when facing colon cancer, or fully
recognize our fears and losses, and share them with others so
that they might offer support and comfort?*

YIZKOR IS NO TIME FOR POLITICS. And I'm not going
to talk politics. But I'm going to share a thought about
President Reagan—I'm thinking of his illness and colon
surgery.

This past year the President found out that he had cancer,
went through surgery, had part of his intestine removed, came
out, recuperated, and has had some small recurrences since.

And through it all, the President and his administration
acted as if nothing consequential had happened. Suffering
and vulnerability and weakness were taken out of the official
vocabulary.

Nothing that you or I heard from the President gave any
impression of anything but cheery optimism. It seemed like an
aftermath of the attempt on Reagan's life a few years ago, when
he joked on the way into surgery and afterwards as well.

Now of course we respect the personal bravery he showed and admire the physical ability to bounce back. But—and I quote Andrew Purves: "Here surely was a man confronted with vulnerability and suffering, yet 'officially,' he seems not to have experienced such normal facts of human life. He has managed to act as if suffering has not touched him deeply. His mortality has been suppressed." And I would add—he could have taught us all a better lesson if he had not shown us only his optimistic, jaunty side, but if he had publicly recognized the fears that must have been with him, thus permitting us to be concerned for him, and to find mortality as much a reality in the White House as in our house.

For when we experience a loss, even one by surgery, we are pained. It helps us, and lets others know they can share the feeling with us. It is unnatural not to be affected by suffering, not to mourn losses.

And the losses for which we mourn are not only the deaths of loved ones, though such losses are uppermost in our minds right now. The truth is that you and I are acquainted with loss from the beginning of our lives. Losses occur at every stage in our lives, in different forms from the time we leave that pre-natal bathtub of our mother, to when we first realize that we will not always have our mother's full attention. Throughout life, starting very young, we experience loss and must mourn.

Judith Viorst captures all of this in her book *Necessary Losses*. I'm going to be quoting from that book for a few moments.

Viorst writes: "We confront these lifelong losses when we become aware of these inescapable facts:

> ... that our mother is going to leave us and we will leave her.
> ... that our mother's love can never be ours alone.
> ... that what hurts us cannot always be kissed and made better.
> ... that we are essentially on our own.
> ... that we will have to accept—in others and ourselves— the mingling of love with hate, of the good with the bad.

… that no matter how wise and beautiful and charming
a girl may be, she still cannot grow up to marry her dad
(and write that with gender change for boys).

… that there are flaws in every human connection,
including marriage and parenthood.

… that we will not only have to let our children go, but
also our dreams for our children.

… that we are utterly powerless to offer ourselves, or our
loved ones, protection—from danger of pain, from the
inroads of time, from the coming of age, from the
coming of death."

These are necessary losses. Necessary because they just must
happen; necessary if we are to keep growing.

Can you think back to a very early childhood loss? If you
can't, just watch a ten-month old, or a three-year old, desperately
wanting his mother, and you can feel all over again how it once
felt. It is complete panic—the mother's absence which, while one
hour on your watch, is eternity to the child's internal clock. Viorst
says, with great insight, that in such cases, "Absence makes the
heart grow not fonder, but frantic."

And what about having to share a mother's love? Viorst says,
"Inside our heads we kill our brothers and sisters for having
more—or even some—of our parent's love. And when the new
baby comes home from the hospital, the older child covers up the
smash-the-baby impulse in many ways like denial, saying—'She's
OK. But who will be *her* mother?'"

A necessary loss—like the loss of the dream that marriage will
be like Snow White and Prince Charming, happily ever after. We
mourn for that loss often. Viorst says, "The bad news is that no
two adults can do each other more damage than husband and
wife. The good news is that love can survive the hate." I think
she's right both times.

Loss of youth—we mourn for that. Viorst has an earlier poem
about lost youth, in which she says:

"What am I doing with a mid-life crisis?
This morning I was seventeen.
I have barely begun the beguine and it's Goodnight Ladies
Already.

While I've been wondering who to be
When I grow up someday
My acne has vanished away and it's sagging kneecaps
Already.

Why do I seem to remember Pearl Harbor?
Surely I must be too young.
When did the boys I once clung to start losing their hair?
Why can't I take barefoot walks in the park
Without giving my kidneys a chill?
There's poetry left in me still and it doesn't seem fair.

While I was thinking I was just a girl
My future turned into my past.
The time for wild kisses goes fast and it's time for Sanka.
Already?"

We begin to experience loss from the beginning of our lives—
and we mourn for the things we lose, but somehow we get beyond
the mourning. And losses are not just the death of loved ones. An
abortion is a loss, no matter how much it may have been the right
decision. The child that might have been needs to be mourned.

Divorce is a great loss for which we must mourn. Too many
of us know that already. And so is your child's going off to
college, and so is the marriage of a child, and so is a friend moving
away—all losses for which we have to mourn.

At the end of her book Viorst says, "My youngest son is
waiting to hear from the college of his choice. He'll be leaving
soon. My mother, my sister, too many friends, are dead. I'm
taking calcium to save my middle-aged bones from osteoporosis.
I'm living on Lean Cuisine in a last-ditch effort to defeat my
middle-aged spread. And although my husband and I have

maintained our imperfect connection for twenty-five rich years, full years, the bombs of divorce and widowhood are falling all around us. We live with loss."

And she concludes, "We cannot love deeply without becoming vulnerable to loss, and we cannot become separate, whole, responsible people, connected people, without some losing and leaving and letting go."

You all face those ark doors. They tell the same story about loss, and how we live through it.

There is a wealth of images on those doors, but included prominently are lions, birds, mother and babies, nests, eggs. There are three types of lions, the proud male with the crown, pictured twice, his mate, the lioness, the one suckling her young tenderly, and then that same mate out stalking prey, giving a very fierce stare and roar.

There are three nests. In one there are eggs. In another there are baby birds, to which the mother is bringing food. A third nest is empty, and the roaring lioness stands over it, one paw resting on the empty nest itself.

What really happened? How are we to understand these images? Did the baby birds leave the nest before the lioness found them? Is she roaring in frustration, having lost them, or has she already fed them to her young?

In either case—whether the baby birds have been killed or they have flown away—they will not return. The mother bird has lost them.

And yet, above that last empty nest at which the lioness stands, upper left, the mother bird lifts her wings and her beak and her voice towards heaven and sends forth a note. As I look at her, I almost hear that note, with something of the agony and ecstasy of the *Shofar* in it—a note which sounds bereavement and loss, acceptance and hope.

Her loss was inescapable. Necessary. Yet she is still able to sing again.

Her story is our story, too.

We have been acquainted with loss and mourning since we first opened our lives to the light in a delivery room. We have mourned and panicked and we have come through the losses. We are still coming through them. At *Yizkor*, it is good to know how experienced we are in surviving them.

Sacred Field
of Dreams

Rosh Hashanah Morning, 5750/1989

---

*MSS often managed to work his favorite sport—baseball—
and his favorite team—the Chicago White Sox—into his
High Holiday sermons, usually alongside themes of pain,
frustration, and unmet expectations. In this sermon, he turns
to baseball as he discusses "awesome" moments, specifically
to "Field of Dreams," a magical movie about baseball. He
tells us how watching that movie became a sacred experience
for him. While he noted that he often sees people cry at the
end of movies, in this movie, he realized that—for the first
time—it was men doing most of the crying.*

A T THE END OF THIS SERMON I'll be talking about the
movie *Field of Dreams*. Even if you haven't seen it you
probably know that it's about baseball.

I know that some of you think I play a little game at the High
Holy Days every year, trying to get a baseball comment into a
sermon, sort of the way Alfred Hitchcock tried to get himself into
all his movies for a cameo. I promise you that I won't be talking
about *Field of Dreams* just for the baseball. As you know, if
there were any year for an ex-South Sider to leave baseball out of
things, this would be the year.

What I really want to talk about is Awe. They call the High
Holy Days the "Days of Awe." Abraham Joshua Heschel wrote
about the feeling of Awe, and to get myself in the mood for the

Holy Days I always go back and read some Heschel.

He says that we experience Awe when "we are stunned to find more meaning in reality than the mind can take in," like parents and grandparents being stunned to find that newborn child evoking emotions in them beyond their understanding.

That is awesome. Usage has made the word "awesome" less than awesome these days, but real AWE stuns us with how filled with meaning the usual can be.

Heschel says that if you have experienced Awe you are potentially a religious person. Yes, you, even if you're not much of a Temple-goer, even if the peak of your Jewishness has so far been searching for a piece of *gefilte* fish like your *bubbe's*. Yes, you are. In the Bible a religious person isn't called a ma'amin, a believer, but rather "*y'rei Adonai:* one who stands in awe of God." And if you have experienced AWE you are potentially a more religious person than you think.

Do you feel Awe on these Days of Awe? That you're involved in something bigger than just sitting here and turning pages? Maybe the Days of Awe leave you cold. I can understand how that might happen. You worry about seating, and parking and logistics and babysitters and cooking. I empathize. I worry if all the participants will show up, will the mics function well, will I step on the choir's lines or they on mine?

No, I think it is more likely that you will feel Awe at a different time.

And Heschel, who knew about Awe, knew that too. He said, "Awe enables us to sense in small things the beginning of infinite significance; to sense the ultimate in the common and simple—to feel, in the rush of the passing, the stillness of the Eternal."

So I want to tell you when I have seen you feel Awe, at some slightly smaller events than the High Holy Days: maybe at the wedding of a friend or a friend's child; or when coincidentally you witness someone becoming a Jew by Choice in Temple… and even in the movies.

At a wedding. You know, rabbis have the best sight lines at weddings. Some of my colleagues like to appear from the side at the last minute, but I like watching everyone come down the aisle, with their expressions: the bridesmaid biting her lip in hope that she won't trip on the long gown as she goes up the stairs, the parents who can't believe it's their little girl dressed as a bride, the groom trying to look cool and in control, but who never does.

And from my spot up there I see everybody else sitting out there. And I see when the handkerchiefs come out, when people dab at their eyes—men, too, giving a furtive eye-wipe. Not just your sentimental aunt who even cries when they sing *God Bless America*, but people who didn't think they could be touched and are surprised to find themselves in Awe at the infinite significance of that not-so-unusual moment.

If you ask them why they're crying, they won't talk about Awe. They'll say, "Oh, the bride is so beautiful," or even more honestly, "It reminds me that time is passing so fast."

I think it's even bigger than that. I think people are touched, even stunned, by the sacred nature of the moment. For as you look at a couple under a *chuppah*, time can stop and open up to past and future. And for a moment you see beneath the *chuppah* the living and the dead, those who are there and those who would have wanted to be. You can also see the unborn children one day to spring from this bride and groom, God willing, whom this bride and groom will one day escort to the *chuppah*, too.

It gives you a shiver. You hear ordinary flesh-and-blood people vowing that they will make it work in the face of all the difficulties that we know only too well. You sense a moment bigger than both of them, when finite creatures reach the infinite, and try to make the words "I do" into a vow that will carry them till death. And your eyes mist as you realize that you are praying God will touch them and give them the strength—that God will give you and those you love best—to make your love grow and endure and survive.

That is feeling Awe. That is, I think, a religious experience. And it does happen to you, sometimes without the tear.

Maybe this explains why I have such *mishagass*, why I seem to be so idiosyncratic, about rules for photographers and video camera operators at weddings. I am on their black lists, I know, because I've been unwilling to have weddings turn into photo opportunities or look like they're being staged for cable news. It's true that I have become a bit less restrictive since I realized how much people say they enjoy that wedding video. Yet Awe is a fragile possibility, and if people at the wedding feel it is a performance, or find themselves concentrating on a cameraman, then the possibility of Awe evaporates, like a dream forgotten. Awe does not live at media events.

So, if you have ever sensed something bigger than the details at a wedding, then you know Awe, and you have the potential to be a religious person.

And sometimes it happens here on a Friday evening. I hope it happens often here on Friday evenings, but it seems especially likely to happen when we are welcoming new Jews. Not baby naming. Those are new Jews, too, and there's some awe around them also, but I'm talking about when we have ceremonies of *giyur*, conversion, during Friday night services. If you haven't shared one, you've missed something.

I never used to do it this way. I just assumed the person becoming Jewish would be very self-conscious standing in front of the whole congregation, and that it should be a private ceremony instead, the only people attending being those invited by the new Jew.

But then the Reform movement began to rethink the process of becoming Jewish and how the ceremony should feel to those going through it. And we realized that a public ceremony has a great impact upon the person coming into Judaism. It's good to feel like you're entering the people of Israel if you become Jewish in the presence of the people of Israel, at least those of them here that evening. So we offer people a public or private ceremony, but urge the public one, and more and more people opt to go public.

But I didn't realize that people watching that ceremony could be touched by its power and feel Awe until I was talking to an old friend. He had witnessed a *giyur* here and he said, "All of a sudden I had tears in my eyes," and he's not a crier. And often, out of the corner of my eye, I see glistening eyes here, too.

I know that I feel some Awe during those ceremonies, especially when the new Jew takes the Czech *Torah* scroll, saved from the Holocaust, and holds it while receiving a Hebrew name. I think of all of those Kolin, Czechoslovakian Jews whose family lines came to an end in the *Shoah*, and of this new Jew being the link between those families and the future, somehow their child. And I am amazed at how moved I am when I say to them, "It is good to find out that when all of us stood at Sinai, you were there with us."

More important, I know that many of you have been moved, often to tears. You say so. Sometimes a person can't put his finger on why it was awesome. They say, "Well, I've never seen that before," or "She really had to work hard for that."

I think it's bigger than that. I think people are awed, stunned by the ultimate significance they find in seeing a non-Jew choose to become a Jew. It reminds them of how proud they are of their heritage. It says to them "in spades," *Am Yisrael Chai*, the People of Israel will live. Those people watching them are reminded that they too stood at Sinai and at that moment they can almost remember what it was like.

It is a bigger moment than we can express. And some of you feel, with me, Awe at such times. Which means you have the potential, Heschel said, to be a religious person.

All right, what's it all got to do with *Field of Dreams*?

The characters in the movie experienced Awe as a lost world of ballplayers came through the Iowa corn to play on that ball field. But to me, even more awesome was what happened in the audience at the end of the movie. Men were crying. Lots of us.

If you don't know the story, here's a capsule. Ray Kinsella and his wife try to keep their '60s dreams alive by buying and working a farm in Iowa. Their life is interrupted when Ray hears a voice in the field saying: "IF YOU BUILD IT, HE WILL COME." And he has a vision of what he must build: He is to plow under acres of his corn to build a baseball field, with lights. As minister and writer James Wall said, "it will look as senseless to his neighbors as Noah must have looked when he listened to God and started to build the Ark."

"IF YOU BUILD IT HE WILL COME." But who will come? Ray thinks it may be Shoeless Joe Jackson, his late father's favorite baseball player, coming back to live again and play on that field. And Jackson does come with more of the Black Sox with him.

But *Field of Dreams* goes further. It turns out that the Field exists so that others will come and complete what was incomplete in their lives. So an author comes, who always wanted to play ball, and an old doctor comes back as a young man to get his one at-bat in the majors. They leave. Shoeless Joe leaves too. And as Ray stands there alone, the one for whom the field was built does come. It is Ray's father, John, as the young minor league catcher that he once was. John had already seemed to be a tired and sour old man to his son Ray-the-teenager, and they had fought and never really became friends again. But they meet in that Field of Dreams, and do what fathers and sons do to bond, at least in America: They throw a ball back and forth.

Ray, having trusted in a voice, found something that went beyond the rational, and stunningly had time stand still so he could be reconciled with his father.

That happened on the screen at the end of the movie. But what was happening in the audience was also important. A movie critic said it this way: "Usually at the end of emotional films the women have tears in their eyes and need to sit a few moments to collect themselves, while their husbands are on their feet, ready to go. At *Field of Dreams* the men remained in their seats, surprised to be crying, needing that few moments of credit-rolling to get it under control again."

And what was the Awe that brought tears? I think we all know; maybe men know best. We cried, imagining a game of catch with our fathers, which might mean saying to him all the things you never did say or never have said, bonding with him in some ultimate way. We sensed that moment of connection between parent and child to be a moment of Awe, a holy moment.

And it is. In Iowa and in Northbrook.

Let me personalize it. I don't know if the males in your home expressed affection physically for one another as you were growing up, but it didn't happen in mine once I was more than very little. Kissing or hugging a son was not what my father did. I guess it was an inability he learned from his father, who didn't kiss his son. So we would stand at half arm's length, and sort of smack each other on the back. Until one year, thanks to some wise counsel, I kissed him. Bells did not ring, *shofars* did not blow, but inside me they did and I later found out inside him, too. It was a small but stunning moment, which had ultimate significance.

Bonding is Awesome.

And by the way, rabbis know about bonds that come apart in families. We know how much estrangement there is in families because we see people at their family events. I know there is no cold shoulder frostier than a brother can give a sister, no chasm more bleak than the one that keeps parent and child from making peace with one another. So maybe this is the year to let *Field of Dreams* happen in your life, to express the love beneath the garbage we've piled on it, to let a child know that he is loved unconditionally, with no regard for performance.

And that will be a moment of awe too, worthy of the Days of Awe.

Maybe some of you are surprised that I talked about the Awesome and never mentioned nature. Some of you are hooked on natural views.

Well, let me tell you. A few of us went on a six-day rafting trip through the Grand Canyon this past summer, sixteen of us, nobody a kid, roller-coastering over rapids, hiking into side canyons, camping on sandbars.

And the views from that great rift were spectacular. The night view of stars so clear was almost as powerful as the daytime sight of all the wonders of rock against sky.

And I did feel some Awe on that trip, but honestly, nature wasn't the main source. The awesome shared moment came thanks to a lady on the trip. She hadn't liked roller coasters, water, or heights. So what was she doing there? Probably looking to challenge herself a little. She got a new courage somewhere, or found old guts, and she rode rapids on the front of the raft, climbed gullies, explored waterfalls, and toward the end of the trip, on a high, she said, "I think I've outlived my fears."

Shofars should have blown. I think they did, inside her. I think I heard their echo.

Awe is more often what happens with people than even in the greatest postcard views of nature. At least to me.

And you can feel it, too. Which means that this year you have the pre-prerequisite for being more of a religious person than you were before. For you can sense the stillness of the Eternal in the rush of the passing.

No, you and I are not *Chasidic* folks. Far from it. For we live with beepers and laser printers and cash station numbers and none of that seems very sacred.

But the movie was right. Sacred moments occur away from heaven.

Shoeless Joe, in awe of what he had found, asked Ray if the field was in heaven, and Ray said "Nope, it's just Iowa." Iowa is just as good for feeling the Awesome, maybe better.

And so is the wedding you didn't think would move you, or the darkened movie theater or a moment in a brick circle building just north of a Union 76 Station.

You get a shiver. You cry. You are touched. I believe you are touched by God. And you know that you know the deepest secrets behind all of the prayers.

Yes, I think you do.

Shulayim: Ira J. Wise, DJRE

I remember getting notes from Rabbi Shapiro that came off that old manual typewriter he kept on the shelf behind his desk, under the Steinsaltz Talmud. I still have the one he sent when I graduated HUC. So it was a tectonic shift when he posted for the first time to the "I am a Jewish Leader and Mark S. Shapiro was my Rabbi" Facebook group.

He was commenting and praising those of us who have been connected with BJBE during his watch and have pursued careers as Jewish professionals. There are 32 of us—that we know of—including two children of ours who are beginning their own paths.

I think of Mark as our Jewish AAA. He introduced us to a variety of choices and role models to help us plan our journeys, gave us some maps, told us about great destinations and then sent us on our ways to find our own paths.

Reading through these sermons, I was struck by his theme of Awe in "Sacred Field of Dreams." What grabbed my attention was his reference to Abraham Joshua Heschel, telling us that he reads Heschel to get himself in the mood for the Holy Days.

I first met Heschel's ideas in confirmation class in 1977, but I returned to Heschel not too long ago when I began studying via Skype with another Heschel fan, Rabbi Mark Borovitz.

With this other "Rabbi Mark" we're studying Heschel's "Insecurity of Freedom." And every week, I feel MSS over my shoulder reminding me of something I had learned long before: "Radical Amazement." When we live in Radical Amazement, we are aware of and appreciate our connection to ourselves and to others.

Wow. I am back at BJBE in Room 10 with Steve and David and Larry, Leslie, Maureen, and Heidi, and a bunch of others. Then, I am in the darkened sanctuary with our Confirmation class as we write ourselves letters and try to decide if we want to receive a blessing from the rabbi or just talk baseball.

Is this heaven? Nope, it's 901 Milwaukee Avenue.

I have been radically amazed for much of my

life. And Rabbi Shapiro helped us become that way and begin to understand how that changed us.

Ira Wise is Temple Educator at Congregation B'nai Israel in Bridgeport, Connecticut. He received his Master's in Jewish Education from HUC-JIR in 1991, and was confirmed at BJBE in 1977.

What Time is it?

Erev Rosh Hashanah 5751/1990

Something significant was happening in the early 1990s—just as, generations earlier, many of our ancestors had come to this country in need of a home, Soviet Jews by the thousands were finally allowed to leave Russia. They were coming into our communities in need of jobs, money and community. MSS, who had visited Soviet refuseniks some years earlier in the USSR, spoke about the importance of this time in our history, and the opportunity to give back by helping this group of new Jewish immigrants.

OCCASIONALLY HANNA AND I FIND ourselves awake in the middle of the night. Because the clock on her side of the bed is much easier to read than the one on my side, I will say to her, "What time is it?" And she will say, "What time do you think it is?" And I will guess.

You know what? I'm quite good at it. And occasionally when I'm the only one awake I'll do the game by myself. I'll guess what time it is and then grab the clock to see, and when I come within a half-hour, I'm delighted.

A lot of the time I know what time it is without looking.

And I think you may, too.

Different times feel different. Our body can let us know that it's a sacred time. That Hebrew word *Kadosh*, usually translated "holy" or "sacred" really means "different." So the essence of a time being sacred is that it feels significantly different from an ordinary time.

You may say that you're not a person who feels that certain times are sacred, but I think you're wrong. In that basic sense in which sacred means different and highly charged, we all know sacred times, feel them in our bones.

What about birthdays? Aren't you always aware of how old you are and how soon the next digit will click in? I am. The number 55, to tell the truth, is never very far away from my consciousness. Don't you know subconsciously how far away your birthday is? And when it arrives, doesn't it feel like a different, high-charged day? And if you say it doesn't, then test it by how you feel when everybody really does forget it.

Sometimes you feel the significance of a date without any conscious knowledge of its meaning. Quite a few months after my father died I woke up on a Sunday morning feeling terrible, out-of-the-blue depressed, for no reason, which is unusual because those of us who experience depressions know that they usually build up slowly. I couldn't get out of bed and had no idea what it was all about, until I turned on the radio and heard the announcer say, "Happy Father's Day to all you fathers out there." My insides had known what my mind had blotted out about that highly charged day, the first Father's Day without a father.

We do sense how significant some times are.

And that strengthens my conviction that you and I also feel this Jewish New Year, deep inside.

The mark of a Jew is living by Jewish time. No, you can't accomplish it by getting one of those cute watches with Hebrew letters in place of the numerals. Living by Jewish time means feeling the uniqueness, even the sacred nature of time like this beginning of a year.

I know you feel it because you are here. Most of you don't come that often but now you're here.

I also know that you feel that this is the REAL New Year, not the winter one, because those of you who make resolutions about trying to change yourselves in important ways are much more likely to do it at *Rosh Hashanah* or *Yom Kippur* than on January 1st. And more likely to succeed.

I know that you feel these days are different and of high significance, and that translates as "sacred," something with an "ought" about it. That would explain something interesting—that would explain why it's so emotionally important to have your children come on the High Holy Days too, even when they would rather not, and even if you're a parent who usually doesn't say "you have to" about Jewish obligations.

But let your child say, "I just don't feel like going on *Rosh Hashanah* this year, it's so long and doesn't do anything for me," and you are saying, even if it's out of character, "You're going." That script has played out a few times in our house, too.

And I know that it is the time that moves you, not just a feeling that your kids should be in Temple occasionally. Because if your child says, "Dad I've been in Temple a lot lately, I was there for the last three Saturday mornings, for *Bar Mitzvahs*. Isn't that enough for a while?" you still respond "You're going."

And what about the old custom of buying new clothing for the New Year? I've heard all the snide remarks about people coming to services to show off new clothes and maybe years back I also looked down my nose at those who had to have something new for *Yontiff*. No more.

Though *Rosh Hashanah* isn't about new clothes, it is definitely about self-renewal, becoming refreshed, which just means "like new again." That is exactly what this time has always asked of us, to cast off the old, to feel this time replete with new possibilities, for us and our lives. So I don't believe that we buy a new garment to impress people on *Yontiff*, I believe we are responding in the most tangible way we can to this oldest message of a New Year— be renewed, you can change—outside and maybe even inside.

It's supposed to go beyond new threads, granted, but the new clothes tell me that you are already connected.

Jewish time does tick inside us. That's why we keep chasing these High Holy Days on their confusing march around the autumn calendar, always later or earlier than we might have thought, and yet we get here on time. The cicada just knows when it's time to emerge. And so do you.

I had wanted to share two truths with you tonight and that's the first—that in the cycle of each year we do feel the sacred nature of the New Year.

And now let's tell the other truth about what sacred time it is right now. Pull the camera back to see this one. Back far enough to get a look at the ongoing 4,000-year march of our people through history. There have been sacred times on that journey, and I believe one is now.

I am sure that every rabbi is telling people about it on these Holy Days, and I mean the exodus of masses of our people from the Soviet Union to Israel and some to the United States.

Somehow, we did it. That's egotistical, but nobody seems to know for sure just why the Soviets opened the doors for our people, so those of us who have been working for it for years might as well take some of the credit.

Yes, we did it. All the "we's" of Jews around this country and the world who wouldn't let world leaders forget about Soviet Jews, who wouldn't let other Jews forget about Soviet Jews... all those who twinned *Bar* and *Bat Mitzvahs*, who went to rallies and wrote letters and sent wires and went to Russia and listened to those who had gone to Russia, and all of us who put up signs on the front lawn that said "Save Soviet Jews" Let's take credit. We did it.

They are coming out, and the numbers are staggering.

When the doors opened it looked like there might be 10,000 leaving the U.S.S.R. every month, and then it was 15,000 per month and now the reports from Israel and transit points say that the number is already up to 20,000 a month. That will add up to at least 200,000 in 1990, of which 150,000 will go to Israel and 40,000 to the United States.

And there are, right now, 700,000 Soviet Jews in the pipeline, which means that they will have applied for papers or already have their papers and are just waiting for a seat on the plane.

A reasonable estimate is that before you are five years older than today, a million Soviet Jews will have been transplanted to Israel, 40 times more than came out of Egypt with Moses.

It makes me think of the old Cecil B. DeMille *Ten Commandments* movie, and its Exodus scene—that great wide shot of the Jews coming out of Egypt into the desert, wave on wave on wave. But now, not on donkeys and foot, but in the bellies of jumbo jets from Finland and Vienna and one day very soon from Moscow itself direct to Tel Aviv.

Yes, it is proper to call this Operation Exodus.

We and our Israeli cousins have wanted this so much we could taste it. More than half of all the *B'nei Mitzvah* youngsters' original prayers, spoken from this *bimah* for years, have included various pleas that God might help us free Soviet Jews.

The prayer has, amazingly, been answered. Maybe God heard, or Gorbachev heard or the world. No matter. They're leaving there, they're coming out. And they are coming COD and HOD. Cash on delivery and Help Needed on delivery, too.

COD. We knew they would come COD. When we prayed for it we knew it would be enough for them to be let out, we knew God couldn't give each family the twelfth chair of the Mel Brooks movie with the Czarina's jewels hidden inside.

It costs to fly them to freedom, to give them a place to live, to tide them over with food and clothing, to teach them Hebrew there or English here. We don't have to buy them out of slavery but we have to pay their way to freedom.

The Jewish United Fund has mounted Operation Exodus in Chicago. To do our share, this metropolitan Jewish community has to raise $53 million over and above normal JUF pledges. I think each one of us should be a part of that.

Now I know that when Jews raise funds from other Jews, yearly, for all the good causes, the speakers always try to make the need seem especially urgent or challenging. And when there isn't a crisis, Jews can imagine one, so we sometimes call a problem a crisis or a difficulty an emergency. But this year I have no trouble with those words, no trouble saying them myself. Yes, it is a crisis and emergency surely in Israel. It is a wondrous opportunity and I believe it is a sacred time in Jewish history.

They come COD. If you care about payback, I think these Soviet Jews will give it all back, more than pay it back, given a few generations. They'll have a positive impact on Jewish life in Israel and America for years to come. American Jewry needs new flows of migrating Jews, and Israel desperately needs the kinds of minds and culture that these Soviet Jews and their children possess, to say nothing of their sheer numbers. We knew it was COD. The name of the collection agency is Operation Exodus of the J.U.F.

And it is also HOD—Help on Delivery. For those Soviet Jews who come to Chicago, only you and I can give that help on delivery. What kind of help? What kind would you have wanted if you had come from Kishinev in Soviet Moldavia to Chicago and felt like a greenhorn?

Put yourself in your great-grandfather's shoes when he passed through the great hall of Ellis Island the way it was then. "So, little refugee, what kind of help do you want?"

"Ah, you want a job, very soon. You want a chance to learn the language, to speak it and understand people on the street. You'd like some American Jewish friends for yourself and for your kids, people who feel like family, who can guide you through the customs of a new land, like knowing that if someone invited you for brunch you'd know what it was."

Now here's a big difference: Your great-grandfather didn't need any help in understanding his Jewishness. He probably knew all about that, but these new Soviet immigrants haven't even got that. They need to be gently introduced to Jewish culture and holidays and synagogue and Jewish education for their children. Most of them will only shy away from that well-intended, aggressive Orthodox effort to herd them into Orthodox life when they don't even know basics, not even *Chanukah*.

In sum, they need friends like you and me and our families.

They need us to help them get jobs. So if you have a job for someone, or could manufacture a job for a new Soviet Jew in Chicago, you would be offering help on delivery. And you should be calling Jewish Vocational Service or our Temple's Soviet Jewry Committee, or your rabbi.

They need you to be their friend… to help them feel wanted, feel American, feel Jewish, and have the pride in it that you have.

They are coming to Israel and Chicago, COD. HOD. Thank God!

There's a wonderful passage in the *Shabbat* morning service that usually is read by the *Bar/Bat Mitzvah* youngster. It says: "Lord, You are our God, even as you were the God of Abraham and Sarah, the God of our fathers and mothers, the God of all the Ages of Israel."

They are our past as we are their future. Abraham and Sarah depend on us to keep it going, us and our kids and their kids, and these new American Jews knocking at our door.

If all those ancient fathers and mothers, the Abrahams and Sarahs, were beamed into the future to stand here now, could I reassure them that we are a decent future for them to have? Could I just point to us here?

Please God, let us be that future. Because we are the only future they have right now. It's not just Abraham and Sarah who depend on us, but also the Vladmirs and Olgas and Borises... from Minsk and Odessa and Leningrad, now of Tel Aviv, Rogers Park, and Morton Grove, and Glenview. We are also the only guarantors of their Jewish present and future.

In the middle of the night sometimes I just know what the time is, and I think I know what time it is now. It is the time to "be" history again. A new year and a new exodus are underway. Maybe we are here for just such moments. And I think it's time!

Shulayim: Rabbi Leah M. Herz

For me, hearing the simple words "Close Your Books" when uttered by Rabbi Mark S. Shapiro was akin to hearing an illusionist say, "Abracadabra." You just knew that magic was about to take place.

Together with my parents, my brother and sister, ours was a family that was at Temple often and therefore I had the opportunity to hear Rabbi Shapiro preach hundreds of times. As a youngster, I may have gotten the gist of what was being said without perhaps understanding the deeper meaning. But as a teenager and then as an adult, I remember that I couldn't wait until I heard those magic words. Now that I was able to understand the smaller details, the tiny brushstrokes if you will, and the messages took on a much greater meaning. Hearing Rabbi Shapiro's sermons was always the highlight of each service for me and that experience was magnified during the High Holy Days when the gravity of the message was that much more significant.

Rabbi's sermons were often a topic for discussion in my family.

I distinctly remember another famous MSS phrase that elicited anticipation whenever I heard it: "The following reading is not in your books." I loved that! What a wonderful way to get the congregation to look up for a few moments and not to be leafing through the text, attempting to follow along with something that wasn't there! Among the myriad things I have learned from Rabbi Shapiro, this is one that I still practice when I lead services today.

Leah Herz is Director of Spiritual Care and Religious Programming at The Communities of Menorah Manor in St. Petersburg and Clearwater, Florida. She was ordained by HUC-JIR in 2005, and confirmed at BJBE in 1970.

The Real World

Yom Kippur 5751/1990

Which is the REAL year, 1990 or 5751? And as long as we're
discussing the answer to that question, what are the REAL
values by which we are to live our lives? For some, those most
cherished values might include 'possessions' or 'profit.' But in
this sermon, MSS considers what those real values should be,
not only for Jews inside the synagogue, but for the rest of the
world as well.

IF YOU DRIVE SLOWLY YOU MIGHT BE ABLE to read the new
sign at the church across the street—the sign that announces
"High Holiday Services."

Yes, it's a free country, free for "Jews for Jesus" and everyone
else too. They might even have sung *Kol Nidre* over there last
night as well. But most Jews will know not to be fooled, for we're
the real Jews and they're not. Agree?

And yet—I told a bunch of 3rd graders that the year would
soon be 5751. A few of them asked "What about 1990?" And
I said that was the other year. One kid pressed on: "Which is it
really?"

A good question. Which is the "more real" year? And if I had
to choose, I'd say that 5751 is the real one. And not just because
we're in a synagogue. I mean it just that way. The world of Jewish
values is the only real and true one, as real as the house you live

in. And the world of today's values is often as false as the props in a stage play.

I think our prayer book is more real than *People* magazine.

Does it sound as if you heard this one before? Another "Jewish values" sermon?

You're right. I'm not protesting Supreme Court appointees today or trying to analyze the Persian Gulf. I'm talking about what is really REAL. I believe that the world we talk about in here turns out to be the real one. And this is what I mean.

For starters, let me tell you about the four new rectangular brown columns at the rear of the sanctuary. They are frame panels on which four fabric pieces will be attached when the artist finishes her work.

What a Jewish lifetime opportunity—to choose what each panel would say! We could artistically display our four top Jewish principles. Letterman had his Top Ten, we would try to do it with four.

The possibilities were staggering. My mind was racing, getting silly, too.

What would we put there? Maybe "Hebrew goes from right to left," or what about "First the cream cheese, and then the lox," or "Stay through confirmation." Or maybe number one: "Don't save seats."

Then I got real. I thought about the values of the 1990 world, and thought we'd have to put up these signposts. Fun, Leisure, Expensive Possessions, and Popularity, with Profit trying to jostle out the others.

But what Jewish words would we put up there? It seemed obvious. We had just decided on *Bar/Bat Mitzvah* project goals which youngsters would be expected to fulfill. Three were: *Torah* (study), *Avodah* (worship), and *G'milut Chasadim* (deeds of loving kindness). To these we added a fourth, *Tz'dakah* (giving help to others).

These will be our Top Four. Study, Worship, Loving Deeds, Giving.

I believe that those words and values are not just the "inside the Temple" thing—I think they represent the most real of all worlds.

Larry Kushner said it well. He said, "*Shabbes* is more real than Wednesday, Jerusalem is more real than Chicago. The *Sukkah* is more real than a garage. *Tz'dakah* is more real than income tax, standing close to God is more real than being far from Him." So we have to fill the less real world with the values of the more real world. How can we ever do that?

Let's think about Fun and Leisure, as well as Flow. (I owe much of this analysis to Dennis Prager's essay "Happiness is a Serious Problem.")

When Professor Adin Steinsaltz first visited America he said that he heard a word that couldn't be translated into Hebrew. The word was "fun." He heard it everywhere—"It's fun to go to the ballgame, that's a fun place to eat, she's a fun person. Let's have fun!" You can say "pleasure" or "enjoyment" or "recreation" in Hebrew, but to say "fun," Israelis had to borrow an Arabic word—*kef*.

Of course there's nothing wrong with fun. It's a great way to spend some time, and I wish all of us some fun this coming year. But it has little to do with happiness, and if you think it does, that will get in the way of finding real happiness.

Dennis Prager tries to get at the difference between fun and happiness. He says, "Fun is something that happens during an activity, happiness happens afterward." And you might want to add that what is fun while you're doing it seldom brings happiness afterward.

Some of us think riding a roller coaster is fun. Does it lead to happiness? No—it just leads to a desire to keep going, and having fun, which is why the little kids inside us yell, "Just one more time!" Because when the fun is over things seem a bit empty.

Prager points to all the interminable talk about a sporting event, introducing and dissecting plays, replaying the event, until even the avid fan says, "Enough already!" There is a desperation about losing the momentary fun.

So, what does make for happiness? Some say their children make them happy. And if you're lucky, that can happen. But is the process of raising them fun? That's not the first word to come to mind.

Many say that lasting relationships bring happiness, but only with effort.

So, fun, like cotton candy, is not a pillar on which to build your world.

But what about leisure, that catchword for a huge industry? The impression the world gives us is that the more leisure, the more happiness.

But leisure can feel empty if filled only with fun, and many of us long to get back on schedule and get home.

What's really good for us?

Let me tell you about the research of a Hungarian professor named Mihaly Csikszentmihalyi. In his youth, he says, he liked to watch rock climbers and he would marvel not only at their total absorption in the task, but also at the deep and abiding satisfaction that came to them from doing that same thing over and over. He later noticed the same thing about artists, many of them would lose interest in a piece after they finished it, though during the creation they were totally absorbed. Csikszentmihalyi began to call the feeling these people were experiencing flow, and he identified this as an optimal experience, wondrously gratifying.

Have you ever experienced flow? What about the book you couldn't put down? Or the last task that so absorbed you that you lost all track of time?

And was that experience of flow deeply satisfying? It may have been, because flow envelops you. Was it not more real?

I believe that your Jewishness might be a source of the flow experience for you.

When you touch a part of your Jewish self, you touch a whole civilization, a whole way of life—and there is always more. The *Torah* is more real than *People* magazine. And it never grows old.

I wish you some fun this year, and surely some leisure, too, and some deep moments of joy and learning—and moments of flow which are so real that they never run dry.

Make it real.

Exposé

Given at Temple Jeremiah for the Installation
of Rabbi Marla Subeck
November 1991

---

*MSS was invited to speak at the installation of Rabbi Marla
Subeck Spanjer, whom he had known for most of her life,
as she assumed her role as rabbi across town at Temple
Jeremiah. In the sermon he gave, he spoke primarily to Marla,
allowing for the rest of the congregation to listen in to this
exposé about what kinds of challenges and opportunities she
should expect from a lifetime in the rabbinate.*

THIS WILL BE AN EXPOSÉ. I want to tell you the truths about rabbis, senior and assistant, about their longings, about their inner life, and about what congregants really want from their rabbis... the kind of stuff that is bound to make the *National Enquirer*.

Now I have to make this sound a little sensational because I already have a few strikes against me. It's a truism that the longer the guest speaker has to travel to get to you the more important he must be and the more attention you'll give him. And I've come all the way from Glenview. I can get here in 16 minutes when traffic isn't bad. So what I lack in cosmopolitan appeal I figure I have to make up somewhere.

Let me set the mood by telling Marla Joy Subeck, henceforth to be referred to as MJS, the hardest thing a rabbi has to do. Someone comes up to you and begins to tell a joke that begins: "You're gonna love this one, rabbi." And it turns out, more times than not, to be either the oldest chestnut ending with... "What kind of job is this for a Jewish boy?" Or perhaps it's the slightly more modern but just as overdone story about the rabbi who gets a hole-in-one playing golf on *Yom Kippur* and then whom can he tell? Now here's the hard part: if you realize early on in the joke which one it is, you can head it off, but if you wait too long the joke teller has a head of steam up and you're caught, having to squeeze out a chuckle at the end. Harder than THAT it doesn't get!

Which leads me into the rest of this exposé. I want to tell MJS what the real behind-the-scenes-frustration in the rabbinate is, the truth about how much easier the senior rabbi's life is once there are two rabbis... and finally the real truth about whether this is a decent job for a Jewish girl.

People think this is a frustrating career. And it can be, but generally not for the reasons they assume.

Congregants think that the hard part is—to put it bluntly— that people don't want to buy a whole lot of what we have to sell. They imagine us being very frustrated when there are empty seats at services, when people care more about the *Oneg* than the *Shabbat*, when people want to know how little they can get away with and not how much they can do.

I don't think that's the frustrating part. Every rabbi who has herself grown up in a normal congregation—and ours is more normal than most—knows all these things, expects them, and they decided to be a rabbi because of the challenge of these things, or in spite of them. I grew up in a synagogue on the South Side which my parents stayed away from for years. I remember my childhood rabbi, G. George Fox, *zichrono livrachah*, approaching my dad and me outside the Temple one day, and because my father thought the rabbi was going to ask him to do something or join something, he pretended he didn't see him or hear him calling as he walked the other way. I didn't have any illusions about how easy it would be if all the congregants were like my family, at least at that time in their lives.

The frustration, to me, MJS (and congregants—you can listen in), is this: We feel pulled in two different directions, both of which are crucial to being a good rabbi, and there is no time to do both well, and also eat and sleep and live and see a ballgame now and then. We are pulled by the books and pulled by the people. I sit in my study at Temple and feel the force fields at work. Behind me and next to me, are all the books, the ones I've read and forgotten, the ones not opened yet, the ones I might use and the ones I gave up on already. The books call to me with siren voices which sound like the voices of my teachers at rabbinic school and they say: "Shapiro, you were smart enough to have become more learned than you are. Here, on our pages lies your first loyalty, do not leave us." And out there, beyond the door, sometimes knocking on the door are all those people to whom I am pledged to be accessible. And there is no end of things I could be doing for them and no end of untouched books. And if you have my tendency to obsess about the things you're not doing which you think all the rest of your colleagues are, then the rabbinate can feed that obsession and paralyze you.

MJS, all that is born of being a real rabbi, but it is a real frustration. Somehow you've got to combine the voices, do both, and feel okay about it. I don't think it's a problem that goes away, not even for senior rabbis.

And now an exposé on senior rabbis.

People say, "Now that we hired him an assistant, things should be a breeze for Shapiro."

Here's my real story, and you'll have to ask your own senior rabbi if it's his, but if there aren't similarities I'd be very surprised.

I resisted having an assistant rabbi for a long time because I probably liked being the only act in town. And the first time I heard somebody around the Temple asking for the rabbi and it didn't mean me, it felt like the older kid feels when the new baby comes home from the hospital.

The truth is that having another rabbi means more things can be done for the congregation. It means that groups we weren't reaching might now get touched. But it doesn't mean life gets easier for the senior rabbi.

Let me say it this way. When we have a service in which other people participate—Sisterhood Shabbat, Teachers Shabbat, people say to me: "You had the night off." We had the night off? NOT!

It's always harder when other people are doing it. You worry about whether they'll know the cues, about whether it is getting across to congregants, about if or when to intervene and help. And you worry about the participants feeling good about themselves and not thinking it was a major flaw if they stumbled a little. That's harder than usual.

And just so, a good senior rabbi cares about the growth of the younger rabbi and about how much responsibility to give her and when, about whether to warn her about certain problems or whether there will be more learning if she doesn't have the answers out front. You want your young colleague to succeed and feel good about herself. That might not make your life easier.

But it's right that your rabbi decided to become a senior rabbi, even though it didn't make his life easier. Effective rabbis who carry out their calling with skill and humor and love have to be the teachers of young rabbis. Rabbis who like being rabbis should teach our young colleagues. That's why it is right that Bob Schreibman now be the teacher for my former student Marla Joy Subeck.

And for those of you who say, "At least it cuts the pastoral calls in half," let me tell you: if the assistant goes and the senior doesn't, the man in the hospital says, "Oh, I'm not good enough for the senior rabbi, huh?" And if the senior goes and the assistant doesn't, the same man says, "The senior rabbi had time for me, the assistant couldn't make time?"

Am I telling you that the old joke may be true... that this is not such a good job for a Jewish kid?

L'hefech, not at all. I have found being a rabbi wonderful. I thought I would, and I have. I think Bob Schreibman thinks so, too. I am pretty sure MJS agrees already.

A bright attorney in my congregation said to me the other day, "I could never do what you do." I looked at him with a question mark. "You know," he said, "the sick people, the dying people, the funerals and the mourners and the sadness."

I can't tell you I get *naches* out of any of that, yet I feel most like an authentic rabbi in some of those situations, giving empathy and support.

You see, a rabbi lives in the world of values. We get to deal with Judaism and values full-time.

It's hard for me to imagine what it would be like to have success measured by how many lines of advertising I sold, or how many orders I had filled for the fall line, or how many hours of legal advice I could bill. Rabbis can know that whatever they are doing in the course of their rabbinic duties has some relationship to their ultimate values.

Of course the rabbinate produces stress. But when I talk to professionals and business people in synagogues I find that their stress is also great, and not only do they have to produce tangibly, but they can't close their eyes at night and know for sure that what they tried to produce was worthwhile. Rabbis can. Even on bad days. The older I get, the more that is worth.

I recently had the honor of being alumnus-in-residence at Hebrew Union College. I was sharing a seminar on homiletics— sermon writing—taught by the dean of the school, who happens to be here tonight for this occasion. A young woman student rabbi looked at both of us and said, "I just want you to tell me that these words, these sermons, do get through to our people, that they make a difference, that people listen."

MJS, the answer is yes. You will get through to them because of what you will say and who you are.

I know it because I know your parents and grandparents and family, and I recall when you fell in love with being Jewish, and what a romance it remains. I know that you believe there is something true-beyond-true about this Jewish heritage, that you believe *Torah* is the best possession, that you feel in some deep way that we were all once together at Sinai, that the Jews have an obligation to be a light to the nations, that we have to ask not just, "Is this good for the Jews?" but "Is it simply good and right?" That God is very real and does say to us in each generation, "You do not have to finish the task, but neither are you free to desist from it."

And when she teaches you *Torah*, you are going to listen and be moved.

For she will say it as one of us, as a young lady who might well have been a success in any of the professions she had chosen, who grew up very much like your sons and daughters. Yes, she was raised in a family with a special gift for knowledge and for language and for listening too, but she is of this world, our world.

And when the old words of Sinai are spoken through the smile and enthusiasm she brings through the warmth and heart she possesses, you might hear them better than ever before.

One of the jokes in Marla's family was that she earned a letter for each year in rabbinic school. After the first year, R. The second added A. She had become RAB by the third, and the last B and I were added in years four and five. Five years, five letters. And what you have done here at *Jeremiah* has underlined each letter.

If I can add anything in these words, let it be an exclamation point. For you deserve one.

I don't know exactly how to "install" a rabbi, but I think that giving a blessing from her rabbi might convey what I feel.

Shulayim: Rabbi Marla Subeck Spanjer

"C'mon in," my rabbi would say warmly, as we approached the *sukkah* or piled into the sanctuary for a religious school assembly. Rabbi Mark S. Shapiro, "MSS," as he sometimes called himself, did not simply deliver sermons; he invited us into them.

Often, Rabbi would draw us closer by stepping off of the *bimah*, sighing softly, and joining his hands just at the fingertips. He would ask us questions during the sermon, and punctuate a point by raising his eyebrows, giving us a moment to absorb the concept or consider the question raised.

Rabbi used his voice masterfully. He would stretch out the word, "If," while drawing an upward arc with one thumb, and it was as if he carried us physically through the logical progression of thoughts. How many of us hear in our heads to this day certain words of *Torah* in Rabbi Shapiro's distinctive voice? "*Avraham, Avraham!*"

Campers and staff at OSRUI were privileged to hear many an MSS sermon, whether by a tree-trunk ark or in less lofty settings like the infirmary, where Rabbi's entire sermon consisted completely of his most welcome presence.

When I began my rabbinate, Rabbi told me in one sentence just how to deliver an effective sermon. "You will get through to them," he said, "because of what you will say and who you are." That was—and remains—the true mark of an "MSS sermon." It has never been just about the words; it has always been as well the beloved man who speaks them.

Marla Spanjer, ordained at HUC-JIR in 1991, was confirmed at BJBE in 1979. In addition to Temple Jeremiah, she has served congregations in Lombard and Chicago, Illinois, Winston-Salem, North Carolina, and Fort Wayne, Indiana.

As Good as Zusia
Could Have Been

Yom Kippur Kol Nidre 5756/1996

MSS's father, Marvin Shapiro, always liked the story of Zusia of Hanipol. MSS used that story to lead into a discussion of expectations—the expectations we have of ourselves and the expectations others have for us. Along the way, he wonders about Jewish obligations—what exactly are they, and do we choose THEM or do they choose US?

Here's a *CHASIDIC* ANECDOTE THAT LOTS OF PEOPLE know and like.

Zusia of Hanipol was dying and his students gathered around his bed. "Master," said a young very intense student, "Aren't you afraid of God's judgment in the next world?"

"Yes," said Zusia. "Oh, I'm not afraid that God will ask me why I wasn't as good as Moses or as wise as Solomon or as courageous as Akiba. I'm only afraid that He will say to me, 'Zusia—why weren't you as good as Zusia should have been?'"

We like the story. It assures us that we only have to do what we're able to do, that God doesn't want outside standards to be imposed on us. The story, seen that way, supports all those who hate it when others tell them what their obligations are. We will be as good as we (Zusia) can be and God knows that is good enough.

Let's apply that to a real-life Jewish situation—for example,

Ethiopian Jews in Israel. We got them there but the second part isn't going that well. The Ethiopian kids feel out of the mainstream. Many of them have been put in boarding schools with the toughest elements of Israeli society, put on vocational tracks no matter what their I.Q., and *de facto* segregated from most other Israeli youngsters. So the danger is that Israel may be creating a racial underclass for the future, and we know only too well how wrong even unintentional discrimination is, and how hard it is to turn around its effects.

But we wouldn't stand for even an ally like America demanding that Israel meet its moral obligations to the Ethiopians. Don't tell us, "You Jews ought to do this better." No, that's an obligation we can choose all by ourselves. Israel doesn't seem to be as wise as Solomon and create a social workers' dreamland by integrating those kids immediately—but we know that Israel should choose to be as good as Zusia, as good as Israel can be, and that means pretty good. That means doing a wise and compassionate job of integrating these kids into Israeli society. We should urge ourselves to do it well, because we are good enough to do it well.

So there are some obligations we Jews should choose to accept.

Except we also think that obligation is a dirty word. We also think that ought is a dirty word. Two dirty O-words, which most of us would like to replace with an o-word we like better—options.

When we call around looking for a Temple that's right for us, people don't still say, "What are the requirements here?" They ask "What are my options?" Can I get the early service if I take the late *Bar Mitzvah* date? Can my kid get a tutor for Hebrew while he's in soccer season, but when he does come back can he be in class with Andy and Laurie and Brad? Don't I get the option of one-day-a-week Hebrew school? I know a temple someplace has cut it down to that? Can we have *yahrzeit* when I'm planning on being there anyway? What are my options?

I'm not surprised that people ask this of liberal synagogues and Liberal Judaism. The car dealer gives you options on the equipment and the lease, the computer is all options, right there on the screen. And if we can figure out these options, we like it that way. We even tend to think that the options we choose give us our personality, our identity.

I'm not so happy with the options approach. But I know that this era is not one in which anyone can impose obligations on other Jews. I know that people who try to impose them will be, at best, ignored.

So, will there be any obligations left? Yep. The ones you choose. There is a chance of a jellyfish getting a spine only if you and I will choose our obligations.

And that's really what the story means! I'm only afraid, says Zusia, that God will not think I did as well as I honestly could, by taking on no personal Jewish obligations at all. But even though many people think that those O-words—Ought and Obligation— are dirty words, I believe you know how much you need to choose some anyway.

I believe this because you all want to be here at *Yom Kippur*, for *Kol Nidre* especially, when the opening song is about trying to keep the commitments we have chosen to make.

Unusual. This generation, which wants nobody to tell it what it should be doing, shows up in droves for the holiday that says, page after page, "This is what you ought to be doing—did you? Why not?"

You may say that the rabbis planned it this way, almost like a sting. They knew you'd all be coming for *Yom Kippur* so they shifted all the heavy obligation prayers to that day so they could bury you in them.

Not true. We Jews decided which holiday we will consider the most important and therefore show up for. And from the beginning, of all the possible holidays, Yom Kippur has had the market on heavy obligation prayers.

You come, with a great sense of "I must be there," to observe the day when the prayer book is loaded with "you ought to" prayers, when the rabbi will probably talk about Ought and Obligation because it's in the air. And if the rabbi lets you off the hook, the *Machzor* won't—if you miss *Ashamnu* on one page you'll get *Al Cheit* 15 minutes later.

What must this mean? That you are hoping, somewhere, that one year you will be moved by all of this to take on some obligations and say to yourself, "I ought to"... giving the jellyfish of options a spine?

Some folks think that our *mitzvah* day was such a big success last year and will be this year again, because of the great number of options we offer.

And we do. This Social Action Committee is ingenious. Last year there were 20 options, and this year 30! I'm excited to see them. This year you can clean Milwaukee Avenue, plant here and there and almost everywhere, feed, and visit. You can brighten a day for the blind, the ill, the elderly, the new immigrants, the homeless—you can even walk dogs (and cats, it says). I'd like to see you try to walk our cats. That would be a miracle, not a *mitzvah*.

I know it seems as if the large options list may ensure success.

Ok, it helps. But the key, I think, is that many of us look at the list and just respond with "You know, Zusia, I ought to do that." Thinking how much fun it could be to do it with friends, and how nice you would feel at the end—that's all icing. So many people come out because they realize that these *Mitzvot* are doable and simultaneously they say, "I ought to be part of this." Choosing to feel and be obligated—that is the power of it.

No rabbi or leader can put obligations on you in this era—that won't work; we can only urge you, Zusia, to choose what your obligations are.

But could I lobby for some?

Like coming to services even when you don't have to.

Last year I told you that we were working on a way to make worship here renewed—make it more inclusive, personal. In the process I criticized the way services have often been—too cold, too much of a show, or not a good enough show, alienating instead of inviting.

A lot of people liked to hear me say that. I get the reports. Quite a few turned to their spouses or friends and said, "See, the rabbi said what I've been saying all along—it's boring, so don't make me come!"

Well, I wouldn't take back a bit of what I said, but that confession has another side to it—coming to services should be one of your oughts, one that you choose.

Does it feel really good to anyone here to know that Jewish attendance at worship services is so far at the bottom of the American chart when compared to Protestants, Catholics, Muslims, and almost everybody else? I know the reason isn't that their services are always enticing while ours are always boring. It must be that more of them have decided they ought to, and you could, too.

Can I keep lobbying? I suggest you finally consider making *Tz'dakah*—giving—your mitzvah. Some of us really do, and some think they do and some know you didn't.

But I mean real giving. Not just a buck in the box when you come for yahrzeit. I mean a decision to give a percentage of what you make to causes that you believe are worthwhile.

You see, if we middle-class Jews, we ordinary earners, aren't making our appropriate ordinary contributions to Jewish causes in greater numbers than at present, then this whole fabric of American Jewish philanthropy, "taking care of our own," as we proclaim, is in jeopardy.

For who is dying out? It's that group of multimillionaire immigrants who made their fortunes and who gave fantastic amounts to Jewish causes over the years.

If you weren't giving your tens and hundreds back then, their thousands kept it ticking. But they are dying out and not being replaced in those brackets, and I wouldn't bet on their heirs.

So <u>your</u> giving to Jewish causes—all of us Jews, doing it at a respectable level, if not 10% of income adjusted gross then five, at least three—is now crucial. You should choose a favorite *Tz'dakah* that you give to, over and above, and urge on others.

And your giving to BJBE is equally crucial. I never mind hearing the Appeal on the High Holy Days anymore because it tells the truth and it is *Tz'dakah*, too. And I have changed my mind on this. I used to think that giving a synagogue support beyond dues wasn't exactly *Tz'dakah* because *Tz'dakah* is giving to the needy, and giving to Temple seemed just like giving to ourselves.

But I was wrong. Synagogues are a *Tz'dakah* because here we uphold the commandment of caring for people who have had a bad year or a run of bad years... caring for people who simply need us... making sure that *Torah* is available to everyone, even the one down on his luck. That is *Tz'dakah*. And you know that a synagogue can concentrate on things like *Mitzvah* Day and Searchers Groups only if we don't sell those out by constantly having to program fund-raising time.

I know you know that. So if you are ready to choose something you believe you ought to do, then consider more than token *Tz'dakah*... for the needy, for the Jewish community, and for the Temple, which is still where it all starts and ends.

Rabbi, I come to Temple to feel good, or at least to feel better. Not to think about more obligations.

I know. I want that too. You should get strength and renewal from your religion. That's why we are trying to re-invent some ways. *Misheberach* is one—bringing the ill to consciousness when we pray.

Another reinvention is the service of healing we'll hold every month—for those who are ill, or troubled, the caretakers, the families, for mourners, for people who need hope and healing. Of course you want that hope and healing and strength from your religion and it will be here regularly.

But I think you can get healing and strength from your religion only if you treat it as your religion—not just your option.

What did your most old-fashioned teacher say? Mine said, "You can't get out more than you put in."

Actually you can. At least here in Temple and Jewish life. Because part of the strength in your religion was put in by our ancestors and part comes from God. And that you don't have to put in. But a lot of the strength of your Jewishness will only come from your saying, "I ought to... I ought to show up and make this 'ought' stick."

For that chosen obligation is the energy that gets recycled along with God's goodness and can come back in healing and renewal.

Just be as good as Zusia can be. You don't want anyone telling you what you ought to do. But Zusia, you can tell yourself. You ought to.

Shulayim: Reb Irwin Keller

When Mark Shapiro would, three-fifths of the way through the service, after a silent prayer and a song, step up to the lectern and say, "Close your books," you could feel the energy shift. People would both settle in and sit up. The room would fill with anticipation. We couldn't help it. It was Pavlovian.

Because for years we had come to experience our lives—our challenges, our sorrows, our aspirations, and our love of Judaism—as having a kind of interpretive soundtrack. And the voice of that soundtrack was Mark Shapiro's.

There was no fire and brimstone here; no preacherly elevation. Rabbi Shapiro would speak in a voice that was equal parts childhood friend and gently persistent conscience. His sermons were colloquial. With humor and poignancy he would treat earthly subjects—politics, justice, being a good person. He would stay solidly at the center of human characters and human experience: the people in, with their hopes and doubts, and us with ours.

And yet at the same time, like a conductor before an orchestra, he was able to cue in depths and heights that you hadn't seen coming. The depths had to do with our shared Jewishness.

He made us feel linked to our ancestors, to our history, and to each other. And the heights had something to do with God, or with awe, or with holiness, even though he wasn't, and isn't, one for mystical abstraction. Still, as he stood at the podium, and would bring us to some important point—something unforeseen and deserving of being spoken—he would, in that sublime moment, lift up on his toes as if he were taking flight, as if while his body gave over the words of the sermon, his spirit, his *neshomeh*, was leading all of ours in *kadosh kadosh kadosh*.

This book isn't meant to be an homage to the person, but an introduction to his thought. So it would be out of place here to address Rabbi Shapiro's kindness, the genuine caring and attention he showed to countless congregants and friends, the *pintele Yid* that he fanned from spark to flame in so many of us. Instead, I'll just say that it is a rare circumstance to have the same rabbi for 51 years and counting as teacher and role model—and a privilege to have this one. Distance and time are of no concern. Mark Shapiro is, was, will always be my rabbi.

Irwin Keller is the spiritual leader of Congregation Ner Shalom in Cotati, California. He is studying for the rabbinate through the Aleph Alliance for Jewish Renewal. He was confirmed at BJBE in 1976.

Three Sizes of Judaism

Rosh Hashanah 5758/1997

Just as the Shofar blows out short, medium, and long notes, Judaism gives us small, medium, and large experiences, from the grandeur of the High Holy Days—the Jewish version of homecoming—to individual practices of prayer, meditation, caring for others. All sizes can be powerful, MSS tells us, and all play a role in helping us to express our own Judaism.

S HOFAR BLOWERS ARE OFTEN DIFFERENT SIZES. *Shofars* themselves come in different sizes. And the basic *Shofar* notes are different sizes, too. There's the major blast, *t'kiah*—a good large long sound, then *sh'varim*—shorter sounds, medium length. Then *t'ruah*—short little pops, then *t'kiah g'dolah*—the summary which seems to include all the sizes.

Shofar notes thus come in three sizes—large, medium, and small. These are also well-known clothing sizes. The scale may have moved a bit for some of us, and the realistic choices might now be M, L, and XL. (M used to mean medium, now it means "maybe.") But whether it's clothes or *shofar* notes or popcorn boxes, there still seem to be three sizes you are offered.

I think there are also three sizes of Judaism, three sizes of Jewish experience that you can try or buy. They're not perfectly comparable to clothing sizes. For Judaism large-size is big but not so roomy and often not so comfortable. Judaism medium-size has more room than large size, though not quite as much appeal as the big size. And Judaism small-size is what everyone says they wear, but it's hard to find it in most closets, though it's slowly coming back into fashion.

This is not a puzzle. You all know what this means. Judaism large-size is like the High Holy Day service we are in right now. Judaism medium-size means all the possible smaller than giant-size groupings that go on in Jewish and particularly synagogue life. And Judaism small-size, the personal size, is of course "you and your Jewishness" and what you do with it.

I want to tell you what I personally think about these three sizes of Judaism. In a way you might say I have an inside view because my job is to help provide them for all of us. But the people who really decide which size will sell are never the rabbis but only the Jews.

We are—at this moment today—in large-size Judaism. Statistics say that this is the size everybody wants, even if they don't buy anything else from the catalog.

We act like we're in love with this large size. "I've got to get there for the BIG holidays, the HIGH Holy Days, got to get my tickets, get home from the office early, make all the arrangements, get on the new clothes, got to get there to join in the parking lot game and the Milwaukee Avenue lineup game and the hunt for seats and the subtle, "how can I save seats without looking like I'm saving seats" game. You all want to be here for the big size, even though it's not roomy.

Why? Because this is the reunion. This is Homecoming! And you just want to be here for it. Being here is the big experience. Yes, I think that the prayers are meaningful and the place looks good, and there is something of a spiritual nature floating here and there on the High Holy Days. But even if you don't quite get much of that, you still get a lot out of just being at the homecoming.

Coming to Homecoming is a declaration of solidarity: "I'm still an alum. I still care about those old *shul*-days. This is still my team. God, I'm still alive and I'm still Jewish!" And God is probably saying, "Thank God."

I absolutely don't mean this sarcastically. For there is power in this large size and the reunion-homecoming experience. Having all of you here gets my adrenaline rising, too. Singing the *Sh'ma* so that the *bimah* vibrates a little gives me a joyous rush.

Most of those who go to the biennial conventions of the UAHC, Reform Judaism's homecoming event, say that there is at least one event at those sessions that has a great emotional impact on them. It's when all the delegates, sometimes 4,000, have Shabbat morning worship all together in the hotel's largest space, and pray and sing in unison. People love the feeling of that many liberal Jews gathered in a service, the way it makes you feel part of this historic Jewish people, standing shoulder to shoulder before the Ark and Mt. Sinai, each knowing he belongs. You just get lifted up by being part of that and you never come quite back all the way down.

So I don't look down my nose in the slightest at Judaism large size. It is big. Except that if it's all you have, it probably doesn't feel as big as it really is.

Let me give an example from another area of life in which I am also emotionally involved. I know that many of us suffer from Chicago baseball, and I say us, for in my objective moments I admit that North-Side suffering could be as agonizing as South-Side suffering. But I digress. In 1993, my team was in the divisional playoffs, and everybody wanted to be at Sox Park. My family and I were there, too, and the place was jammed with people who hardly knew where the place was but who wanted to be there for the big size—the playoffs.

And as I sat there watching my team lose, I wondered, "What are some of these newcomers getting from this big game?" Not quite as much as I am. For I realized that you have to be at the small and medium sizes to appreciate the large sizes, you had to be there with 8,000 in the seats on a cold day or with 15,000 in the seats when they come back to win a game even though they're mathematically out of the race. Being there for those medium-size, even tiny times, gives the big days their special thrill. I felt sorry, well, a bit angry, but mainly sorry for those who had bought just the big size, the playoff size. If that was all they had, the big size wasn't as big as it should be.

Which is why I think that a lot can be said for medium-sized Judaism. What can seem boring in the big size Jewish experience, like these High Holy Days, can be very engaging in a medium-sized group. Take some of these same prayers, sit in a living room with a dozen or so other Jews and talk about what these prayers really could mean, or what they remind you of in your life, or whether you agree with them, and then it almost always gets interesting for just about everyone.

There's a new book by Gil Mann which shows how true this is. I think you're going to hear a lot more about this book. It's called, *How to Get More out of Being Jewish even if you're not sure you believe in God, even if you think going to synagogue is a waste of time, even if you think kosher is stupid, even if you hated Hebrew school, or all of the above.*

That's the title.

Gil Mann describes himself as a successful marketer who is intrigued by his customers' behavior, and who came to feel that as far as Judaism is concerned, "the product is quite good but sales haven't been so hot."

He decided that he needed to form focus groups to give him material for the book. So he got names of Jewish people from friends which led to other names. He wanted to find unaffiliated or non-active Jews. He hooked them by calling them on the phone and telling them he was writing a book titled, "How to get something out of being Jewish even if you think keeping kosher is stupid," and many laughed a little and said, "That sounds sort of interesting, I'll just come to hear what the other people have to say."

Gil Mann says that his first focus group happened the day after *Yom Kippur*. Four of the six people there were not even aware that *Yom Kippur* had just occurred. "Not a very tuned-in group," he thought, which was just what he wanted. But in spite of this, he says, it turned out that all had very strong feelings and opinions about Judaism and being Jewish.

People opened up; they told stories of their Jewish backgrounds. The group was supposed to last two hours at most. After two-and-a-half hours he tried to bring it to a close. Everyone made a final comment and he says the gist was: "This is the first time in 20 years I've talked about some of these things, and I can't believe how comfortable I felt here tonight."

In other words—everyone wanted to talk about and share thoughts on their good or fair or bad Jewish education, their beliefs, their doubts about beliefs, their hopes about beliefs, their Jewish souls, and their Jewishness. And they weren't bored at all. It was fascinating and even addictive. They didn't want to stop.

That was medium-sized Judaism. And medium-sized Judaism is almost always that way—engaging! It lets the real product come through. So the smart money has been going toward medium-sized Judaism.

Are you ready for this year? Medium size covers quite a territory. Our Searchers groups are all under 20 people. *Chavurot*, the same. Discussion study groups are the same... the Saturday *minyan* is the same size, retreats are larger but still very medium size. Medium size lets the Jewish magic come through, not with the blast of *T'kiah*, but with the more approachable smaller notes, ones which leave lots of room for you between their sounds.

And then there's Judaism small size.

I mean the personal size—acts, attachments, feelings that just happen inside you or between you and God or between you and your past and your inner life.

This hasn't been such an easy part for modern Jews. We are a people who so prize community that sometimes it seems un-Jewish just to be off by yourself trying to do and be Jewish.

And of course small-sized Judaism can be a cop out. It has often seemed to me that people who talk about their inside Jewishness were just making an excuse for their lack of involvement, inventing a category of Jewishness that adds up to *gornischt*.

Do people still tell you that they're Jews at heart? We used to hear that a lot. You don't see me much, I don't do much, I don't give much, I don't need much, but that doesn't mean I don't care much because at heart, boy, am I Jewish!

It's an easy cover-up for inaction. And the proper response always seemed to be—the Jewish God cares about what you do with your hands and not how you feel in your heart.

But authentic, small-sized, personal Judaism doesn't have to be a cop out. It is making a comeback, and it is making a big difference to many people, not just as an excuse, but as a fulfillment.

You can now meditate Jewishly. And people are doing it. You can now exercise Jewishly. And people do it. Reb Zalman Schachter Shalomi taught us years ago that you can do appropriate body motions with prayers that combine psyche with soma, and now his students have gone much farther.

I get into it some, too. I used to ride my bicycle outside and *daven* the morning or evening service. I do it out loud so it helps the breathing and the breathing helps the davening and the exercise. When I swim I try to breathe in and out to the letters of God's name, *Yud Hey Vav Hey*. I like it. It feels good. Few other swimmers at the Lattof YMCA have the same mantra...and those who see me "mouthing" as well as breathing on the backstroke probably think I'm daffy, but it seems right.

We are just beginning to explore, seriously, this whole personal Jewish area. And our *K'hillat Shalom* group, which is working to make BJBE into a community of wholeness, will open this up even more as months go by. Personal renewal of body and spirit is Jewish, and more of you will make that connection, from exercise to silent meditation to yoga to Renewal of Spirit Services, and the smallest-sized experiences.

I know that Judaism in this small size is powerful. And it was evident this summer when members of this year's adult *Bar/Bat Mitzvah* class took their *Torah* scroll home.

Phyllis Steiner's *Bar/Bat Mitzvah* classes had to meet over the summer to prepare, but Temple was undergoing renovation so they met at their homes for class. They needed a *Torah* from which to work. So they took one and let it travel from home to home to home over the summer. And they kept a class journal, written by individuals, of what this personal contact with a *Torah* scroll had meant for them and their families.

Phyllis was to have told you about this at one of the *B'nei Mitzvah* services, but time ran out. Here's a taste of what she would have said:

"In a manner of speaking, the *Sefer Torah* was a houseguest in each of our homes. For a houseguest you set out fresh towels, but what do you do when a *Torah* moves in? How does it affect you personally?"

In every home, Phyllis says, a specific place had been prepared for it. Many felt there was another person in the house, one class member said, "I kept a light on in the room so it wouldn't have to sit in the dark."

And the impact on people! They said in their journals things like "Having the *Torah* was a source of unbelievable strength for me and my family." That was, says Phyllis, some power. Imagine it, the *Torah*, coming to you personally. To your door. Small-sized Judaism, microchip Judaism with more power than I could ever have imagined.

Rabbi Memis thinks we should just let one of these *Torah* scrolls keep moving from house to house in the congregation, but your turn might be seven or eight years away, so do something of a personal small-sized Judaism for yourself this year.

I like all the sizes. I wouldn't give up any of them…for the small and the medium make the large much larger.

We are working on a Temple project that is like a dream, which could, like *t'kiah g'dolah*, combine all the sizes.

We are hoping to send a small- to medium-sized group of teenagers to Kolin in the Czech Republic next summer… to be in the synagogue building from which our Holocaust scroll comes: to have services there, to bring some needed clearing and elbow grease to the town's Jewish cemetery and Holocaust memorial wall. And those teens will connect with Jews in Prague and they'll experience a bit of Terezin concentration camp. Sisterhood is helping them and I hope you will too.

This trip will contain all three Jewish sizes at once.

It will be large, a trip of many miles and significant cost, a trip large in symbolism as American Jewish teens "come back to Kolin."

It will be medium-sized, for these fifteen or so teens will bond, and share what they feel as a *chevrah* about walking in Jewish history themselves.

It will be small, personal-sized also, for each one may consider himself not only a child of suburban Chicago parents, and a kid from BJBE, but a personal descendant of those who lived there, a private *Bar/Bat Mitzvah* student or confirmand of Rabbi Richard Feder, Kolin's last Rabbi.

That is a dream that <u>can</u> come true, with all the sizes, like *T'kiah G'dolah*.

There are three sizes of *Shofar* notes. There are three sizes of Judaism. Can you try on, this year, a size you haven't worn before? I think it would feel good. I think it might fit as if it were made just for you.

What about the *Shul?*

Rosh Hashanah 1999/5760

After 35 years as rabbi at BJBE, MSS announced that he would retire in the summer of 2000. In the last Rosh Hashanah sermon he delivered prior to his retirement, he spoke about the future transition that was in store for him and for BJBE, outlining all the reasons why he was confident that the congregation would live on very well after he moved on.

MOST SERMONS I DON'T SAVE, but High Holy Day sermons I do. Some time ago I started marking them with a title at the top and in the upper right hand corner I type RH or YK, the secular year, the Hebrew year, and then "MSS" and "BJBE".

When I typed that at the beginning of this sermon it felt strange. Because MSS and BJBE won't ever be in quite the same relationship again. As you may know, I'm retiring on or about July 1st of 2000.

Of course this has made choosing sermon topics easy. This year I have to talk about us— about you, me, my family, and this congregational family.

These really are conversations for the family—for extended family and friends and cousins. Many of you are like cousins. I have cousins I only see once or twice a year and some of you I also see once or twice a year.

If you are just entering this Temple I want you to know that you've entered at a very interesting time, a time such as this congregation hasn't experienced in years. This is a point-of-passage year, when things are momentarily malleable enough to be shaped into even better configurations before they harden again, but also a time when apprehensions are walking hand in hand with these new opportunities. Transitions always bring such fears, but always open windows for worthwhile change...as when you leave home, or a child leaves home, as at a Bar Mitzvah or wedding, or funeral, or when you move...as at the retirement of a rabbi from the place it seems he's been forever.

So this morning I want to talk about this congregation and on *Erev Yom Kippur* I want to stay on that topic, and also answer some questions about me.

"Vayeilchu Sh'neihem yachdav." (Genesis 22:8). "And they went, the two of them, together." We just read that in *Torah*. (I hope you liked the way we read it.)

Abraham and Isaac, walking right into a life transition. And they will walk three days to get to this mountain. But will they be <u>ready</u> for what is to happen? Probably not. It will turn out to be a real transition—after this encounter their relationship won't be the same. They will even descend the mountain separately. But they seemed to know that if they trusted one another, God would "see to" their getting through it okay.

I don't want to push the comparison too far. Neither of us is carrying a knife to "do in" the other. And even though Abraham chooses a wife for Isaac two chapters on, your new senior rabbi will not in any way be chosen by me. Only by you.

So—what's going to happen to us when we don't come down the mountain together? I think it will be like Abraham and Isaac—scary on occasion, but with a good ending which will become another good beginning... just as in the story.

Here's what I think about this Temple. It will survive, get even better, most everyone with good sense will stay and new people will come. I believe it because first—it's in our genes, and second—it's in our people. Third—it's in your best interests!

First, we are genetically disposed to stay healthy. It's in the genes, especially those that come from the BJ side. Do you know the story about that part of the family? It is a story of successfully defying death twice, and it's tangibly part of us.

Bohemian Jews came to Chicago in the 19th century and settled on the near southwest side. When some got more affluent they moved out along Washington Boulevard and built Washington Boulevard Temple which became Oak Park Temple. But a number of Bohemian Jews remained in a synagogue they had started at 1920 South Ashland Avenue. They liked the neighborhood, so they stayed. They had some 250 families in their heyday, many of whom were cousins or in-laws of others, but they took newcomers also. They served Bohemian rye bread with cream cheese at *Oneg Shabbat*, and had earning fund dinners at Old Prague and Café Bohemia, and the food was all beige. They produced a few rabbis and had great youth groups.

They did it all in the 1950s under a big handicap. Most of the members decided they were leaving that area, which had gone through an ethnic change. And they moved to… well, not one specific area, that was the problem, and the kernel of the survival, too. Many went to Berwyn and Cicero and Riverside, out west. Some went north to Rogers Park and Skokie. Some went south to South Shore but nobody stayed within eight miles of *B'nai Jehoshua* on Ashland Avenue. The place stayed alive through the late '40s and '50s because people travelled back to their old *shul*, just because they liked it and one another. They also had a number of good rabbis, and that helped; the names included Karl Weiner and Arnold Jacob Wolf. But they didn't drive or take the streetcar eight miles just because they liked the rabbi—they did it because they liked one another.

Even so, by 1964 they were almost dead. The demographics had finally swamped them. Fewer than 100 families, mainly old timers, 23 kids in school and most of those only because they took children of non-members for nothing. They had a decent young rabbi whom they liked and who liked them, but you've got to pay the bills.

And then came the miracle on 20th Street, the unexpected

revival of the patient in hospice. This congregation, BJ, which had survived everyone's moving away, only to be at death's door again 20 years later, shape-shifted into a merger with *Beth Elohim*, a young group in Morton Grove/Des Plaines. The story is fascinating, but for another day. With vision from BJ's Leon Rabin and BE's Arnold Preis, and many more, they sold the building on Ashland Avenue for $75,000, bought this land in '66 for most of that money, and had to take the young rabbi in the deal. So Hanna and I went from a dying congregation of 85 elderly families to one with 150 very young families with at least 250 more kids, almost overnight.

So *B'nai Jehoshua* survived its second difficult transition and was reborn into BJBE. That was in '65 and the rest of the story so far, yours and Hanna's and mine, has been lived out in these past 34 years.

See? We have the genes to survive here. Since '65 we've also survived a waiting list, and a too-small building, and a lack of big givers (with a few significant exceptions). And I think we've learned a lot from surviving each one of these hurdles.

So—it's in your bloodline to keep going, even stronger. You are BJBE, out of BJ, by BE. That's the way they give the lineage of racehorses. You are thus like Citation, out of Bull Lea, by Whirlaway, which promises both "early foot" and "stretch-runner."

And if bloodlines don't convince you, then just be convinced of the future because this is such an attractive congregation… the people, the staff, and the program.

Our professional staff met in August, for the first time under the chairmanship of Sandy Robbins, our great new educator. I started the meeting by talking about each one at the table and how lucky we were that they were here, and what it meant for the congregation. And I felt a pang of loss, that I would work together with them for only one more year.

Go around that table with me. For the first time we have a "Temple product" in our professional leadership. Our new Hebrew school principal is Rabbi Deborah Gardner Helbraun, who grew up here from kindergarten, was in youth group here, went to OSRUI from here, became ordained, and who came back to Chicago not so long ago with her husband who is rabbi at Beth El on Dundee. What a great development. Debbie Becker leads the Early Childhood Center and there couldn't be a better person. Larry Glickman, creator of the Quest for Kolin, is not only our senior youth advisor, but also our high school principal—talk about a role model! Jason Kaiz, who is almost as young as he looks, is 8th grade coordinator, junior youth advisor, and member of the Board of Directors. Hedda Schless is the ingenious and indefatigable family education programmer, and she doesn't get tired easily either. Shari Bauer is unflappable as our executive director, and nice, <u>and</u> bright, and is on the cusp of her FTA degree. Rabbi Memis does more and more every year for more people of all ages, with increasing wisdom and her special flair. She helps me stay organized too. And Cory Winter is not only the best cantor around, in my opinion, and most fun too, but has taken what was a very good *Bar/Bat Mitzvah* training program and turned it into something beyond our dreams.

See—they're not going anywhere so why should anyone else?

I have a fairly extensive once-a-year conversation with a member who doesn't come around too much, but who cares about BJBE and whose business sense is superb.

He said, "If your school really works, and if kids really learn things here, then people will know that and they'll want to have their kids and themselves here. Quality still counts."

This congregation will stay healthy because we have that quality.

I think that, most of the time, we are even a "Formula" congregation. The formula, devised I believe by Larry Kushner and Arnold Wolf, says: "Add up the number of member hours spent in Jewish text study plus hours spent in support groups and *mitzvah* and *tz'dakah* and worship groups, then add up separately the number of member hours spent in synagogue business meetings. If there are more of the first than the second, the congregation is healthy. But if there are more business meeting hours, then the congregation has a poor immune system and cardiac insufficiency and can't take the stress." When I add up the figures—searchers groups and *chavurah* meetings and support groups and the *minyan* and all the classes—I think we are just on the good side of the formula, though it's always a struggle to stay there.

We have things the Temple of my youth never even thought of, like a growing group for young singles and couples: This year, they'll make it! A Renewal of Spirit service which helps people, an affiliation with United Power for Action and Justice of which I am so proud. We're bringing on a congregational nurse. We have a great empty-nester fellowship potentially in our post-carpool group, and they will take it in their hands to make it happen regularly, I believe. We have an amazingly successful singles friendship group for more mature singles.

And we have new interfaith activities on a scale beyond anything ever done here, building a connection with Glenview Community Church and with the Islamic mosque in Northbrook. We are beginning an Interfaith Travelers discussion group half-BJBE, half-GCC. Call the office to register because this one will fill up.

This place is <u>that</u> alive and <u>that</u> attractive. If you're Jewish and breathing, who wouldn't want to be here?

So BJBE will thrive because of its genes, because of what it is, which will draw people to join, <u>and</u> people will remain members because it's really beneficial for them to stay here.

It is. What produces the most stress? Change, loss, displacement. Who would want to create more of that for oneself by not staying with their Temple?

Sure, this congregation has its idiosyncrasies, its *mishagass*. But so does every place, churches and JCCs too. Here you at least know what the *mishagass* is already. That's the glue in many good marriages, right? You're comfortable with the other person's shtik, it doesn't surprise you. Here, too. You know the things that could be changed and the ones that probably won't ever be changed. Like the "don't-save-seats" *mishagass*, when the supposed rule is one thing and practice is another. But don't laugh too much because you probably couldn't figure out a better answer either.

You know this place. You know how to read the bulletin, even if it isn't desktop organized yet. You know the phone numbers, and what time to get here, usually anyway.

You know where people generally sit. You also know where people used to sit... and on these Holy Days, as you do, I look around at the sections where people I recall and love used to sit.

That spells community. And being and knowing a community is what most of us need so much, even if we don't come around all the time.

It's not just being a group of good friends, because lots of you are unknown to lots of others. It's that being here connects you, beyond close friendship, to the larger Jewish world, to Reform Judaism as a movement and philosophy you can honestly support, with integrity and without hypocrisy. Being part of this congregation actually connects you to a still living but ancient transcendent community. It gives you a real address in the world, which is more than even a bridge club or a gourmet club can hope to do.

But we do have some worry-warts here. They sidle up to me and ask, "Rabbi, don't you think that some people whose kids belong elsewhere are going to join where their kids belong now that you're retiring?"

Maybe, but most of them, on considering, will realize that it's not such a good idea to go off and do that.

Of course family is important. But if our children and extended family are in the Chicagoland area, I just assume that you are with them often and regularly. But you don't change your community to be a part of your child's community, because that for you would be, I think, a significant loss.

We need our peers—our comfortable group. Who would really trade that for the stress of attempting to live Jewishly through your children's lives?

No—I think most people will stay here, where they belong, in a community they've built, to watch it and help it recreate itself, and be part of this drama of new beginnings. Nobody walks out just when the plot thickens, do they?

A photographer named Sophie Calle has an exhibit of her

work now at the Jewish Museum in New York. She went around Jerusalem and asked people to take her to any public place in Jerusalem which they also considered a private personal space of their own. Then she photographed the places and hung them next to the stories people told about those places. I quote Valerie Steiker's article about the exhibit.

"A photograph of a nondescript bench hints at the story of a youthful love that never happened... a view of some ordinary city pavement emerges as the site of a horrific bus accident in which a child lost a leg and the now grown-up child is quoted as saying, "In a strange way I consider that piece of street mine." A section of stone wall is revealed as the woman says in the story next to the picture, "I still skim that wall lightly with my fingers when I walk past, as if to touch what's still alive."

You may have a place in this building which you consider private and maybe even sacred to you personally. A casket rested here, a kid chanted there, a baby gurgled there, you felt something of God over there.

Yes, it's only a semi-public space, belonging to a big congregation. But if you have already privately made it yours, then I think it's home, no matter whose name they list as Senior Rabbi.

At least I hope so.

This congregation will be fine. It's got survival in its genes and in its people... and staying here will just be good for you.

Happy New Year, for now and all the new years to come.

Shulayim: Hanna Shapiro

It was *Erev Rosh Hashanah* in 1999. I was sitting in the congregation waiting for services to begin. The choir had just marched into the room followed by the rabbis and cantor. My sister-in-law, Barbara, stood in the first row of the choir, facing me, and as we looked at each other we both started to cry at the same time, realizing that this was the beginning of the last High Holidays at BJBE with Mark as rabbi. For the rest of the services over those Holidays, we cried whenever our eyes met. I had to avoid looking at her.

There were several reasons for my tears. In some ways I was afraid of Mark's retirement. It would mean so many changes for our lives—changes that would affect both of us. He had spent so many years working so hard for the synagogue—what would he do now?

Also behind my tears—I realized how proud I had been of Mark's presence on the *bimah* for all those years. I was proud of how he led the congregation, proud of what he said, and especially proud of how people reacted to his sermons. I was sad—as so many people were—that I wouldn't get to see him in that role much longer.

As things turned out, it wasn't the last time I sat in a congregation with Mark leading services or giving the sermon. His continuing work as a rabbi gave us a wonderful opportunity to travel.

We spent four years in congregations in Hawaii, two years in Alaska, and he would lead services on many cruises. And, of course, Mark returned to the BJBE *bimah* many times in the ensuing years.

All in all, it was less change than I had feared. Retirement meant that Mark and I got to spend more quality time together. Better yet, we now get to SIT together in the very same congregation. And we have the *naches* of being joined by our children and grandchildren. Retirement? Not so bad!

−Hanna Shapiro

Tell Us About Yourself

Erev Yom Kippur 5760/1999

Of all the stories that MSS told over the years, the story of Jack was one of the ones that really happened, and perhaps the one that people remember best. In the context of a retelling of "Jack," he spoke about his lifetime of experiences at BJBE, lessons learned along the way, and shared some of his plans for the next stage in his life.

I USUALLY LIKE TO SPEAK WITH A BEGINNING, a middle and an ending, letting the organizing show through. Tonight it may be bumpier. So let me give you the roadmap ahead of time.

I'm going to start with the story of Jack. Then I'm going to respond to questions which people have asked me. I'm going to share two ideas I think are important, one about seriousness versus playfulness, and one on the well-cooked heart. I'm going to tell you why I'm thankful, touch on *Tarzan of the Apes*, and end with Jack. It shouldn't take longer than usual, and I hope I'm through talking before you're through listening.

The story of Jack. Hanna experienced it with me, as did our former cantor Steve Sher. It happened some 20 years ago, right here. I have told it before, so don't tell the ending to your neighbor if you know it already.

It was a Sunday night in April. We had just concluded second

Seder here at Temple with a big crowd. Hanna and the cantor and I were closing up the place about 9:40 p.m. We came up from downstairs, and sitting out in that foyer, near the doors on the landing, on the large column ashtray, was a big man with a scraggly beard, dirty, carrying a kind of a knapsack. He said he was walking north on Milwaukee, but had a bad leg and couldn't quite get up over the hill on Milwaukee Avenue just north of here. Could we give him a lift, he asked? He spoke softly, but with confidence, not like a beggar or someone we should fear. We looked at one another, sniffed him a little—I didn't consciously think about Elijah—but we said, "Okay. How far are you going?" He said something about heading for the Randhurst Mall area. And he told us that his name was Jack.

"I'll drive," I said to Hanna and the cantor, "but you two come with me." I had a little two-door Ford Fiesta. The cantor and Hanna climbed in the back, Jack sat next to me, and the Fiesta tilted his way. We drove over the hill, up Milwaukee Avenue, and when we approached Lake Street he said, "Let me out right here at the corner, it's fine." I pulled into the Shell station (that used to be there), which was dark, and Jack heaved himself out and said thanks. We went back south on deserted Milwaukee and headed back to Temple so the cantor could get his car.

I was relieved to have him out of the car, but as we drove back toward Temple one of us said, "Randhurst? Randhurst is closed. It's Sunday night—everything is closed. How can he walk that far?" We made a U-turn on Milwaukee, went back north to look for him, but he was gone. We had let him off just 90 seconds before, he didn't walk too well, but he was gone. And we all went home.

I have wondered—if Elijah were Jack, coming to test us, how did we do? We did fair, but not well enough. Probably a grade of B-minus. And maybe Jack or Elijah decided that the three of us, and all of you by extension, were worth working with, though with lots of *rachmones* yet to learn.

That is the story. It really did happen here. Because you are partners in BJBE, the story belongs as much to you personally as to Hanna and me and Steve Sher. So I thought you should know it to see what you make of it.

I am surely not Jack, but I have decided to go on from here, too. In the process, I am getting lots of help and affection from the people here. Some of you want to know where I'm going and what I'll do and more. So I thought I would answer some of these questions while you're looking around for the footprints of Jack. It is a bit narcissistic to think you want to hear me talk about Hanna and me and our family, but indulge me—I've indulged a few of you over the years. How did you decide to retire? How does it feel? What will being Rabbi Emeritus mean? Where will you and Hanna live, and what will you do? That's enough.

Why did you decide to retire? A colleague once told me he knew it was time to retire when he was working on a project at Temple one day, and a congregant called, and he realized that he resented it as an interruption. That began happening to me on occasion. You need a rabbi who doesn't feel that you can be an interruption.

I also knew it was time when meetings that I had often enjoyed for their potential or at least for their sociability seemed to be not a joy at all. And I was also finding that I didn't know the kids, and that didn't feel right. So it was time, and we're fortunate that I'm able to retire.

How does this feel to Hanna and me? Well, she can answer for herself, but much of it we do share. It feels mixed. For example, I always shop in supermarkets rather slowly and if we shop together too much I'll drive her crazy. But the new possibilities for travel and recreation are attractive.

I was at first elated when I decided to retire, then became quite depressed over it as I began a sabbatical last January. But with some help, I've come to a balanced happiness at the prospect. I know this year will be fun and sad, too. We will feel loss, maybe me the most. And I hope I can let myself feel those feelings. And I hope you will too.

What does "emeritus" mean? That question probably translates as: "Will you still be our rabbi?" No, I will not, after next summer, be your rabbi as I have been for so long, and will not even be <u>one</u> of your rabbis in that former way. "Emeritus" is to me a bestowed and earned title, not at all a job description. Will I be officiating at life cycle ceremonies? Not in a scheduled way at all. I might share some words at a wedding or funeral if I'm in town and available, which I probably will know only at the last minute, and will do that only at the invitation of the Senior Rabbi and only for families who are members of BJBE at that time. Being retired means not having to make long-range commitments other than to family and very close friends and to personally chosen projects.

I will be officiating at weddings through next August, and we don't know where we will be for the High Holy Days next year. We plan to stay in Israel for an extended time after the Interfaith trip to Israel a year from this October, and I will try to be smart enough to be very scarce around here that whole first year in retirement. But this will probably remain our congregation, and we'll be sitting out there with you listening to sermons.

Where will we live? Somewhere around here, I expect. We like the area, our family is mainly in Chicago, we know our way around, though I still get lost sometimes without Hanna in the car.

What will you do? Hanna will keep doing her travel agent work, supporting me, she's much younger than I.

And I? Well, the White Sox have not asked me to be spiritual advisor to the kids who are trying to play—I even found out that most of them are gentile! So that's out.

I'm not trying to plan it in too much detail yet. I think I'm trying to listen to what God has in mind for me. That is partially a cop-out answer I guess, but partially the real truth.

I think I'll try to do the things I like. Many of these overlap with things I've done as your rabbi, and some don't.

I'll study and learn and take classes and read, in lots of different areas, and do some teaching though maybe not right away. I may continue doing personal counseling and maybe some chaplaincy work with hospice.

Two projects attract me at the moment. One is helping create a network of congregations which have Czech *Torah* scrolls, and the other is volunteering to work in the cause of more stringent gun control legislation.

I also want to swim more, try to stay healthy... I may play more golf although I have to be sure it's not bad for my mental health, and golfers all know just what I mean.

These are some of my plans, but retirement means they don't have to be promises.

And now, because I may not have the attention of so many of you for who-knows-how-long-again, I want to tell you two things I have learned which might be of benefit to you. One I learned from a classmate colleague and the others I recently learned from a younger colleague. I believe both insights are winners.

Here is the first. Problems get worse when you go at them too seriously. Things often seem to get better when you can be more playful about them.

I think I've known this instinctively for a long time, but it was the late Edwin Friedman, a rabbinical school classmate, who made me think analytically about it and who piqued my interest in family systems theory and therapy.

Let me give an example of Edwin Friedman talking about being playful in a paradoxical way. He wrote in his book *From Generation to Generation* the following:

"A rabbi came into his Sunday school one morning to find teachers, parents, and the principal terribly upset. There was to be a big celebration that morning, with many outsiders invited. All were upset because an eleven-year-old had written out the Anglo- Saxon four-letter word for "feces" in Hebrew letters and vowels all over a very visible auditorium blackboard. Parents and teachers were talking about the psychological meaning of the child's actions, about whether this was really profaning of the Temple, about what to tell the parents and how to punish the child. But instead of entering into that heavy discussion, the rabbi noticed that the child had spelled out the word mistakenly, with a long "ee" sound, instead of the short "i" sound. The rabbi lectured the kid about not paying more attention to Hebrew vowel phonics and told him he could join the festivities later only after he had spelled it right one hundred times."

And Friedman concludes: "some may hear this as gimmicky or just reverse psychology—but that would be too serious a way of listening. The major effect of playfulness with a twist of paradox, is on the person who is being playful. It makes you less anxious and that change in you can affect the emotional weather around you, and in others."

If you need a different example, try this one. Some folks at BJBE were seriously worried about Reform Temple *Beth El* opening on Dundee some years ago. They worried *Beth El* would be cheaper, or would undercut us by offering one day a week Hebrew. A few approached me—"This is a real threat, what do you think we should do?"

Accidentally I gave a good response. I said, "What, us worry? I hear their *Oneg Shabbat* doesn't come close to ours, so how are they a threat? Besides," I added, "aren't there a few members we'd really be happy to send over there? Let's make a list!"

Did that solve what some saw as a big problem? Not really. But it kept me and maybe them from being too anxious over something we couldn't control anyway. And the anxiety over the problem was potentially far more debilitating than the problem.

Now if you think this talk about the merit of playfulness and the pathology of seriousness isn't appropriate for serious *Yom Kippur*, then you have another think coming. And I can prove it from the High Holy Day music.

Of course I believe that repentance is serious, that good and evil are serious and that Jews are to be dead serious in choosing one over the other. These are not jokes.

But—the *Ashamnu* echo, the "we have sinned" chant, has a playful lilt you might not expect. And when we sing *Un'taneh Tokef*, that great piece about judgment, which turns me to water, the refrain, paradoxically enough, is like a little dance. And the *Ya'aleh* is playful and even swingy.

That playful relief helps us imbibe the serious music more

fully, the way that Jewish irony and humor has kept us from being so uptight that we add to our own *tzorres*.

See—take important things seriously, but without deadly seriousness.

Second thing I've learned… or just found the way to verbalize in proper Jewish terms:

I studied some Jewish spiritual writings with a teacher of *Kabbalah* named Elliott Ginsburg, whom I'm bringing here to teach a weekend next spring. He called his workshop, "The Well-Cooked Heart." The title was based on a quote from Rebbe Nachman of Bratzlav. Listen to it, please: "Even more than God wants the straw fire, God wants the well-cooked heart."

So what does this mean? Well, what's a straw fire? Most of us think that's what a spiritual moment feels like… chills up and down the spine, all senses alive, tears in the eyes, or pounding of the heart, mouth hanging open in awe. Like the blazing straw fire which lasts a moment.

But, says Rebbe Nachman, more than God wants the straw fire, He wants the well-cooked heart.

That's different! Slow cooking is simmering. You must find ways to sustain the warmth so that it's a part of you. The trick is finding things you can keep doing which keep the fire alive. Maybe it's candles, or studying, or going on retreat, or *tz'dakah*—but it has to be something you can keep doing for a long time, regularly, which eventually cooks you to a tender heart of wisdom.

So—what are you doing—what am I doing—that I can keep doing and that keeps the flame alive inside?

Let me add—if none of this now makes sense to you then it is enough, for now, to make sure that the simmering flame does not go out. You can do that by supporting the synagogues and all the stoves of *Torah* around to make sure they keep cooking, and that will link you to the warmth as well.

So—thank you.

I am so grateful. BJ and BE have done more for me than I have ever done for either. And that is really the truth. *B'nai Jehoshua* was a nurturing presence for me and my family at a difficult time in life. They helped me regain confidence as a rabbi, and gave me and Hanna and Steve unconditional love, as Eliot, David, and Natalie and those they loved have received it from you as well. *B'nai Jehoshua* called me rabbi, at age 27, and helped me live up to it. And then the exodus from Ashland Avenue to Glenview, our coming to this new congregation was like a miracle for us.

When Hanna asked me what I'd like to do for my birthday this past July I said, "Let's go see the movie *Tarzan*. We did. *Tarzan of the Apes* was one of my first and best-loved series books. But only this year did I realize that I had lived out a theme of the story. No, I don't swing from vines, nor did I ever say, "You Hanna, me Tarzan."

But I now see that the Tarzan story is about someone born with a double heritage. Tarzan has been raised by apes, has been comfortable in ape culture, and then realizes that another heritage is in him, too. He finds the cabin of his dead parents, and begins slowly to examine the books, and figure out the funny bugs on the picture book page, which were print. And the rest of his life, through all the plots that Edgar Rice Burroughs drew for him, his quest was to integrate those two parts of himself, both wondrous treasures, into one whole person.

I see a bit of that in my life so far... being born into the American secular world and loving it, but discovering that there was a place with funny writing which held the wisdom of an ancient people and which was equally mine.

And what about Jack?

We haven't seen him for at least 20 years. Could he return? And if so, what would he say? Maybe "keep it up." Or possibly, "Do it better."

I imagine him saying, "Don't dismiss the Jewish stuff so easily." Or maybe—"You've got a job bigger than the one for which you're paid. That job is being the best Jew you can be." So, just keep an eye out for Jack and an ear out, too. You never know when...

Shulayim: Patti Frazin

I lost my father before I became an adult. It was a loss of a guide, a navigator, my compass, that light within. And then I met and married a rabbi's son. Rabbi Shapiro was a classmate of Rabbi Frazin and we became members of BJBE.

Newly married, we were welcomed to Rabbi and Hanna's home. I admit I came somewhat reluctantly. If we were to embark on a conversation about God—the God that took away my guide—I would have no part of it.

Rabbi Shapiro saw in me that *pintela yid*, that divine spark, I thought had been extinguished. That evening he asked me to join a group of congregants who made and delivered meals to the hungry. My path illuminated... my Jewish journey began.

And he nurtured that spark, inviting me to join a new social action initiative. From there I chaired our social action committee on my way to becoming president of BJBE. It was and is that opportunity to "pray with my feet" though that has shown me the way to my closest friends, provided our children a grounded path, and is the place I go when I need to be reminded of that divine light within me and within all of us.

Rabbi, thank you for seeing in me, in so many of us, that *pintela yid*.

Patti Frazin, assistant vice president for the Jewish United Fund of Metropolitan Chicago, joined BJBE in 1989, and served as the Temple's president from 2009–2011.

Not For Myself

Congregation Sukkat Shalom, Juneau, Alaska
Rosh Hashanah 5764/2003

---

*After he retired and became Rabbi Emeritus at BJBE in
2000, MSS spent several years serving as rabbi over the High
Holy Days—three years at Congregation Kona Bet Shalom
on the Big Island of Hawaii, a fourth in Kauai, and two at
Congregation Sukkat Shalom in Juneau, Alaska. Leading
services in our country's 49th and 50th states meant that he
needed to introduce himself to an entirely new community,
but it also meant that he could recycle parts of some of his
favorite sermons from over his years at BJBE.*

LET'S GET ACQUAINTED. To you, I'm another rabbi of
the moment, just passing through Juneau. I'm 68, Rabbi
Emeritus at Congregation BJBE, wife Hanna (don't call her
rebbitzen), much younger. Three sons, two daughters-in-law, one
granddaughter and one grandchild on the way.

You're my fourth congregation as a rabbi: First Buffalo, then
suburban Chicago, then in retirement Kona, Hawaii, and now
Juneau. Happy to be here, yes, though I will be sorry to be far
away from baseball and my White Sox.

Speaking of baseball, a great Jewish reunion occurred in
September of 1999. Actually there are two slightly different
endings. Here's what happened. The Jewish slugger Shawn Green,
then a Toronto Blue Jay, now a Dodger, came up to bat. The

catcher was Jesse Levis, also Jewish, a second-string catcher for the Indians. And the umpire was Al Clark, also Jewish.

Here's version #1 of what happened then: It dawned on all of them what an uncommon event this was—to have a major league home plate and its environs populated exclusively by Jews. And umpire Clark proposed that they all recite the *shehecheyanu*, and they did.

Well—not quite. What actually took place, we hear, is that it was Shawn Green who first caught the coincidence and simply said, "Hello *Yids*," at which point they all wished each other a happy new year because it was just a few days before *Rosh Hashanah*.

So we can look around and say, "hello, *Yids*" but, yes, *L'shanah Tova* is better.

A bit more about me. I grew up in a Reform synagogue in Chicago, wasn't *Bar Mitzvah* until I was 20, but was confirmed with my class at age 15. We all had parts in that ceremony. I had a short reading part and the honor of lifting up the *Torah* after it was read. My rabbi showed me a technique for lifting it. I'll try to display it this morning. But my reading part was a quote from Hillel in the *Pirkei Avot*, and here is what Hillel said and what I spoke: "If I am not for myself, who will be for me? But if I am only for myself, what am I? And if not now, when?"

I don't think I quite got it all when I said it at Confirmation, though I liked the rhythm of it. It seemed almost like a bit of blank verse—poetry you didn't have to understand.

And even when I thought I understood the dialectic between the first two lines, I was never sure how the last line fit in.

"If I am not for myself who will be for me? If I am only for myself, what am I? And if not now, when?"

Let's unpack that a bit.

If I am not for myself, who will be for me? Sounds like—take care of yourself because no one else may care as much as you do. That's a modern thought. People say: "I have to learn to take care of myself" and they usually mean mental or physical health, or both.

But I think Hillel wasn't just speaking of us as individuals—he was talking about us, in the plural. I think he meant: "We Jewish people have to take care of, and stand up for ourselves, because if we don't nobody else will." And you can make a good argument from all the later Jewish history between then and now that he was right.

Compare it to a family. The younger generation is often encouraged to "care about your family—your grandparents, your siblings, cousins—people outside the family won't be there for you the way *mishpachah* will be." Families even drop a little guilt on family members to "support the family and be there for them."

It's an important lesson to learn. My 30-year-old cousin Reni, just ordained a rabbi last May, said it so well at a family event in August. We were all at a young cousin's *Bar Mitzvah* and at the service Reni said to the youngster these words: "I want you to know the most important thing about our family—we show up and we keep showing up!" Our extended family will be quoting Reni for years as we try to keep showing up at family events, no matter where we start from. If we are not for ourselves, who will be for us?

Big events bring the Jewish people out. Big moments make most of us show up. At crises in Israel—which means all the time, big celebrations, major holidays, it happens all over the world— we show up. There must be some great stories about this in Southeast Alaska and the rest of the state.

One of the best such stories I know is the story of two trekking American Jews in Nepal at *Seder* time. They had packed one box of matzah. The Israeli embassy in Katmandu had no food or space for them but gave them six *Haggadot*. They hung a notice of their *Seder* on the "notice tree" in downtown Katmandu and 40 Jews from who-knows-where signed up, including one who had packed a bottle of *Pesach* wine, and a dozen or so young Jews from the Buddhist monastery up the hill. They had their Seder, under the protection of the Nepalese army.

"*Im Eyn Ani Li Mi Li?*" If I am not for myself, who shall be for me? The Jewish default position seems to be caring about our group, wanting our group to survive. As I heard it said once, "Loving all the other Jews even when we don't like some of them."

But what does Hillel say next? *"Uch'sheani l'atmzi mah ani?* If I am only for myself, what am I?" And what are the possible answers to that? Insulated? Isolated? Selfish? Self-serving? Not very Jewish?

Maybe. I just know that our other Jewish teachings about justice and mercy and how to treat the strangers, and how we must do *tikkun olam*, repair the world's environmental ills, social ills, and economic ills, these ideals of NOT being only for ourselves have lit up my Jewish heritage for me.

And for many others, maybe for many of you.

I know that the best of our kids, the best of our teens and young adults especially once they learn a bit, desperately want a Judaism that gets beyond just ourselves and beyond what's good only for the Jews. They really would like to believe in and try to live out the commandments of social justice—as most of us wanted to do before we got busy with life. As a rabbi involved with teens for so many years… and as a Jewish boy who grew up through Jewish youth groups and Jewish camps, I know the flame that Jewish justice work can light inside. Hanna and I were house leaders of a *mitzvah* corps of teens in the 1960s who lived together in Chicago and went out every day to work in the inner city serving mainly black kids and families. They felt it was Jewish work. I know that the best programs we did for younger teens in camp was to take them into town to do *mitzvot* like visiting the sick, entertaining in community elder residences, or demonstrating with Cesar Chavez. And I know that programs like American Jewish World Services are living examples of the *mitzvah* of *tikkun olam*, a core precept of both the Conservative and Reform movements, all of this representing the living response to the second half of that quote. We will not be only for ourselves, not make Judaism into just another interest group.

Of course you can care about justice for all and also stand up for our Jewish family and Jewish survival. Most of the time there's not much conflict. Most of the time one helps the other. But there are times when there's a tension.

Two examples—one easy to discuss, the other less comfortable for some.

First—years ago Rabbi Harold Schulweis began a project for feeding the hungry which he called *Mazon* (Hebrew for "food"). He suggested that families that celebrated events like weddings and *Bar* and *Bat Mitzvahs*, take 3% of what the event cost them and give it to Mazon to be distributed among organizations that feed the hungry. Great idea—it caught on. *Mazon* is a growing organization by now, collecting $15 million every year and doing good with it.

Some donors soon saw the lists of the neighborhood organizations which got the money for feeding the hungry projects and said, "How many of these will feed Jewish poor people?" And it was less than 50%. A discussion began—what should the proportion be?

Yes, Jews were giving this money. Did it make a difference who got it? Lots of talk. What would you have said? The decision was, Jewish causes get not less than one-third, not more than one-half. Good example of putting "If I am not for myself... If I am only for myself" into practice.

An interesting issue.

But the more uncomfortable issue relates to Israel. If all of us agreed that whatever Israel does is by definition just and right and wise, then there would be no tension. But we're not all agreed on that. And thus the mixed feelings.

Some say Jews should always stand up for Israel; nobody else will if we won't. It's family. Don't criticize. You may need an Israel someday.

Lots of truth in that. It's the default position. If we're not for ourselves who will be for us? And Israel is definitely inside our "us."

But many, including many Israelis, think we can't leave our Jewish beliefs in justice and peace behind us when we think about Israel. Some believe we only help Israel if we try to influence it from the outside to make social justice decisions about the future with the Palestinians. For if we are only for ourselves, what are we and what is Israel?

Avraham Burg is a credible voice in Israel. He was speaker

of the *Knesset* for four years, chair of the Jewish Agency, and an Orthodox Jew of the more mainstream religious party. Here's a bit of what he wrote in the Israeli press recently:

> "The Zionist revolution always rested on a just path and an ethical leadership. Neither of these is operative any longer. This 2000-year struggle for Jewish survival comes down to a state of settlements, run by an amoral clique of corrupt lawbreakers who are deaf both to their citizens and their enemies. A state lacking justice cannot survive."

So says Avraham Burg. He's talking about survival as well as justice.

If I am not for myself, who will be for me? If I am only for myself, what am I? A tug of war at times. And maybe the only authentic resolution is—no matter which side you think is most important, feel some of the pull of gravity of the other side.

And if not now, when?

What a strange ending! A Woody Allen line. It should give us an answer to the two above questions, or a way of deciding which is the most important...but all it says is if not now, when?

Maybe it means this: Don't get paralyzed. Should you care most about the family? Should you care most about injustice for everybody? Make a choice, make both choices, take a little from column A, a little from Column B, and do something, for our Jewish family, for justice, but do it now! Get un-paralyzed, get unstuck. Do important Jewish business, this year! Now! If not now, when?

Like Green, Levis and Clark, we're all at home plate... *Rosh Hashanah*, the beginning of the Jewish yearly run around the bases, back to home plate again as we were last year. I'm glad we're here with you. As the three Jewish ball players said to one another: Hello Jews... Happy New Year. It's good to be with the family to talk *Torah*.

And if not now, when?

Rabbi Reacts Columns

MSS enjoyed writing columns for the monthly BJBE bulletin. Over the years, he wrote hundreds of "Rabbi Reacts" columns, which he almost always signed: "Sincerely, Mark S. Shapiro." According to legend, then bulletin editor Sandee Holleb once wanted to put together a silly Purim edition of the Bulletin, along with a column entitled, "Rabbi Overreacts." Many of these articles were about current activities or people in the synagogue. Some covered programs, events, or projects of specific interest to him. He selected a few of his favorite columns for publication here.

Rabbi Reacts
September 5, 1986

Four of us were on an extended auto trip, and we had already played 20 Questions and Ghost. One of us suggested a very serious game—could we think of any family, known reasonably well to us, which was not living with some significant problem?

We could not. Not a one. Some had job or money problems, but most were family situations—recent bereavements, illnesses, aging parents, in-laws, children, married and unmarried.

I'm sure that you would come to the same conclusion if you thought of the people you know reasonably well. It's become very clear to me after a number of years as rabbi in the same congregation. Most every family appears to be relatively free of deep wounds—*until* they feel comfortable enough to share the deeper stuff with me.

And it may be good just to *know* that, so we don't feel singled out by crisis, so that we realize that we probably wouldn't trade our problems for those of others. Just *knowing* that can help.

And having the right expectations can help too. Family living can be joyous and fulfilling, but it doesn't come without the same effort and difficulty that our jobs demand of us. We like to think of the family as an escape from the anxieties of our work world, a place to relax and be refreshed. But the family often makes even greater demands on our time and our energy than the work world. Parenting is frustrating work much of the time. It is a picnic only on rare occasions, which are to be savored.

When we ask God to inscribe us in the Book of Life for a good year, we should know that it's the book of *ordinary* life, not carefree life. That could make us much more easily pleased by the prospects, problems, and occasional blessings of that ordinary life.

Sincerely,
Mark S. Shapiro

Rabbi Reacts
February 27, 1987

The theme of our exchange weekend with Congregation Beth Shalom of Northbrook was "Jewish Life in 2037." Rabbi Wolkin and I both made some predictions. In case you missed mine (the weather was bad that night), I'll share a selection of those predictions:

- Because it will also be a problem to find Jewish mates in 2037, almost every synagogue will have revived the institution of *Shad'chanut*—marriage brokering. It will come with your dues. Some synagogues will work with members on a committee, some will have staff professionals hired to make the matches. Synagogues will give gifts to the brides and grooms, but no guarantees.

- In 2037, CBS will have its first woman rabbi, an assistant rabbi whose name will be Stacy. It will be considered an old fashioned name. BJBE will also have come to a similar milestone. We will have had 4 women assistant rabbis prior to 2037, but we will have just installed our first woman Senior Rabbi. Her name will be Charlotte. It will be considered an ordinary Jewish name.

- In 2037, the following will be said in both our congregations: "Why can't we attract the kids to come to Temple when they're in college and afterwards? Why do we lose them? Why do they only come back when they marry and start having children? We've got to do something about it!" (And they will be unsuccessful, just as we are.)

- In 2037, a new Jewish protest group will arise, for men only. It will be known as GaMBLIS - Get Men Back Into Leadership of Synagogues! 80% of synagogue offices will be filled by women. There will be suburban synagogues which have never had a male Temple President. GaMBLIS will arise as an underground synagogue organization, and will try to sneak at least one extra man onto every synagogue nominating committee.

- In 2037 people will be getting their child's Bar/Bat Mitzvah date 2-1/2 years in advance. They will be heard to say as the day approaches, "How will I live through all this aggravation? Can't s/he run away and get *Bat Mitzvahed*?"

- It will be as much of a rite of passage for parents as for children. Children will still be nervous and mothers will still cry. The rabbis will be urging *simple Bar/Bat Mitzvah* celebrations, but some will not be listening. The favorite party themes will be Horses, Baseball, Marbles, and Aliens from the 4th Galaxy. The most lavish party of the season will include a visit by an *actual* alien from the 4th Galaxy who will lead the *Kiddush* and *Motzi* by thought waves.

- When asked about their congregations in the year 2037, both Rabbi Stacy and Rabbi Charlotte will respond by saying, "Those who feel their Jewishness the most deeply are those who sense in it something bigger than they are, more purposeful than they are, something *Kadosh*, something holy, something of God." They will not be surprised to hear that their predecessors had said much the same thing in 1987.

Sincerely,
Mark S. Shapiro

Shulayim: **Eliot M. Shapiro**

Those of us lucky enough to hear MSS deliver a sermon knew that we were listening to a masterful speaker. His ability to say the right words in just the right way certainly was a strong influence on my career journey. For the past 20+ years, I've been a presentation and communication coach, helping people learn to communicate more effectively during meetings, presentations, and speeches. When clients ask, as they often do, "Who's the best speaker you've ever heard?" I'll often reply, "My father." As cliché as it sounds, in this case it's absolutely true.

What do I remember most from listening to MSS-the-speaker" during my lifetime? Two specific areas:

The murmur. Before High Holiday sermons, there was a distinct sound that rippled through the congregation. It was the combined whispers of those sitting nearby.

"Here he comes."

"Do you think he'll mention the Sox this year?"

"This is my favorite part."

And of course, "Is he going to say it this year?" (A reference to the title of this book.) Everyone knew something good was coming, and the anticipation was palpable. Then, as MSS finished and walked back to his seat, there was an even louder murmur, a cacophony of whispers that had been brewing as he spoke.

"Wow."

"He's SO good."

"How long was that?"

"We're so lucky."

"That was even better than LAST year."

It was like a collective sigh, exhaling the breath we'd be holding the entire time.

He spoke to YOU. Following a High Holiday sermon, I admit that I often sat in my seat feeling a bit ticked off. I'd find myself thinking, "There he goes again, choosing Yom Kippur as an opportunity to deliver fatherly advice. Why did he have to call us out in front of the entire congregation?" As I grew older and actually listened to those around me, I came to realize, as others have recounted in these pages, that EVERYONE felt the same thing. Whatever the topic, each congregant was able to personally connect with his message and find relevance in their own life.

Specifically, though, what made MSS such a dynamic and inspirational speaker, and helped congregants remember the impact of his remarks long after the folding chairs were cleared out? As it turns out, they're the same skills I encourage my clients to work on as they seek to make a better connection with their audiences:

- **He was conversational**. Many rabbis and pastors write sermons as if they were magazine articles, reading them to their congregations. The style tends to be stuffy and formal, using SAT-type words rarely heard in casual settings. MSS had the unique ability to deliver his sermons in the same tone he used while speaking to you in his office or teaching a class.

- **He incorporated dramatic pauses**. Silence is a powerful speaking tool, and MSS was a master at using it for effect. During that silence, you couldn't help but feel the impact of what he'd just said.

- **He used vocal variety**. MSS never spoke in a monotone. At times he'd shout certain phrases (*"Avraham! AVRAHAM!!"*), followed by a dramatic whisper (*"Hineni."*) He was also well known for adding a musical quality to his delivery, often singing the words he delivered in order to convey the feeling behind them.

- **He used purposeful body movement**. Though MSS always spoke from behind the lectern, he never stood still. He would turn his body and reach out to the audience, making people in the back feel just as connected as those in the front rows. He'd often take a step backward while speaking, allowing him to then take a strong step

forward to drive home his point. He'd tap
the lectern with two fingers, gesture with
both hands, occasionally adjust his glasses,
rest his hands in front of him or lean on the
lectern, always keeping us guessing as to
what would come next.

Long-time congregants remember all of
these characteristics, along with his sense of
humor, his use of repetition, his creative openers
and his willingness to be vulnerable. Yes, many
have called him a "rabbi's rabbi," but just as
significantly, he was a "speaker's speaker."

Eliot Shapiro was confirmed at BJBE in 1980.

Rabbi Reacts
May 30, 1988

I think a Jew should come to services. I also think a Jew should
know some *Torah*, give *Tz'dakah*, perform deeds of kindness, and
be a mensch.

But coming to services doesn't run second to any of the others.

My grandmother Lena Shapiro was the *Shabbes*-service-goer
of my youth. She went quite regularly, sang along with the choir,
held the *Tz'dakah* basket, and knew most of the people there. We
never talked about whether she still believed in God after she lost
a 32-year-old son, or what she got out of attending services so
often. But she did tell me that we "ought to go to Temple."

Lena was right. Now that I'm 52 I understand how right
she was. There are lots of ways to encourage people to come to
services, like talking about the warmth, the food, the teaching, the
fun, the nice chairs, and *none* of them work, because you can get

all those things elsewhere and in spades. Reasons are irrelevant.

The truth is a Jew shows loyalty to being Jewish by coming to services with at least some constancy. It doesn't have much to do with God (Do you think everyone who comes regularly is a devout believer? I don't...) or with knowing Hebrew. You don't have to enjoy it, though you may, or get much out of it, which happens only once you're coming often. Being at services simply renews your commitment to the Jewish people, who are together regularly for worship and study.

Being at services with no reason (like *Yahrzeit*, your cousin's *Bar Mitzvah*, a special speaker or other bells and whistles), shows the most loyalty to your Jewishness.

I don't know why so many nice Temple members never think of coming to services. But I do know they ought to.

So when you say, "Being a good Jew really doesn't mean being at services most of the time," don't look to me for agreement. I'm with Grandma Lena, whose ought-to's aren't old fashioned. You ought to be a mensch, you ought to give *Tz'dakah*, and you ought to be at services.

Sincerely,
Lena's grandson Mark

Rabbi Reacts
March 30, 1990

When it comes to the public school I think that some of us suburban Jewish parents do weird things.

We foolishly roar like lions to get the public schools to close on our Holidays, but curl up like tabby cats when the activity and sports coaches play the tyrant with our family schedules and values.

Some Jewish parents consider it a great thing to get the public schools to close on *Rosh Hashanah* and *Yom Kippur*. Frankly, I can't imagine why. Do we believe that the public schools ought to be closed for every major religious holiday celebrated by some of the students? And what about Muslim holidays, and the Buddhist, and the Hindu? Our pluralistic society could get kids lots of days off if we extended that principle fairly to all.

Rabbi Karl Weiner *zichrono livrachah* understood this very well. He urged that we leave school boards alone on this issue. If the number of students absent on a High Holy Day makes them feel it is better to close the school (attendance is tied in to funding, after all) let them make that decision solely on those grounds. That principle can be applied equally to any religion's holiday.

Yes, the school should try not to penalize youngsters who are out for religious holidays, should offer reasonable makeup opportunities, and ought to try to keep major events off major religious holidays. But that's all.

And for purposes of Jewish education I would much rather the public schools were open on our Holy Days. There is a lesson in Jewish commitment in having to miss school, in having to be different, even in having to spend a few extra study hours tomorrow because you were in Temple today.

We've been pretty aggressive on that issue, mistakenly so in my opinion.

But we play dead when the soccer or drama coach plays god.

They really seem to have our number. Parents tell me that their kids must miss lots of Hebrew School, or Monday night class, or Shabbat services because the coach says, "One absence and you're off the team," or "out of the play." And arguing with the coach may get their child in the doghouse.

Who let coaches make those rules, especially when it means interference with the Jewish commitments we make for our kids? When did we tell them we approve of completely inflexible rules for non-academic areas? Why don't the public schools compromise in these areas? And why do we let them get away with it?

Here's an issue on which we should be roaring.

Sincerely,
Mark S. Shapiro

Rabbi Reacts
April 24, 1992

Sometimes you say something out loud and find out that many were thinking the same thing, hoping that someone would speak out.

That is happening now in our community, and the topic is *Bar/Bat Mitzvah*. A few rabbis and synagogue members have said that they believe *Bar/Bat Mitzvah* celebrations are out of control. And wherever that is said, most people agree and hope that something can be done about it.

None of this is meant to embarrass anyone. People have a right to spend exorbitant sums if they want to. I can't judge someone else's values just from looking at the kind of *Bar/Bat Mitzvah* celebration they put on.

But I can say that the totality of what these parties has become is an embarrassment to the Jewish people and absolutely the wrong Jewish message to youngsters.

I believe that many families think so, too. They don't want to spend a fortune, or invite the whole class, or make a child's Jewish event into a gala that no one appreciates except the caterers. And these families need support, because they are right.

A coalition of members from many synagogues is setting out to change our culture. It is a big task. But so many of you agree with us already that we might be able to do it, and maybe soon. We want to proclaim that *it is not fashionable* to "keep up with the Goldbergs," that less is really more, that celebrations which have a theme other than Jewish values are comical and tasteless.

The vandalism has opened a lot of eyes. Our nice Jewish kids are trashing hotels and destroying property. They are often out of control and seem to think it is okay. I think we have taught them that, by celebrations which are wasteful, vulgar, and out of control.

We need to change the culture. Soon. And I think you think so too.

Sincerely,
Mark S. Shapiro

Rabbi Reacts
August, 1998

Some Israeli kids taught me a swimming pool team game that
begins with a frightening yell:

"Who's afraid of the big white bear?"

"Not us!"

"But what if he gets <u>close</u>?"

"Let him get close!"

"But what if his claws rip?"

"Let 'em rip!"

And then one team swims off to try to tag the other team.

Aside from yelling, there's nothing to be afraid of.

That's much the way our BJBE travelers felt about their two
weeks in Israel. Despite a few apprehensions before they left,
they never <u>felt</u> or <u>were</u> in any danger at all—not at the Lebanese
border, or in the Arab markets, or on the roads in the West Bank.
(I can give you 22 names to call for verification.)

Only once did we experience a touch of anxiety. That came on
Friday, June 26, at sunset at the Western Wall in Jerusalem where
we held our *Erev Shabbat* Service. And there wasn't an Arab in
sight.

Let me back up. Hanna and I have now led BJBE Israel trips
since 1977. Our custom has always been to bring our own Reform
prayer books and have *Shabbat* services as we stand in our own
circle in the large plaza in front of the Western Wall. We don't go
too close to the Wall. That marked-off area is designated as an
Orthodox Synagogue and our group of men and women would
be an *"in your face"* provocation if we stood there. So we always
choose a spot in the middle of the Plaza, close enough to see and
feel the Wall, yet appropriately far (as I see it) from the designated
Synagogue area.

Hanna and I have always done it this way. We don't do it
to provoke a confrontation. We do it because the words of our
Reform *Siddur* take on extraordinary new overtones when spoken
in sight of that Wall, overtones which people can take home with
them to BJBE worship.

Occasionally, we've been heckled by a few of our least tolerant
brothers and sisters, who frequent the Wall and the plaza. Once

we had to compromise and move back 15 feet for the sake of peace.

I thought it might be less easy this trip. Large groups of non-Orthodox Jews on "official" missions have recently been physically harassed or been restricted to the farthest corner of the plaza while holding a service. Orthodox strength in the present government has made some of them even more aggressive against us and our increasing presence in Israel has also made some dig more deeply.

We got as far as *"V'shamru"* with no disturbance.

Much of what follows is based on what others in our group later told me. I was just trying to concentrate on the service and <u>not</u> look beyond our circle of prayer. So I saw little.

Someone tapped me on the shoulder, and a voice said, "Who is the group leader here?" I ignored whoever it was. It turned out to be a Jerusalem policeman assigned to keep the peace in the plaza. Our Shelley K. stepped between me and the policeman and told him, "You can't disturb him now... he's praying. That worked till about *Yism'chu.* And now I could hear the commotion near us. The policeman's two-way radio crackled. Loud shouts of *Chutzah*—"Get out of Here"—were coming from about 25 of those less tolerant Orthodox men and boys gathered <u>very</u> close to us now. A lady yelled at Natalie C. telling her to "get out of here." Normally gentle Natalie lifted her voice to respond: "Stop bothering us—we're having a service here." The noise got louder and we began to pray louder.

The policeman stepped into the middle of our circle. I couldn't continue to ignore him. He said, "You can pray here but only if the women stand on one side and the men on the other. That's the law here." I was prepared to ignore the request, knowing it wasn't the law and being more afraid of our ladies' reaction, than of the policeman. But Hanna had sized up the situation and urged us to do it. She saw that four policeman (and a few soldiers who had joined them) would protect us if only we gave in on that one point. And she was right.

We separated men from the women while keeping the circle whole and continued the service. And then we saw that our group of 22 was increasing in size. By the Silent Prayer (try three

minutes of that while being yelled at), we had more than 50
people standing with us—other American Jews and Israelis who
encouraged us by saying, "Ignore them, you <u>should</u> be standing
here," and "We're not <u>all</u> like them."

Before *Aleinu* I think I said something like this to our group:
"Please don't judge Orthodox or Traditional Judaism by those
people. *Torah* teaches love of the Jewish people. Most Traditional
Jews know that even better than we do. We are not here to hate
the Orthodox just because they have an intolerant fringe group of
crazies here."

I don't know if I convinced them, or even you. But it's the
truth!

We finished *Aleinu*, said *Kaddish*, and sang *Ein Keloheinu*
with great fervor. We had become much more numerous and
louder than our detractors. We felt good, maybe too good. But
we had only done what we always have done, to pray in sight
of the Western Wall, maintaining self-respect, without acting
confrontational. If that spiritual act was taken as a political
statement, so be it.

The service ended. The people who had joined us introduced
themselves all around, we milled and kissed Shabbat Shalom, and
couldn't stop talking about how it had felt.

The original policeman approached me. He wanted a private
talk. We went off a few paces. (Hanna thought they were leading
me away.)

"Are you the rabbi of this group?" "Yes, I'm Mark Shapiro."
"What is a Mark Shapiro?" "It's my name." "Okay—you
understand I just have to do my job. I have to keep peace here." "I
understand completely. Thanks for your help." "Have a good trip
in Israel and think well of us, and come back again soon." And he
initiated a handshake.

So we got in cabs and went to our hotel for Shabbat dinner.
Hanna's elation (she called me a tiger) shaded into anger. You can
read what she has to say at the end of this report.

Characteristically, I wondered if it had been the right thing
to do. We could have gone to Friday Night Services at *Kol
Han'shamah* Progressive Synagogue instead and met Israelis who
are building Liberal Judaism in Israel. The worship experience

there might have been less fragmented, though with less adrenaline, too.

Who's afraid of the big white bear? Not me! What if he comes close and his claws rip? Let 'em rip! The chant is bloodthirsty, but the game is tame.

Traveling in Israel is like that. There is absolutely nothing for a tourist to fear while traveling in Israel. You <u>feel</u> safe and you <u>are</u> safe. Sometimes there's some yelling. We can live with that. Especially if it means your wife calls you a tiger!

Sincerely,
Mark S. Shapiro

Hanna's Addendum

I wasn't frightened while traveling in Egypt or Jordan. We've stood at all of Israel's borders without feeling a twinge of fear. But on *Erev Shabbat* at the Western Wall, I was afraid—afraid of Jews. And that makes me angry!

I couldn't concentrate during our service at the Wall. We were praying very quietly in our small circle. I was looking around anxiously—watching for trouble. Every time a "black hat" walked by, my heart would pound more. When the yelling began, my concentration unraveled completely.

My back was to the police and the hecklers and I didn't want to turn to look at them—giving them the satisfaction of getting my attention. I know that there were about four policemen and it sounded like about 20 or so hecklers. I hear them yell *chutzah l'America*—"go back to America!" And there were voices of children too.

Suddenly we were being joined by friendly faces, as if the louder the hecklers yelled, the more people wanted to join our service. One man standing next to me, holding his child, said, "I'm Israeli and I want you to know that we welcome you here and <u>THEY</u> are a minority." The more shouting came from hecklers, the louder we sang and prayed—many voices together.

When the service ended, we were elated! One of the women that had joined our group even wanted to sing *We Shall*

Overcome.

But after the elation, came anger. On Friday night at the Wall, in Israel, I had been afraid of other Jews.

–Hanna Shapiro

Rabbi Reacts
November, 1999

Only a pope can speak ex cathedra, but a Reform rabbi could at least give it a try. So here goes.

I declare that Charlton Heston no longer holds any title to being Moses.

He was okay when he played Moses in *The Ten Commandments*. And I never before regretted that his face came to mind when I tried to picture Moses.

Until... he became honorary chairman of, and major spokesman for, the National Rifle Association, the NRA.

Mr. Heston, you can be Mr. NRA and work for proliferation of guns, or you can stay Moses. But not both!

Yes, Moses did have his own problems with violence. He was a murderer in his Egyptian days and never got over his tendency to hit with sticks instead of talking things out. But God kept correcting him, and telling him to legislate for the sanctity of human life. And the tradition that Moses has come to symbolize is, as I read it, strongly in favor of strict gun control.

Some people do think that the NRA is right. More firepower to them. But I think the vast majority of us want the government to be VERY strict about gun manufacture, sale, and possession, so why are we being blatantly ignored?

President Clinton met with Jewish leaders recently to discuss issues regarding Israel and other Jewish interests. He hasn't always told the truth, but I believe that what he said at the meeting is true, namely that Congress is so beholden to and afraid of the gun lobby that they <u>just don't care</u> what the rest of us think.

We simply haven't made enough noise yet, or played hardball. So if you are for strict gun control, let your Congressperson know and tell them that it will make a big difference at the ballot box.

And please, if you haven't done so yet, sign the petition started by the American Jewish Congress which has been going around BJBE.

John Huston can have Noah, Victor Mature is still fine as Samson and Buddhist Richard Gere is probably as good a David as anyone around.

But Charlton Heston can't be Moses anymore.

Who says we Jews can't play hardball?

Sincerely,
Mark S. Shapiro

Rabbi Reacts
(Date Not Known)

Tradition says that "the seal of God is truth." Acting publicly for the truth can be an important form of Jewish social action.

In 1969, a well-known Jewish bank owner was to be honored as "Man of the Year" by a large Jewish organization. Such honors were habitually given to people who had given the most money. One of the early BJ rabbis, Arnold Jacob Wolf, taught me that such "honoring" of the money men wasn't worthy of our Jewish community, so I had worked against such events taking place at BJBE.

But this gentleman, in my opinion, also had his own dark side, reflecting racism. He had spoken out strongly against Martin Luther King's work for integration in Chicago, followed by his refusal to close his bank on King's birthday, which had been proclaimed a national holiday.

Of course it was his right to do so. But it was our right to tell the truth—that such a man was not worthy of a Jewish honor. It seemed worth protesting. I could feel the adrenaline.

So I asked our small Confirmation class to join Frank Kon, our Social Action Chair, and me to go protest. Eight teenagers joined us and we gathered on the sidewalk across from the Sherman House Hotel where the "honor dinner" was taking place. We protested by carrying signs which said "This 'honoree' is not our Jew of ANY YEAR." It was cold. Some invited banquet guests entering the hotel asked us what it was all about, and our kids, well-prepped by Frank and me, told why we felt Jews honoring such a man was a sham.

A high point, for me was when an editor of the Jewish Sentinel News, which had co-sponsored the event, heard of our sidewalk protest, charged out of the hotel and confronted us, saying, "What are you guys doing? Making these kids Communists?" I think he helped our youngsters understand how an establishment can try to overcome the truth by name-calling.

The banquet went on, of course. We took the kids out for dinner and then drove them home. They joked that we were "all Communists." We hadn't put much of a crimp in the dinner or the honor. But there was a small sympathetic newspaper article, and the Jewish Council on Urban Affairs made protests as well.

I hope that our actions in standing up for the truth as we saw it became a part of the lives of those youngsters, now middle-aged and older. But no matter—it was exciting to stand up for the truth—the truth of which is God's own seal.

Sincerely,
Rabbi Mark S. Shapiro

Rabbi Reacts
2015 for Dedication of New Sanctuary

Rabbi Larry Kushner wrote, "*Shabbat* is more real than Wednesday, Jerusalem is more real than Chicago." I would add, "A sanctuary is more real than an office." A synagogue's sanctuary has a mystique. Even as a youngster I understood that you wouldn't bounce a ball or eat a snack in the sanctuary. It was a place set aside from other places. It was more real because it "personified" the intangible yet real values of Jewish life, then, now and yet to be.

English teachers speak of "unpacking" a book. They mean finding the below-the-surface themes and insights. If you could somehow unpack a sanctuary, you would find that the items built into it—*Bimah, Ark, Torah, Ner Tamid,* candles—all point to the covenant made long ago that we would somehow be an eternal people. The sacred becomes real in a sanctuary, comes out to meet us, in silence or in the bustle of kids—children are named, bride and groom are blessed, children (now almost adults?) read *Torah*, the ill are in our speech or silence, the names of our loved ones on our lips.

All this can happen anywhere, and does, but like a crystal, the sanctuary gathers the light of all these and sends it back to fill the room, and us. And that, I think, is why we didn't bounce a ball or eat a Hershey bar in that place.

The closest Hebrew word for sanctuary is *Mikdash* (from *Kadosh*, holy). It referred to the innermost chamber of the Temple, the place where God met with us through the person of the long-gone high priest. Although that moment of meeting could occur in any place, a sanctuary reminds us of what that moment might be like.

Larry Kushner (again) wrote that the youngest children in his congregation were taken by their teacher to see the sanctuary. She asked them what they thought was behind the ark curtains. Kushner writes:

> One kid thought it would be empty. One kid (a devotee of TV consumerism) thought it would be a new car. One guessed rightly, that it would be *Torah* scrolls. But one kid said, "When the Rabbi opens the curtains there will be a big mirror."

A nice thought. It puts you and me right into the thick of things, giving, receiving, and reflecting the best, the most real, of the Jewish way of life.

Leave the candy outside our sanctuary. There's plenty of sweetness inside.

–MSS